LIVING
WITH
HONOUR

A PAGAN ETHICS

First published by O Books, 2007
O Books is an imprint of John Hunt Publishing
Ltd., The Bothy, Deershot Lodge, Park Lane,
Ropley, Hants, SO24 0BE, UK
office1@o-books.net
www.o-books.net

Distribution in:

UK and Europe
Orca Book Services
orders@orcabookservices.co.uk
Tel: 01202 665432 Fax: 01202 666219 Int. code
(44)

USA and Canada
NBN
custserv@nbnbooks.com
Tel: 1 800 462 6420 Fax: 1 800 338 4550

Australia and New Zealand
Brumby Books
sales@brumbybooks.com.au
Tel: 61 3 9761 5535 Fax: 61 3 9761 7095

Far East (offices in Singapore, Thailand, Hong
Kong, Taiwan)
Pansing Distribution Pte Ltd
kemal@pansing.com
Tel: 65 6319 9939 Fax: 65 6462 5761

South Africa
Alternative Books
altbook@peterhyde.co.za
Tel: 021 555 4027 Fax: 021 447 1430

Text copyright Emma Restall Orr 2008

Design: Stuart Davies

ISBN: 978 1 84694 094 1

A CIP catalogue record for this book is available
from the British Library.

Printed in the UK by CPI Antony Rowe

O Books operates a distinctive and ethical publishing philosophy in
all areas of its business. It has no central office. The publishers are
a group of people who work together globally, doing something
they enjoy.

As far as the production goes, no trees were cut down to print
this book. The paper is 100% recycled, with 50% of that being
post-consumer. It's processed chlorine-free, and has no fibre from
ancient or endangered forests. This production method for this print
run saved approx. 3 trees, 1400 gallons of wastewater, 1500 pounds
of solid waste, 300 pounds of greenhouse gases and 550 kilowatt
hours of electricity.

LIVING
WITH
HONOUR
A PAGAN ETHICS

Emma Restall Orr

BOOKS

Winchester, UK
Washington, USA

CONTENTS

Part One :   Finding a Perspective   1

Chapter One :   Defining Pagan   9

Chapter Two :   Natural Paganism   36

Chapter Three :   Defining Choice   62

Chapter Four :   Defining Pagan Ethics   96

Chapter Five :   Natural Pagan Ethics   122

Part Two :   The Pathways of our Choices   148

Chapter Six :   Human Relationship   154

Chapter Seven :   The Value of Human Life   189

Chapter Eight :   The Value of Nonhuman Animals   219

Chapter Nine :   The Value of the Environment   257

Chapter Ten :   The Value of the Web   288

Part Three :   Walking the Path   318

Chapter Eleven :   Integration and Integrity   320

Bibliography   345

Index   351

Dedication

This book I offer to my gods,
to their wild winds and gentle breezes,
thick mud and sweet soil,
rose petal and thorns,
endless darkness and sparkling light
in thanks
for their company upon the journey, and for each step along the way.

ACKNOWLEDGEMENTS

With regard to how and why this book was written, I'd like to acknowledge in particular three souls with my thanks: Mark the Polecat, who gave me the initial confidence that I not only could but should write this book; Piotr Seven Pebbles, who encouraged me throughout its writing, and moused each chapter for gaps and errors; and David, my beautiful husband, whose wisdom and energy inspires me to walk with strength and integrity.

I would like to thank Ronald Hutton, whose own pondering upon virtue in Paganism had led him to pose as pre-eminent the values of courage, generosity and loyalty. His input, so close to the beginning of this project, was deeply appreciated, allowing me to journey along the paths of my research, distilling ideas and possibilities against that touch-stone. That my own philosophy, crafted through the rough process of pulling apart and pondering ideas again and again, came to feel those three words as key is a real pleasure.

I thank too all those who contributed by sharing with me their ideas and convictions, in emails, in long conversations, and in the gatherings I brought together to discuss the hardest issues. I acknowledge the courage of those who shared their thoughts, self-reflecting upon flaws and failings, finding the drive to live with honour.

PART ONE

FINDING A PERSPECTIVE

When I was six years old, I watched a man die. Slumped in the dirt of a narrow street, his back awkwardly propped against a wall, his shoulders crooked, head fallen to one side, he seemed to me simply too tired to keep breathing.

The clamour and bustle of the market carried on, without him - people shouting, pushing, laughing, selling. I remember the sound of my father's voice as he argued with a trader about the price of a cage of birds, little wild birds that fluttered frantically, losing tiny downy feathers in fright. It was the last decade of Franco's fascism, Spain still covered in the dust of poverty. It was my world. And with my fingers curled tightly around my father's hand, I stared at that man, his eyes closed, his skin like old brown leather worn soft over hollow cheeks, his mouth hanging open, a half dozen yellow teeth, black and broken. A tear was sliding slowly down his cheek. He coughed, which startled me. Then he breathed out with a rasping growl.

I turned to pull at my father but he was too busy to be with me, instead disentangling his hand from my grip to count out money and close his deal. I tugged hard at his coat, but he pushed me away, until, giving up my protestations, I turned again to stare at the old man. But something had changed. He looked different, empty, dull. Strangely, now, suddenly, he was no more than a pile of ragged dusty clothes on the street, the eye that had shed a tear half open but seeing nothing. I was bewildered and enraged; in that moment, something had happened, something important, and no one had noticed.

Ten years later, in the glitz of an expensive Tokyo nightclub, high on the cocaine I'd been given by a posse of US marines, I watched an

American girl, younger than myself, fight for her life, weeping for the heroin her body desperately needed. Rake-thin in her petite designer-neat clothes, a working model in the style of the anorexic rich, she lay slumped on the floor in the toilets in a pool of her own piss, her skin yellowish white, her eyes like black hollow tubes crawling with spiders.

Albeit stoned myself, I wasn't old enough or wise enough to help her. Instead, when she lost consciousness, I simply staggered back into the restless lights and thudding music of the club, numbed by confusion. Swaying in my four inch heels, I watched the fat black marine craft more little white lines in his silver box.

Nothing made sense.

As a child, wandering with my parents who were dedicated naturalists, spending time in scrub deserts and the humming of rainforest, travelling on seemingly endless rivers and in the brilliant rage of mountain storms, I experienced moments when I felt myself almost alone in the expanse of nature. And each time we returned to the city, to wherever it was that my father still made his living from corporate America, the caustic and selfish behaviour of human beings was harder to digest.

In my late teens, inspired by a heady mix of Wittgenstein, punk rock and the desolation of the Great War poets, determined and desperate I began my quest to find some sure heroic reason in the human soul, something I could hold to and feel proud of. Perhaps too, as Britain staggered out of its recession, I was seeking hope in humanity's future, and my own. Yet every starving child gazing out of an expensive TV, every figure of authority who broke the law, every parent who lied, every striker with his banner of resentment, spun a web in my mind; and upon those sticky fibres all the contradictions and ironies that flowed my way, the hypocrisies and prejudices, the blinkered and blatant injustices of the human world became hopelessly and heavily entangled.

Turning away from secular culture, which seemed to me to hold nothing sacred but the sating of one's own desires, I sought out the world's sacred texts, diving straight in, at times spluttering, drowning, at times finding currents I could ride and understand.

I sought out honesty, but found little in the love-and-light hyperpositivity of New Age spirituality or Californian pop psychology, nor could I find consistent reason in religions that required blind faith in some supernatural and untouchable being. I turned from Christianity as a faith that preached love yet sanctioned war. Exploring traditions of the east, dissolving into meditation, reaching to achieve new physical and mental asanas, I felt the stretch across cultures invalidating the work. I studied and found value in psychology, yet turned away from its meta-religious practice of psychotherapy, its preoccupation with ego and measures of normalcy. The ubiquitous escapism, the hypocrisy and self-centricity wore me bored and thin.

Yet the raw wonder of traditions that revered nature enchanted me. They returned me to the moments of meaning in my childhood, sitting on warm stone by a river's rushing water, dreaming with geckos in the empty desert, dancing and laughing and hiding in an old forest's golden falling leaves.

So did my focus change. Exploring all I could find, often with reckless dedication, I devoured the philosophies and theologies of animistic and shamanistic traditions. Hungrily I began learning: how to feel connection with the wind and the waves, how to hear the songs of the land and the stories of the ancestors, how to dissolve into darkness and ride the thermals of light. Slowly I discovered how these traditions are still alive, not just in lands that, with a mix of disquiet and envy, Western cultures call primitive and uncivilized. Returning to the islands of my ancestors, with wonder and relief, I found animistic religions in the rolling hills and flowering gardens of Britain.

To my surprise and delight, I found too that here my passion for science was as nurtured as my soul's artistic creativity. There was nothing in quantum physics or molecular biology, or the theories of the physiology of consciousness that could negate my growing understanding and experience of sanctity. I found the power of reason here, naturally inherent within the language of a religion.

Furthermore, the path drew my focus not only upon the world beyond humanity, but upon human nature too. I had in my teens, along with the great British analytical philosopher Bertrand Russell, entirely failed to find any celebration of intelligence in the Christian Bible. In fact, its beliefs seemed to me to require quite the reverse: a willingness to accept without question 'facts' that would more easily sit in a comic book about heroes, their nemeses, and their violence and valiant deeds. Yet in the nature-based traditions, I found the stories and poetry of our heritage celebrated, stories that, though equally violent and magical, were not confused with history. Indeed, the traditions' tenets appeared to encourage an inspiring depth of questioning and wakeful discovery. They revered the weave of instinct and reason, both as essential constituents of humanity, exploring the extraordinary ordinary patterns of the mind.

So did I become a Pagan.

It took a couple of years but, as I grew to be more involved in various communities of British Pagan traditions, I found myself increasingly saddened and disturbed.

In Paganism, I had thought, I would find a community of spiritually sagacious people, dedicated to crafting respectful relationships through their reverence for nature. While some Pagans were committed to walking the path awake, many others simply did not seem to care. Their vision was of personal power, about crafting control with magic; their attitude appeared to be more about rejection than relationship. Less dangerous but more tedious, many were simply concerned with wearing the right clothes and flaunting their accessories. Too often I would attend Pagan events to find overeating, heavily drinking, cigarette smoking individuals, bitching, expressing no more care for the world than the mundane crowd in a shopping mall, chewing on their McDonald's and Prozac.

Of course, there is a difference between those who are trained for the priesthood, or dedicated to study the deep mysteries of any religion, and those whose affiliation is based upon the easy gossip and common ground of belonging to a community; the latter may seldom work to develop their understanding and experience of sanctity. Furthermore, greed, competition and hypocrisy exist in every gathering of human beings. Not many Christians know what is truly meant by 'love thy neighbour', let alone live in ways that shine with the precept. Yet, over time, as increasingly I was asked to stand as a spokesperson for Paganism, and for my own chosen tradition of Druidry, I found myself embarrassed. It is hard to brush off the behaviour of drunken or ill-informed protesters, to explain litter left at stone circles by Pagan visitors, candle wax spilled on ancient tomb shrines. It is impossible to feel proud of being Pagan beside those whose religious expression is mostly theatrical posturing, or whose 'green spirituality' is underpinned by hypocritical consumerism with its casual support of amoral corporations.

At an interfaith conference I was once asked by a Christian minister to justify the basis of my spirituality which to him clearly, without God, had no divine source of ethics. My response was that Pagan ethics are sourced in the individual's acutely sensitive relationship with nature: my words made complete and rational sense to me, and they still do. However, while my previous books have been more of a celebration of Paganism, this one is motivated by a sincere need to understand just how and why its tenets can fail. Consequently, and for me crucially, the book emerges through a need to explore how, as a source of ethics, my religious tradition can and must succeed.

Clearly, where any relationship breaks down, the result is a collapse in respect, but to respond by demanding the relationship improves is seldom helpful. What I seek to explore and express in these pages is the motivation that inspires the momentum that of itself creates the necessary change: the natural reason. For my Paganism is both rooted and nourished in this *reason* that infuses the relationship between the storm and the waves, the reason that silently hums in the patterns of mathematics and the dance of electrons, the reason that shimmers between a mother and her child. This book is an exploration of how the magically beautiful reason, that underlies the natural spirituality of all Paganism, touches and fails to touch the minds of so much of humanity.

Yet I am not righteous in my own position. For I too live as a part of Western culture, fighting to be conscious and accurately informed, doing all I can not to be complicit in the obscenity of unnecessary consumption, crafting relationships with honour through the clumsiness of my human mind. I write this book because I too need to hear it.

In my writing I am also conscious of being in the first decade of the twenty first century, a time when American democracy is acknowledged as farce, when the flood of environmental crises and world poverty has not yet been fully addressed, when the majority of our Western culture lives stupefied on legal and illegal drugs that promote both denial and passivity, when greed is an acceptable norm and ignorance still the greatest weapon employed by those in power. A great deal is destructive in the way that human beings live. Through the arrogance of my human soul, and through my own craving for peace, I need others to read this book too.

Furthermore, it seems to me that too much of humankind is just existing, trudging and stomping through day after day, with a lack of joy. The thick cloak of drugs, of easy sugar and heavy animal fats, of TV and computer games, allows the temporary illusion of escape; the self-focus of psychotherapy is too often a long and self-indulgent route heading nowhere. The difference comes only and surely when we change our attitude towards others - human and nonhuman - and learn to live in relationships that are rich with respect, with honesty and responsibility.

So do I craft here a book about Pagan ethics - for those interested in Paganism, those interested in ethics, and those interested simply in the elusive skill of living well.

This book is divided into three parts, this first exploring the definitions and ideas that provide a philosophical and religious context for later chapters.

Aware that the word *Pagan* can be an awkward creature, for those who walk its paths, let alone for those who don't, I begin in Chapter One with an exploration of the term. Sketching the main strands of its practice, I trace the threads through our history, gathering into the weave influences, priorities and perspectives to craft a sufficient context for the notion of Paganism as a whole. In Chapter Two, I trace the undercurrents, presenting more openly the heart of Paganism as I myself perceive it to be.

The context established, in Chapter Three I turn to define ethics, once again exploring ideas and influences, seeking just how the problem of choice has been considered in Western culture through the past two and half millennia. Chapter Four explores how Pagans have debated ethics, taking into consideration the currents of their gods and the effects of religious persecution.

It is in the final chapter of Part One that I lay out what I perceive to be the critical tenets of Pagan ethics. My hope is to have adequately prepared the reader for the second part of the book, in which these ideas are placed within the practical context of our world, directly addressing the choices we all face, both trivial and fundamental.

Paganism, however, and particularly that based upon deep reverence for nature, is a religious tradition that cannot sufficiently be explained solely through objective observation; ontological discussion is not enough. Throughout Part One, therefore, the text is interspersed with passages that describe the direct experience of Pagan relationship which lies at the heart of the ethical debate. This phenomenological technique may seem to lack philosophical rigour to readers used to academic texts, but my rationale is not to bring to the text the quality of a memoir through a sprinkling of easy anecdotes. If we are to understand Paganism fully, ultimately it can only be through the empirical language of life being lived.

CHAPTER ONE

DEFINING PAGAN

Three yarns intertwine to make a useful rope :
one that encircles, one that binds,
and one that breaks.

The Paradox

There is a mischievous pleasure derived from putting together words that, side by side, create a contradiction in terms. Like a healthy pathology or an honest autocrat, when used in a serious context the mind tends to stall, all the usual connotations failing to apply. As with a Zen *koan*, we must intuit the meaning, accepting that in time the rational significance may somehow emerge: thus though we may never hear, one day we might just understand the sound of one hand clapping.

Within the title of this book is one such term. Struggling like a small boy in a hessian sack, unidentifiable limbs kicking out in all directions, *Pagan* tries to disassociate itself from *Ethics*, and vice versa. In truth, over the period of time that this book has been in the making, whenever I've explained the basics of what I am writing the term has seldom not provoked an eyebrow raised in amusement or concern.

For those who don't understand the word *Pagan*, that I use it seems unnecessarily provocative and self-sabotaging. The most extensively assumed definition describes a person who rejects the widely acceptable religious beliefs, specifically the Semitic monotheisms; and where consciously or subconsciously they connect morality with those religion's teachings, a Pagan is then clearly one who is morally dubious. In addition, because of the universally common presumption that white Europeans, and their far-flung descendants, either hold to one of those religions or have none at all, given the derogatory edge of the word surely I'd be better off using a term like *humanist* or *secular*, for otherwise I am implying the book is about those on the edge of society. Furthermore, because the word *ethics* delineates the often unspoken social rules that underlie a culture, any rejection of social conventions intimates an unwillingness to behave ethically.

Given that both words are so broad, so chronically misused and misconstrued, in order to lay down a foundational context onto which I can build ideas with some hope of stability, I must then begin by exploring the key definitions. Beginning with the word *Pagan*, however, the issues of paradox don't immediately disappear. Even amongst those within Western culture for whom the word describes their religious practice, there are attitudes that readily complicate the term *Pagan ethics*; writing a book that implies a clear moral code is to many modern Pagans a misguided venture. Indeed, that this is such a common response, and one often stated with some pride, reveals a key foundational difficulty.

For just as Hinduism is the name given to the broad spectrum of religious and spiritual traditions originally based around the Indus valley, within the context of this book Paganism covers an equally extensive range rooted within Western Europe and the diaspora of its peoples. Each tradition has emerged through different threads of ideas, histories, landscapes and theologies, each holding its own priorities, its specific religious and practical focus. Its reach embraces those from harsh high rugged mountains to those of fertile valley meadows, those of crowded noisy urban society to those of rural quiet and isolation. Its expression may be filled with the keening entropic songs of the dead, with the sensuous dances of fertility, or with the harvest's sacrifice and joy; it may be twilit in its devotion to the gods of darkness, or always celebrating the gifts of the sun. It may require the undiluted commitment needed for taking devotees into deep esoteric mysteries, or find its coherence and spiritual wealth in the easy sharing of culture and community. And though some of these may be the differing hues of one Pagan group or tradition's interaction with nature, others are less malleable, holding to one focus in all that they do.

Thus to declare a clear definition of Paganism is not easy, let alone to outline an ethics that might emerge from the weave of that vision. Even if I were to set down the parameters of my own understanding, with assurances that the majority with whom I work would agree with my words, were I to imply that declaration in any way definitive I would quickly have a crowd around me yelling their protest. Indeed, it is widely recognized that, in a circle of any number of Pagans, there are often more ideas about what Paganism is than there are people present.

As a collection of what are essentially (literally) innumerable different religions, each thoroughly held within a particular community, tradition or location, Paganism can appear fragmented. Some ill-informed commentators have tried to malign Paganism by calling it a 'pick and mix' spiritual or religious construct, yet for many Pagans there is profound value in the freedom that allows them to draw together all that inspires from any number of sources. To do so generates a pluralism that supports individual exploration; for Pagans seek to create not a religious structure but a deeply personal understanding of life and sanctity. Pagan diversity is thus increased by its very nature, like nature, each individual exploiting their natural curiosity, diving deep into their own vision and growth, and sharing that experience with those of their religious community.

While this degree of diversity is positively encouraged and celebrated within Paganism, it is not always helpful for those trying to grasp comprehension from the outside. And it is not just the theoretical exercise of finding a definition that provokes the search for common ground: many hope for a way of drawing the various traditions together in order to strengthen their position of representation. Working for social and political recognition, dealing with issues such as education, chaplaincy in hospitals and prisons, the treatment of the dead, appropriate care of ancient monuments and artefacts, it is useful to be able to stand with one voice before the benches of a nation's authority. So the task is ever to find the commonalities.

In this chapter, I shall present a definition of Pagan that I feel is both broad enough to be valid, while not compromising that inimitably wild spirit of Paganism in all its richness of idiosyncratic individuality. Finding the core threads, it isn't specific belief and practice I shall focus on, but the roots that have formed and nourished those threads, for my hope is to explore the ideas that have crafted Paganism into what it is today, and thus to understand how codes of behaviour might sit within it.

As each proponent puts forward ideas about what draws the various traditions into a coherent faith community, it is inevitable that within their definition they present their own hopes about what Paganism could or should be. Delving into the complications of Pagan diversity, acknowledging how the traditions found their way into the twenty first century, I am equally at risk of bias, at times this being well beneath my conscious awareness. However, towards the end of this chapter and into the next, that bias will become more obvious, as I make it clear where I choose to leave my own footprints upon its many pathways.

The Gods

The largest non-profit Pagan organization in Europe, the Pagan Federation, defines Paganism as 'a polytheistic or pantheistic nature-worshipping religion which incorporates beliefs and ritual practices from ancient traditions'. Those seeking to join are asked to agree with three basic principles of belief. These have changed over the years, the Federation remaining acutely aware that many cannot subscribe to the distinctions it has laid down. Currently the principles stand as: (1) love for and kinship with nature, reverence for the life force and its ever-renewing cycles of life and death; (2) a positive morality, in which the individual is responsible for the discovery and development of their true nature in harmony with the outer world and community; (3) recognition of the divine, which transcends gender, acknowledging both the female and male aspect of deity.

There are a good number of Pagans who are loathe to join the Federation simply because they prefer to remain uncounted, detached from any establishment even if the organization in question is wholly Pagan; as a distinctly Pagan disposition, this was clearly expressed in the last British population census (2001) when many refused to fill in the box on religion, or ridiculed the question by writing 'Jedi Knight'. However, there are many more who would or do join, but need to bend the words of the Federation's statements in order fully to agree. For myself, it is only the third that causes the problems: deity.

While a tradition such as Buddhism is acknowledged as a religion without a God or gods, when the belief and practice of a religious tradition does include deity it is most often the understanding and reverence for those gods that provides the foundational definition of the religion. This is not true of modern Paganism. The gods are not so easy to define, nor do they come in just one agreed conceptual or experiential form.

For many Pagans, countless of the many gods are the forces of nature: the winds that race through the valley, the valley itself crafted by mud and rock and water, the ancient rivers that flow across and beneath the land, the woodland and meadows, the sun that holds our planet in thrall, and so on. These are the most obvious of the gods, simply because we can perceive them through their physicality, their tangible creativity. Others are harder to see but no less easy to feel: still forces of nature, including human nature, these are anger and lust, hunger, regeneration, grief and change. Like hurricanes and earthquakes, most are clearly more powerful than humankind: at times we may learn how to ride the high seas of love or rage, but many are repeatedly (or indeed always) overwhelmed by such forces.

Other than those who embody the qualities of male and female, as currents of nature these deities have no gender - so do not need to transcend it. At times they may be ascribed a sex in the poetry of stories and prayer, and may even be clothed in some kind of human form; some

Pagans take this anthropomorphization as integral to their perception of the gods, allowing it to facilitate their interaction with powers that may be felt but otherwise have no obvious form. Others perceive this anthropomorphization as simplistic and distracting, preferring to see the gods in their own nonhuman, even abstract, forms.

Most Pagans also revere ancestral gods whose stories, however fragmentary their remains, link them to particular aspects of nature, such as the Irish solar goddess Grainne or the Cailleach of the Scottish Highlands. Most often they appear in vaguely human or animal casts, if sometimes as giants or elusively fey. Other Pagans venerate gods that come more easily into human form, for they have done so for a thousand years or more, not least the mythic heroes like Bran or Rhiannon from the Welsh medieval tales, or Black Annis who hums in the legends of the East Midlands. Raised to the status of deity, the humanity of these gods is a key part of their value, inspiring their devotees towards living more honourable lives.

The concepts of deity differ further because of individual attitudes towards these powers of nature. For example, though I tend to avoid the word *worship* because it implies submission, some use it easily and with pride for it expresses the absolute devotion inspired by a deep love for a particular deity. Although my gods are as merciless as nature, some feel connection with gods they believe truly love and care. Some Pagans are utterly bound to one particular god or pantheon, such as those of their home landscape or family, or through some storm of life experience; others are touched by many gods, offering prayers according to a deity's area of expertise, the time of year and their own situation. Furthermore, there are Pagans who are entirely animistic in their spirituality, perceiving the powers of nature as spirits and not gods at all. And perhaps the most baffling to me in terms of spiritual Paganism, some acknowledge the gods purely as human constructs, aspects of the human psyche and collected mythos.

Indeed, that Pagan deity is so hard to convey to one who has no personal experience further complicates. A Christian might describe his Abrahamic god as a force extant outside of nature, beyond the world in which we live, thus asserting that his deity is an objective reality. Though to the Pagan, acknowledging a force beyond nature seems irrational and irrelevant, to the monotheist Pagan deity can appear irrational. For Pagan deity is never super-natural; existing within nature, as nature, both human and nonhuman nature, the gods are the darkness, the vibrance, the hunger, that we not only witness around us but experience within us. The gods are the cry for justice, the tug of trade, the belly-kick of loss, the bond with the land and with kin that are relayed again and again in the tales of our people and heritage, tales we daily observe in others and feel inside ourselves. The Pagan understanding of deity is therefore *not* wholly objective; he may acknowledge the existence of any or all gods, but each Pagan's relationship with his gods is fuelled by his own critically subjective and visceral experience of those forces.

An understanding of deity, then, not only cannot provide a ready definition of Paganism, but exploring the ways in which Pagans view deity is a fundamental reason for its breadth of diversity. Nor can this variation be ordered neatly into the different traditions that exist beneath the umbrella of modern Paganism; for within each strand are individuals who perceive the gods in any of the above ways.

Though often duotheistic, honouring a Goddess and her divine consort, there are the many different forms of Wicca, from the Gardnerian of the 1940s and Alexandrian of the sixties, to the wholly feminist Dianic, the Faerie and Seax; there is traditional Witchcraft, hedgecraft and wombcraft, often animistic and polytheistic; there are the Heathen traditions derived from Norse, Germanic and Icelandic sources, with their various pantheons of gods; there is Druidry in its many forms, from the Neolithic-inspired shamanistic, through the myth-based Celtic and poetic, to the patriarchal and intellectual of the eighteenth century revival; there are British Paganisms based on the Classical mythology and pantheons of ancient Greece and Rome, on the Egyptian, Sumerian and Babylonian;

some Paganisms are clearly inspired by native American, Mayan and aboriginal antipodean; then there are the traditions that use Kabbala, Gnosticism, and various other sources of Semitic mysticism, medieval occult threads or chaos and quantum theories. The list goes on.

If the gods are no help, being more numerous than the stars, inside and around us, I turn my search for a definition towards the non-devotional aspects of Pagan religious expression in practice. Here too there is significant diversity; even where actions appear similar, such as the offering of a cup of wine to the moon, the underlying intentions may vary. Yet, in order to find sufficient clarity of context before looking at ethics, I shall describe what appear to me to be four distinct threads in modern Western Paganism.

Four Threads of Paganism

The first is the most obvious as seen from the outside, and one that has emerged out of the glamour of television and film. This is Paganism as fashion. Like smoking cigarettes, its principal market is teenage girls seeking identity and autonomy, and a market it is, for it has been nurtured and sculpted by TV shows, glossy magazines and the big commercial publishing houses. Increasingly it has been sustained by a regular supply of crass picture books, describing love charms and spells for dealing with homework, boyfriends and awkward parents, together with ideas about how to look like a 'real' Witch (wear black, buy a cat). Without any depth of spiritual focus, this is Paganism in colourful thick felt-tip pens. Having acknowledged its existence, I here lay it to one side and ask the reader to do the same.

The second, an authentic and ancient thread, is that of magic: many paths within Western Paganism hold the craft of magic as a defining and focal practice. The commonly accepted definition of magic is the ability to effect change by the power of our own will, and while (in my experience and observation) very few achieve the ability to make radical change, some do appear to alter the course of the present, pushing it down one current of potential rather than another. Indeed, even if or when they are not causing or gaining any actual shift, the focus on positivity, often shared within a gathering, is usually beneficial to all present.

Whether we are fighting for the life of one we love, or struggling under the tyranny of an autocratic fool, however real or imagined our situation may be, this belief that an individual can make a significant difference, in a society where individuals so often feel impotent, is an important feature of many Paganisms. There is no doubt that, for aeons, human beings have petitioned external forces for change; in Pagan magic, the understanding is that we ourselves can make the desired change by accessing the power within, or through invoking some external power that we can in some way direct or control.

The vast majority work their magic for what they believe to be the highest good, casting spells for healing, clarity, peace and the alleviation of poverty. Nevertheless, it is a practice based on personal empowerment and control, and the human psyche, fractured with insecurities, tends to bias its vision of what is right or necessary. As the Stoic philosopher Seneca stated in the first century of the Common Era, magic seems rather too much like giving orders to the gods. As such it is not central to all Pagans' practice.

The third thread is almost as old as magic: this is Paganism based upon the quest for knowledge and knowing. Another genuine and authentic thread, many find profound inspiration in the dedicated study of their forebears' writings, teachings and research, some pushing the edges of knowledge themselves. Where deep spiritual experience is hard to achieve, many affirm the validity of their path through extensive learning within a specific field of interest. History, archaeology and anthropology are all manoeuvred into place as foundation stones of spiritual under-standing, as are cultural studies, literature and language, mythology, sociology and any other colours within the landscape of our heritage. Indeed, some such Pagans are hard to extricate from the comfort of their library with its tidy lines of published words and apparent certainties. To the fourth thread getting stuck in a book is anathema.

This last thread of Paganism is clearly the oldest. It is the perspective that appears to be the most rudimentary, the most primitive and elemental, wholly unfettered by justification. Here the core focus is the spiritual power of nature, and spiritual or religious practice requires one simply and physically to get out there, to dance in the wind and rain, with muddy boots, an open heart, a cold nose, and an eagerness to feel.

In reality and entirely in tune with the nature of Paganism, most plait their own combinations of these three (or four, if we include the insubstantial thread of fashion), crafting their own patterns in colour, language and understanding, using only those sources that inspire and make sense to them personally.

Indeed, it is in both the weave of threads, and in their most basic qualities, that we find the common elements within the many different traditions. The essential and idiosyncratic nature of creativity, the underlying importance of community, the acknowledgement of the power of human nature and of nature's forces outside humanity, the necessity and depth of our facility to understand, to choose and to act, and our awareness of just how our actions affect the world around us: all these are not side issues but fundamental to modern Paganism.

To appreciate more fully why, we must look more carefully at its roots.

The Roots

The strongest claim for continuity between ancient or pre-Christian Paganism and current practice is in this fourth thread, woven as it usually is into the cloth of the tradition, as a profound and religious acknowledgement of the power of nature. Providing an underlying stability, this stabilizing root found its form in our ancestors' quest to understand the forces of the natural world that appeared to control them. Even to the most cynical atheist, it is easy to imagine how our ancestors first spoke of the spirits and gods of nature, needing to find comprehension, observing patterns as they emerged, perceiving a sentience in the forces that pushed and twisted their lives, using their own language to bestow them with characteristics and human emotions they could understand. It takes a very strong and determined individual not to do the same when placed in a desperate situation.

We may now use poetic terms to describe the wind's curiosity, the mountain's gloom, the hunger of a plague, the rage of a river's flood, but removing the poetry and, with it, any human projection or anthropomorphization, it is still possible to suspect a pattern exists that, if understood, could help us avoid further struggle. This quest for reason seems to me the most natural craving of humanity, nor has that desire to understand lessened. In our Western culture, the intricate search for pattern is now the work of scientists, the need to control is crafted by our engineers, and the charge of portraying the enormity of the task is taken up writers, poets and film makers. Five thousand years ago, the exploration of the powers of nature was the vocation of the priest.

Our society still delegates its need for answers to the limited few who can do the work for us, and this is as true within modern Paganism as it was in the past: each individual is encouraged to find their own specialist interests and skills, then to feed that insight back into the community as a whole. To modern Pagans, the work is still sacred. Holding central the importance of crafting sustainable and respectful relationship with every aspect of the world, the traditions still ascribe sanctity to the task of understanding the power and patterns of nature.

This quest is crucial to all traditions within modern Paganism. As a central part of my own spirituality, and a tap root of *Pagan*, to a great extent it will be the core current and indeed the inherent bias of this book. However, first it is necessary to explore more recent influences. For while that tap root gives the most stability of continuity, there are many other roots that have nourished and shaped modern Paganism, roots that must be acknowledged before we can turn to explore the notion of a Pagan ethics.

Like shifting sands, assumptions that underlie a culture change as it moves through time. The change can happen so slowly it is hard to perceive, individual minds adjusting, children accepting and rejecting their parents' paradigms, understanding and disseminating ideas and assumptions, a sand dune moving grain by grain in the winds of change. After a while, if we are able to compare the present with past horizons, we can see the contours of the landscape are entirely different. The same is true of human consciousness: the essence is the same, but the position is new.

Spreading that notion over the landscape of many centuries of human culture, we can see how that craving to deal with the forces of nature has brought about the various religious and philosophical standpoints that now turn towards each other, creating the sometimes uneasy coherence of the modern Pagan community.

The Witch

One of the most prominent of those standpoints is the archetypal concept of the 'witch'.

~ ~ ~

With her arm above the fire, her fist clenched tight, she moves it in circles as if stirring a great cauldron, her eyes closed in the trance, her body swaying to the music that fills her soul, as she breathes deeply, whispering the chant to the thumping rhythm of her heart and her feet, at times hearing her own voice lift out of the murmuring into a cry that shrieks with the wind and the rooks in the trees. Another hand clutches hers, and then the third on the top, as all three women find their way to that very moment in time, slipping into the same current, catching the same rhythm, stirring the ethereal black pot that sits upon the fire, brewing and bubbling up their desire.

From a distance, for periods, they seem utterly silent, swaying and stirring, three women around a fire in the centre of an ancient circle of stones. Then into the night, one voice then another rises up like a flurry of leaves in the wind, stirring up a cyclone, leaving a chill in the air, before falling back down into the quiet hum of affirmation, and then slipping softly into stillness. And sometimes the noise is laughter, wild and free, and sometimes their voices cut the air with grief, like the keening of an old yet still brutal storm.

The fire catches at a log and blazes with light, casting long shadows of their dancing across the sheep-shorn grass. As slowly it softens to a reddening glow, one by one they raise their arms to the indigo skies. And a single voice sings to the beauty of the stars.

~ ~ ~

Though many play with the guise and props of the broomstick and black cat, it is the more grounded if idealized image of the village wise one that the serious Pagan is more likely to reach for. Well versed in herbal medicine, living perhaps on the edge of society, this old man or woman worked for the benefit of others, using trickery and facilitating positive change with the currency of superstition, naiveté and the ongoing fear of the power of nature. Still integrated with nature's tides, deeply attuned to and able to communicate with the wild, this enigmatic figure carried an ancient knowledge, one that had been held by the priests of a time long before 'civilization' and technology divorced humanity from nature.

Holding precious such an archetype, it is easy to imagine how the dogmatic ignorance of ruling authorities - the patriarchy of the Roman Empire or Christianity - could be blamed for the tradition's demise. In reality, the picture is not so clean. Such people were not uncommon, and generally very much more human than the image implies. Often known as the cunning folk, they used their vision and magic to help the community, albeit seldom through altruism but as a profitable local enterprise. While many were no doubt wholly invaluable members of a community, not all were willingly helpful; for centuries, many such folk ran what would now be called protection rackets, bleeding money and other resources from locals in return for *not* laying curses on their lives and livelihood. Whether bartering in spells or hexes, witches and sorcerers depended upon the same gullible communities, and their superstitions and fears.

I doubt, nonetheless, whether the Church was hell-bent on their annihilation. Having myself grown up in the majority world of less developed countries, I witnessed local traditions happy to accept Jesus and his band of holy saints on the simple basis that, as spirits, they may have some useful power and be susceptible to the odd bribe or sacrifice. I suspect most cunning folk did the same, and through long periods of the history of our Western culture.

Of course, with laws against blasphemy, should an individual become troublesome to his or her neighbours, or step on the wrong side of someone in authority, it is always possible to use such laws to have them removed from a community, or even killed. Yet Christianity was not the active and long-term aggressor against natural magic that many like to imagine. As important were the shifting sands of human understanding that were changing social perspectives. Ground roots preaching of religious attitudes is an effective way of drip-feeding ideas into any community, but most compelling where people are struggling and in need of hope and change; so did Christianity spread through these islands of Britain, out on the edge of the world. Adding to the mix were the radical ideas and technologies flowing into medieval Europe from the Moslem east, together with the new science that began emerging from the fourteenth century, all of which were contributing to the changing contours of our basic understanding. The demise of the old village witch, then, is most poignantly expressed in the change made to British law in 1736, when legislation against witchcraft was altered to address anyone *claiming* to practise magic: it was no longer widely accepted that such things were real. The sands had changed.

To the modern Pagan Witch, the image of the old cunning man or woman is nonetheless an important one. It remains the key archetype of natural magic, mystical power and community care. It is an image of independence and empowerment, and one of the many roots that continue to nourish the body of modern Paganism.

The Thinker

If the witch, the old cunning one, reflects the strand of magic within Paganism, one that more closely associates with the quest for knowledge is an equally important strand of our heritage. The practice of magic can ease a sense of impotence in a complicated world; the accumulation of knowledge promises to do the same.

By the end of the sixteenth century, literacy was spreading through Europe, the dissemination of ideas hastening the speed of change, and close upon its heels came the broader thinking and innovative courage that brought about the industrial revolution. Yet as the smog grew thicker, vast areas of landscape covered with smoking factories, mills and quarries, bringing the filth of crowded urban living and treacherous working conditions, so came the Romantic movement of poets and thinkers, writing of the exquisite beauty, power, serenity and purity of nature unsoiled by human need and greed. Advocating freedom of the individual through nostalgia for a perfect past, writers such as Blake, Shelley, Wordsworth and Coleridge, Goethe and Schiller also contributed to the shifting contours of human understanding. Wordsworth's lines expressed beautifully this sense of a human world now 'out of tune' with nature, for when nature 'moves us not. - Great God! I'd rather be / A Pagan suckled in a creed outworn; / So might I, standing on this pleasant lea, / Have glimpses that would make me less forlorn'.

Though socially perhaps a long way from the village witch, with the luxury of education and the leisure to write, the Romantics called for a deeper connection with the essence of nature, in the belief that it might provide a critically needed sense of healing. Their words rode a powerful swell of counter-culturalism, rejecting the voracity and pollution of industry and urbanization, reaching for new concepts of value, sanctity and morality, and as such their sentiments fed clearly into modern Pagan thought.

Writing through the turbulence of the late seventeenth century and the English civil war, the philosopher, John Locke is another influence that nourished the roots of modern Paganism. Locke was an extraordinary thinker for his time. His notions of democracy led England to become one of the most liberal countries of the following century, and are credited as a key source of inspiration for the American Constitution. Shifting the sands of assumption, with his then radical notion that nobody is superior at birth, that each life's path is dependent solely on education and opportunities, he influenced writers such as Rousseau and Voltaire, pushing forward the thinking that allowed the French Revolution and inspiring those that followed across Europe in the middle of the nineteenth century.

European adventurers, many no more than pirates commissioned by royal houses, journeyed out to discover (and plunder) new lands and tribal peoples, inspiring the concept of Europe's own noble heritage of nature-loving primitives. In Britain, the idea of a precious ancient inheritance was carefully constructed, much of this concurrent with a renewed interest in folklore. Traditions were sought out, revived or reinvented. From within a newly educated social class sprang an enthusiasm for European medieval mythologies and poetry, and for Classical literature, with old writings being translated, published and made available for the first time. Figures such as the Welsh stonemason, Iolo Morganwg, presented their own beautifully crafted bardic writings as if they too were of some ancient origin, writings that inspired the Welsh Gorsedd and significant roots of modern Druidry.

The Golden Bough, written at the end of the nineteenth century by folklorist and anthropologist James Frazer, was another force of counter-cultural thought whose influence can still be seen in modern Paganism. Aiming to diminish the core myth of Christianity, his book explored the notion of the death and resurrection of the sacrificed god, expounding the concept of regeneration as a part of nature's cycles. Frazer's poetic vision spoke of the re-birthed vegetation god growing into his prime, rising up in glory each year to be cut down once again. This vision of the cyclicity of nature, particularly within the temperate European climate, is now one of the strongest in most Western Pagan traditions.

Contemporary with the Romantics and the liberal revolution, another product of urbanization and the growing middle class was developing, and one that can also be seen as a root that influenced modern Paganism: the craftsmen's' guilds.

Coming to prominence with the increase in work, the guilds tended to be aggressively exclusive, determinedly protecting the secrets of their trade. Lodges, set up to house those working away from home, became meeting places of guild members and, while some were clearly no more than working men's drinking clubs with theatrical and pretentious names, others met in all seriousness, sharing philosophical and alchemical insights. The origins of these secret societies are widely debated even now, some claims reaching back through medieval mysticism and magical occultism, and from there into Classical philosophy and Egyptian sorcery. It was from this source that Freemasonry emerged in the early eighteenth century, together with a branch of Druidry based on Nonconformist Christianity. Another strand still feeds into some elements of modern Paganism: the magickal occultism of figures such as Eliphas Levi, Samuel MacGregor Mathers and Aleister Crowley.

Focusing on mental discipline, the power of human will, harnessing the force of desire, invoking and controlling spirits, entities, daemons, ancient gods and embodiments of energy, the corpus of learning built up by some occultists is both extensive and impressive. Indeed, from the time of the Renaissance in Europe magical tomes were being written, offering an alternative to the power of the Christian Church. The thirteenth century astrologer and mathematician Michael Scot wrote of how to bring into subservience 'fallen angels' that they might do one's bidding, emphasizing the need for the magician to remain pure in his belief in God and goodness.

As Seneca too perceived, the focus on control seems to me a long way from religious Paganism. However, there is here both a fundamental acceptance and significant exploration of nature's power, particularly that of human nature. Furthermore, some trace these roots back to the natural philosophers of ancient Druidry, and their magick is undeniably entangled with that of the cunning folk of our more recent past.

Wicca, sometimes called modern Witchcraft, is in many ways a clear amalgam of the influences upon modern Paganism. Developed in the late 1940s by retired civil servant Gerald Gardner, his religion of the Witches was the first expression of religious practice to claim the term 'Pagan'. Taking elements of the esoteric seership and magick developed within the nineteenth century secret societies such as the Golden Dawn, it mixed them with the muddier craft of the cunning folk, with their herbalism, spells and astrology, creating a richly potent brew. It drew too on the Romantics' image of nature as a mother goddess, together with Pan, the mischievous Roman deity of nature's fecundity. Adding to Gardner's vision, in 1948 poet and novelist Robert Graves published his classic work, *The White Goddess*, a profoundly influential book on the path of Wicca and modern Paganism, bringing to its core the concept of goddess as moon: the waxing maiden, the fullness of mother and the waning sharp crescent of the darker crone.

Embracing the social changes of the last sixty years, as a blend of fertility religion and the occultic focus on personal power, the duotheism of Wicca's triple goddess and horned god was further influenced by the radical feminism that emerged from west coast America in the 1970s. Writers such as Andrea Dworkin, like discredited academic Margaret Murray writing forty years earlier, reinterpreted sources such as the medieval witch trials and papers on archaeological research in order to declare Witchcraft a surviving expression of ancient female power and suppression. So did Wicca take on board the weight of a persecution crisis that was far deeper than the pressure of ridicule and scandal mongering it had been under for the previous score of years since Gardner's first coven hit the tabloid press. Attracted by the idea crafted by these writers of a great mother goddess who had been widely worshipped throughout prehistory, many were drawn to Wicca and wombcraft spiritualities (the spread of women's mystery traditions). Thankfully, both the delusion of a golden matriarchal age and its attendant victim consciousness has lifted a little over the past decade, allowing Wicca to find its feet more securely. The ideas have, however, left their mark on its focus and practice.

The Druid

Druidry of recent times has not suffered persecution in the way that Wicca and Witchcraft have. If we are seeking out persecution, the stories take us back much further.

When Vespasian first drew the force of his armies across the British Isles almost two thousand years ago, bringing with him the conquering rule of the Roman Empire, many Druids believed it would be beneficial to all if they were simply to co-operate. Rome appeared, after all, to be offering a wealth of new technologies, philosophies and opportunities. Needless to say, any Briton, including the Druids, who refused to relinquish their autonomy were slaughtered. It wasn't, however, the Druid religion or philosophy that the Romans objected to. It was their comprehensive hold on social and political power, and that was exactly what the Romans desired. Where necessary they seized violently, together with the economic control that came with it.

As a social framework, Druidry was indeed destroyed, but the basic philosophy was not lost. Retaining a hold in the bardic colleges, in the farthest reaches of the islands not brought under Roman law, in centuries of folklore, music and mythology, in the cunning craft of the working masses, and perhaps most poignantly in the continuing study of natural philosophy and law, Druidry remained alive. For many in the tradition today, Druidry is the expression of the quintessential spirit of Britain and the British, and that (we like to think) could never be destroyed.

Some perceive Druidry to have been a European Iron Age import, a temporary resident in Britain for little more than 500 years, which quickly died under Roman occupation, only finding its rebirth within the patriarchal revival of the eighteenth century. However, to dismiss the centuries between the Roman conquest and this revival, particularly the history and mythology of the later medieval centuries, is to do the tradition a disservice; what happened in the 1700s was entirely an accumulation of all that had been building before.

Fully embraced by its context of that century's Enlightenment, banked by the Romantics' quest for nature's perfect soul and the philosophers' search for perfect reason, the Druid revival was based upon the belief that clear and critical thinking would release society from the darkness of ignorance. As America fought for its independence and France imploded into the civil war of revolution, Druid Orders emerged in Britain, proliferating throughout an age that seemed to thrive on secret societies and esoteric learning. Questing the most accurate and intimate comprehension of the natural world, Druidry focused on finding sources of wisdom in every quarter.

Druidry was particularly inspired by tales from and travels through the growing British Empire and was fully involved in the desire for an idealized ancient past. As Scotland, Wales and Ireland asserted their political importance, mythologies and old poetry becoming more readily accessible, the notion of the wild and perpetually oppressed Celt found its feet and started the glorious march it continues to this day.

Meanwhile in England, a romantic vision of the ancient Druid was crafted. Wearing pure white robes, he was a priest of the light, worshipping the sun and preparing for the coming of the son of light. Fundamentally monotheistic, acknowledging a single creative force that was believed to underlie all religions of the world (and culminating in the perfection of Christianity), Druidry of this period gradually lost its momentum. By the twentieth century it was running out of steam. Pockets of the tradition continued in Britain and Ireland, energized by the social changes that also fed into Wicca, but it wasn't until the late 1980s that it once again found its popularity more broadly.

Appearing in a vision to one of his former students, Philip Carr Gomm, the Druid Ross Nicols instructed him to restore the Order that had passed into hibernation upon his death in the mid 70s. This time, he advised, the Order should address the key issues of the day: the spiritual desire to reconnect with nature. So did Carr Gomm recreate the Order of Bards, Ovates and Druids, a gentle and conservative organization that disseminated gems of inspiration in the form a correspondence course to what became a rapidly growing membership. Inspired by its presence, directly and indirectly, smaller groups and individuals found their Druidic feet, some walking the road of serious monotheistic mysticism, and others - like myself - exploring the wilder paths of shamanistic animism.

Whether Druidic practice is formal and meditative, or based upon trance and ecstatic spiritual connection, or anything in between, the influence of the Enlightenment remains, albeit with a postmodernist dose of retrospective scepticism and balance. Guiding its focus, holding the sanctity of learning and the creativity of passion, Druidry is still a tradition based upon the personal quest for the power of reason and the patterns of nature.

As is the case in many Pagan traditions, its focus of honouring nature includes the forces of human nature. In Druidry, that is most poetically expressed through the love of history, mythology, folklore and heritage: the stories of our land and our people.

~ ~ ~

In the soft light of dusk, her fingers seem barely to touch the strings, moving as if caressing the warm skin of a lover. But her words are not gentle, and neither is her voice, for the tale she tells is one of ordinary complacency, brutally cut short by the violence of waking, and at times she talks in a hurried flood of sharp-edged words, and at times she lifts her voice into song, dancing through notes in the old Gaelic, telling of warnings, of wisdom and wonder. And as each word spills from her mouth, she glows like a fire burning low, surrounded not just by the gathering of students, but also by the presence of the ancestors, whispering through her memories, reminding her that in one way or another this tale has been told before, thousands of times, over thousands of years.

A storm lantern spreads a pool of light onto the grass, flickering warmth over the faces of those listening, and though some are wide-eyed as young children, in others it is obvious they are feeling the current. Their faces in the stillness of trance, they hold to the tale, as its flow of blood and heritage surges through the moment, carrying them on, watching as she scatters, like petals into a river, the sounds, the words and music, her offerings to the gods.

~ ~ ~

It was Ross Nichols, meditating upon all these roots of modern Paganism, who developed the idea of a wheel of eight festivals. Taking archaeological and folkloric evidence from around the islands of Britain and Ireland, he divided the year into a discipline of five to seven week-long chunks, based around the solar and pastoral/agricultural cycles. When his vision was rejected by the elders of the Druid Order who then celebrated only the two equinoxes and summer solstice, Nichols showed it to his friend, Gerald Gardner, who readily adopted it as a key part of the Wiccan religion he was creating. When Nichols left the old Order to found his own, he took this mandala of festivals with him, integrating it into his Druidry in the last decade of his life.

While clearly our ancestors would not have had the resources to celebrate so frequently, the majority of Pagans now hold to Nichols' idea as useful, perhaps essential, and wholly relevant to modern life. Each of the eight festivals provides the pause of a day or two in the midst of a busy world, securing time for us to remember the values of our religious traditions, to re-inspire our creativity, to make offerings and deepen our spiritual relationships. And in an era where the seasons are not so harshly felt, Pagans use the time to realign themselves to the cycles of nature, ensuring they are not pushing against the tide but moving in harmony with its currents of emergence and recession, warmth and cold, regeneration and decay.

The Heathen

One exception to those celebrating eight festivals is a wide swathe of the Heathen community of Nordic and Anglo Saxon Pagans. Looking to the wealth of Germanic heritage, and its spread into Scandinavia and other parts of western Europe throughout the first millennium of the common era, the greatest source of its modern reconstruction comes from the writings of Christian monks in the early medieval period. These local converts, reading the Latin literature of Rome, recognized the value of writing down their own history and mythology, stories which were a part of the oral traditions of the bands of Vikings and Saxons that drifted across Europe, pillaging and settling. Had they not been entrusted to ink, the tales would undoubtedly have been lost; indeed, much of Western heritage was saved in just the same way.

Although Heathens have generally kept themselves separate from the wider Pagan community, the revival of their tradition, forged through the twentieth century, has brought a couple of important influences to modern practice, albeit indirectly. The first is their undiluted polytheism.

In the eighteenth century, the much loved English philosopher, David Hume, stated that the shift from polytheism to monotheism was a natural flow of evolution, and Druidry of the Enlightenment explored this idea to its fullness. The loss of true polytheism globally is poignantly evident in modern Hindu theology, one of the last broad bastions of global Paganism. Indeed, while the vast majority of Western Pagans acknowledge the existence of numerous gods, upon the drifting sands of human consciousness this perspective is sometimes now based upon an underlying assumption that all gods are different facets of one creative force. As the Wiccan writer Vivianne Crowley states, those of her own tradition recognize that 'all Gods are different aspects of the one God and all Goddesses are different aspects of the one Goddess, and that ultimately these two are reconciled in the one divine essence'. Even where Egyptian and Classical gods are revered, the concept of deity is not always that of independent and powerful beings, busy with their own lives. Within Heathenism, however, we find a fully and uncompromisingly polytheist theology.

Polytheism is fundamental within my own animistic religious tradition, and I consider its loss to be profound. The current that dismisses it is one of sophistication, a word which to me is entirely derogatory, originating from the Latin *sophisticare*, meaning to tamper with: to use an old English word, the idea of polytheism was *whittled* down until it became meaningless and was discarded. Indeed, much of modern Paganism has been reluctant to embrace this understanding. Yet true polytheism has evolved into a theology that can comfortably sit within the contours of twenty first century human understanding. Most crucially perhaps, a ramification of the polytheistic perspective is that human beings are neither central nor important to the gods, nor indeed to nature as a whole; they are ideas poignant to what I shall come to describe as Pagan ethics.

The second important Heathen influence is the Anglo-Saxon concept of *wyrd*. The word is derived from *weorpan*, which has no exact translation in modern English; it means to become, yet is held within the notion of nature's ever-turning cycles, thus the term implies the process of constant emergence, transformation, death and rebirth. As such, it brings Frazer's image of the cyclicity of nature into the soul of each individual.

Offering a sense of connection through time, it is extended by the idea of the *web* of wyrd, most popularly presented by the English writer and academic, Brian Bates, in the 1980s: in the flow that is the perpetual process of nature's changing state, everything is constantly affecting everything. Nothing is separate. Every thought, every action, vibrates through the web. Taken by some as a powerful insight into magic, by others simply as an expression of true nature, it has quickly became a core concept within much modern Pagan thought.

Nature Religion

In as much as is feasible within the limits of the space allowed, through the preceding pages I have described the main roots nourishing and influencing the formation of what is now modern Paganism. I shall end this chapter, though, with a note about one more: the Native American.

While some indigenous peoples in the Americas have sought to protect their heritage by isolating it from non-Native blood and cultural influence, many have done the opposite. Admitting how few individuals can now claim undiluted blood, and acknowledging just how much has been lost and destroyed, some Native Americans are keenly sharing what they do have left. Indeed, as can be seen in so many minority cultures, the realization is slowly being accepted in some quarters that the outsiders are often more interested in their language and traditions than their own younger generations.

Furthermore, at times both tribal elders and isolated youngsters have studied Western Pagan heritage and its modern revivals and reconstructions in order to extend and enrich their understanding of their own people's spirituality: to reconstruct what they too have lost. This is not confined to north America, but is also happening in other aboriginal cultures, including those of Australasia, southern and west Africa, south east Asia, south America, and the Arctic circle.

When such sharing has been rich with mutual consent, with respect given for both common ground and significant differences, and interaction achieved without the caustic antagonism of defensive assumptions, the exchange has been enormously valuable. Giving Native people the sense of a broader appreciation for their unique vision and wisdom, it has also provided Western Paganism with another source of understanding.

Although many indigenous nations are primarily preoccupied with the social problems provoked by their decimation and dislocation, perhaps their most potent influence on Western Paganism has been through the urgency with which they express their loss of landscape and heritage. This has touched white European culture, and particularly the Pagan community, primarily in a very simple way: by waking many to a visceral grief about environmental devastation. Indeed, just as environmental issues blazed through the eighteenth century, so are they once again profoundly affecting the sands of human understanding, the idealized image of the Native American spreading through the New Age and Pagan communities, provoking for a while in the late twentieth century the emergence of what was known as the 'wannabe Indian'.

Beginning in the 1960s and finding its momentum by the late 80s, the rapid growth in modern Paganism has been in itself a response to what are now global environmental crises. Many who have only recently come to Paganism perceive their tradition as being - and as always having been - wholly a nature religion.

In Europe, the influence of Native American culture is indirect, but its imagery is powerful. Within the Pagan community, the growing abhorrence and frustration generated by the seeping imperialism of American consumerism, with its plastic, bland and soulless culture provokes an increasingly urgent need to hold onto our own heritage, to explore what we have, to cherish our ancestry. The black and white photographs of the age-wrinkled American Indian that are so often seen, his face worn by sun and wind, yet somehow emptied by so much grief and bewilderment, provide an added impetus to protect ourselves from that dreadful flooding tide of Wal-Mart and Disney.

In the following chapters I shall look more fully at these qualities within Paganism, those inspired by what is effectively a profoundly devoted love of nature. It is this devotion that seems to me to lie at the core of our ancient religious traditions; not as a romantic projection of what nature should be, but a perception enriched with learning, rent wide open with wonder and the appreciation that comes where there is no complacency, acknowledging both the beauty and the brutality of its power. This is nature beloved by Pagans. This is my religion, as a Druid and Pagan.

So does the bias of this book veer towards this perspective. Consequently, inevitably, I am perpetually at risk of implying that these views are shared by all Pagans, that they define Paganism *completely*.

Having carefully explained the wealth of diversity within Paganism, both in its practice and its roots, as a key thread throughout this chapter, I do not wish to compromise or dilute that by the reader at any time sensing that I am speaking for all Pagans. Though I could once again emphasize that I do not and cannot, another half dozen pages won't have passed before the risk rises again. I choose then, instead, to use a trick well employed by many philosophers: I shall minutely bend our language by creating a new term.

Wherever I am referring to a Paganism that is deeply rooted in, informed by and expressed through this devotional reverence for nature, for landscape and ancestry, in as much as I understand it, I shall use instead the word *Pagan. It is *Paganism that flows as an undercurrent throughout the coming chapter.

CHAPTER TWO

NATURAL PAGANISM

Looking over the forest, three worlds are perceived :
a source of wood for the fire, a place to hide,
and a temple in which to celebrate life.

Autonomy

Even acknowledging its many diverse threads, there is one significant attitude that draws modern Pagans together: the unwillingness to accept without question society's norms. No wonder it has been, and to some still is, considered a threat. Not only are the ideals and values of convention doubted but also, throughout Paganism, and *Paganism in particular, there is a persistent unwillingness to abdicate the freedom and privacy of personal autonomy.

Throughout history, as the centralized political authority of monotheisms and secular autocracies has seeped down to affect day to day living, there have always been swathes of society strident in their opposition. Just as these forces of counter-culturalism nurtured the roots of modern Paganism, so do they still: Paganism thrives on a vision that is most often opposed to the easy assumptions accepted by society and propagated by the ruling authority.

We may now be gently stepping away from the eighteenth century Romantics' nostalgia and idealization, but their cry against the use and abuse of the environment still feeds the tap root of modern Paganism. The destruction of life in the name of 'progress' - itself perhaps the most idealized myth - is still held to be wholly unacceptable. Then as now, the rebel cry of environmentalism equally rejects the capitalist culture of rapacious growth, yet society is pervaded by its belief in the need for such growth. As the Romantics did before, so does *Paganism continue to push towards the radical, working to shift the sands of human assumption.

An immediate example is acknowledgement of the spirits of landscapes, rivers, trees and nonhuman animals. Such notions are dismissed as primitive and superstitious, both monotheistic and secular authorities refusing to accept them as valid spiritual perceptions of value, even though they have been held by ancient cultures for millennia. It is not simply semantics. To cherish *all* life is restrictive, disallowing the consumption of nature as a resource, so limiting the wealth and power of those who would claim to own it, or to 'have dominion over' it.

The difference in attitude is not just about utility. Nature is not easy, or tidy or safe. While the desire to reduce the threat is perfectly under-standable, to wish to control it is, to the *Pagan, nonsensical. Yet the belief that we can, or should be able to, is another that saturates our Western world. As we stride into the twenty first century, again and again society turns to question why there isn't sufficient order and control: an earthquake or virus devastates a population and people ask who is to blame for failing to avert tragedy, failing to establish or retain enough power over nature.

After Hurricane Katrina flooded New Orleans, the authorities were declared culpable. Yet the city was built upon a floodplain and a delusion that humankind was powerful enough to tame the old Mississippi. It clearly wasn't. The river goddess rose to dance with the wind, reclaiming her ancient territory, as she will no doubt do again. Nature is both beautiful and brutal.

Following the December 2004 tsunami, a BBC radio programme debated what kind of god would allow such devastation and suffering. The answer is, of course, a *Pagan god: or rather, a gathering of *Pagan gods, of earth and sea and sky. Nature is not merciful. It is not just or compassionate.

The *Pagan acceptance of nature's destructive power is not about resignation, but reverence. Our human attempt to control nature is most often futile and, in its ignorance and clumsy defensiveness, always irreverent. Yet neither is there sense in the act of submitting to nature's power: when we submit to the ocean we drown, to the fire we burn, to anger we suffer from the consequences of our violence. Submission is self-negation.

Instead, the *Pagan's focus is always upon crafting a sustainable relationship with nature. Instead of drowning in the sea, or trying to hold back the tide, we learn to swim with its currents. We listen to what nature suggests is feasible and, when knowingly we push against that, wanting a little more, we don't complain or look for someone to blame when nature comes crashing in.

Crafting relationship is a task often guided by watching and learning to work with nature's patterns and cycles - all of them. So are a great many Pagans students of anthropology, sociology, philosophy, mathematics and the sciences, seeking out those patterns, watching the currents of the gods in molecules and winds, in populations and beliefs.

Nor is there any sense in judging some patterns acceptable, a part of some divine creator's plan, while discarding others as worthless: nature doesn't compartmentalise. Everything is connected. Yet measurable correlations between illness, drugs, violence, diet and environment, are determinedly ignored by a secular society that declares it has a right to easy living. Patterns in climate and animal behaviour, clearly observed by scientists, are dismissed as restrictive to the march of progress and our human 'God-given freedom'. To the *Pagan, personal autonomy means the freedom to live with nature, not free from it.

An understanding of the sun's cycles and the physical power of light has been central to almost every political force throughout time, not least the Neolithic priests who designed temples such as Stonehenge and New Grange, and those of the medieval Christian Church who sought to control the calendar. Western society now takes light for granted, complacent that the authorities will provide the necessary electricity. Access to light, day and night, is now considered by most a human right.

To the *Pagan, that is ludicrous. More consciously aware of the power of light, and all that it allows, *darkness* is a profoundly potent word. It speaks of all that is hard to understand within nature, the infinite space of the universe, the energy of the night, of winter, of release and death, of decay and entropy. There are here no connotations of negativity; darkness is that which necessarily balances and embraces light. It contains those aspects of nature that are not known or not knowable, the void and the density, the mysteries beyond our human consciousness, the world beyond current comprehension. The word expresses all that could happen; in the poetry of *Paganism, it is the cauldron of potential, the womb of rebirth, the rich mud in which the seed germinates.

To venture into this uncomfortable territory is encouraged in *Paganism. For to take our spiritual, emotional and rational quest into landscapes we have not explored is to extend the bounds of our consciousness, either with knowledge gained or simply with rich and true experience of life. Not to do so is considered to live with eyes half open and just half a lung for breath.

More often than not, something tries to hold us back. It may be our own fear of the dark or the unknown, deep animal instincts of caution, or childish beliefs and superstitions. Yet, usually that fear is also nurtured and supported by social convention. Through friends, family, colleagues, the media, a tide of human concern arises to block the way, the flood of emotion washing all around. The collective mind we call society does all it can to hold back the force of change, remaining within the safety of the familiar.

Yet, what has drawn an individual into a Pagan tradition is often precisely this need to find a place that is centred, strong and supportive, which is *not* within the heart of ordinary life. Having failed to gain peace and well-being in the conventional world, their quest is to find and ride a current that celebrates change, and often radical change. Integral to Paganism, then, is a rejection of any construct of authority that would hinder that current. In fact, to most Pagans, the very idea of authority is antipathetic to their spiritual philosophy; once again, autonomy is so important.

Of course, not all radical discovery and change is achieved or utilized without selfishness. There is testament to that in all reaches of human society (not least governments and their military). It is here that Paganism is accused of or confused with Satanism.

Being a Christian concept, it is not theologically possible for a Pagan to be a Satanist. Yet it is easy to see how the perceived threat of a counter-cultural force, working with images and energies of darkness and personal empowerment, can be perceived as Satanic, and particularly by those holding to a hierarchical monotheistic theology based on a metaphor of light, believing in an embodiment of evil. To those who hold authority and are keen to maintain the social *status quo*, any such force would be, at least, an irritation.

Among those dissatisfied with a culture, there always have been and always will be some who rebel through rage without reason, without responsibility or functional relationship. When adolescent anger and impotence provokes such selfishness, to spit back at society by calling oneself a Satanist is icing your cake of rebellious behaviour. But it is not Paganism.

~ ~ ~

I close my book, reluctantly accepting that I can no longer read, and, looking up at the lamp, I sigh. Stiff from sitting for too long in one position, deep in my reading, I stretch and yawn, getting to my feet. But instead of heading to the lamp, I push open the French windows and step out into the garden.

The skies to the west are awash with orange, the horizon still golden where the sun has just set, clouds absorbing the colours and spreading them far out above the landscape. A smile breaks through me, and I whisper a prayer of thanks to the gods before and above me, bowing in acknowledgement, feeling myself a part of another day done and the beauty of its ending. I climb onto the low stone wall, listening to the last of the rooks settling in the forest. A toad croaks somewhere by the pond.

And I watch, opening my soul to the words of my prayers, softly sung to the gods of the night as they come, aware of my perception as it changes, and I smile, knowing that I have no way of explaining what it is that I see, other than through the broad brushstrokes of theology and poetry. For as the twilight softens, the sun's glow dwindling, the world seems to relax, released from the order of light in its straight lines. The molecules of the air seem to wriggle, stretching, waking. The darker it becomes, the more freedom I can perceive. Is there more space and ease between and within all I see, or simply that my mind needs less to identify everything as separate, as tree and gate and blade of grass ... My soul's answer is simple: a little of both. The world has begun its night-time exhalation, and is gently, quietly, falling apart, letting go. If dawn comes in time, form will be reclaimed. Until then, we dance the dance of life's release.

I breathe in deeply, breathing in the dark.

~ ~ ~

Anarchy and Heresy

Pagan: the word comes from the Latin *pagus*, a village or rural community, but my sense of its importance, used to define a spirituality, is in relation to this issue of authority. The *paganus*, the villager, was neither *miles* (soldier), nor *cives* (citizen). The hierarchy of the Roman army is legendary, a very human power filtered down through an established pattern of authority; the *cives*, as a part of the wealth and culture of the city state, looked to the state government for authority, living according to its laws. The *paganus*, however, dependent on the mud and rain of nature for his livelihood and security, held nature as the highest authority.

In our modern world, it is still nature the *Pagan looks to for guidance. Yet this is not a hierarchy of power. I am not seeking nature's laws that I might worship and submit. My quest is to understand the cycles and tides, that I might live in sustained harmony, not fighting the forces that flow through and around me, but riding their currents that we might live together.

In most English dictionaries, the word *pagan* denotes a person who is not a member of a Semitic-based religion. The idea of authority still saturates the definition. Seeking the origin of the English word, as distinct from its Latin context, we look back to the collapse of Rome and the rise of the Holy Roman Empire. A *pagan* was an individual who was not one of the *miles*, this soldier being one of the imperial army of Christ who set out to wage war against the forces of evil. So was the pagan one who did not convert, refusing to bow down to the authority that was the hierarchy of the Christian Church and its construct of an omnipotent supernatural being.

It is a neat option if you can grasp it: evading personal responsibility, and thus culpability, an individual readily gives up his autonomy to a governing authority. In doing so, he clings onto a sense of his own innocence, believing that he will be looked after by the boss (the government, the church, the loving just God) to whom he has given his power.

This makes no sense to the *Pagan. Perceiving the world as an intricate web of connections, ecologies interweaving with ecologies, each flicker of energy is seen to have an effect, each current of intention influencing the whole. We are never blameless. From the moments of our conception until the last dregs of our body energy and memory dissipate away, we are an affecting part of an environment; taking responsibility provokes us to examine every action we take.

The very word *pagan* seethes with connotations of anarchy. Yet anarchy is not about the selfish mayhem that many assume: a disparate gathering of people living with no defining structure of organization. The Australian academic, Rob Sparrow, defines anarchy as a system 'where people govern themselves democratically without domination or hierarchy'. The anarchist does not perceive the state as an effective source of social control, yet he does not crave mayhem. The anarchist does not abdicate responsibility, but looks to craft natural order through sound relationship. *Paganism is naturally anarchistic.

Through the pressure provoked by an ineffective government, and particularly those that claim to be democratic, frustration sometimes explodes into violence, and some of these angry groups do call themselves anarchists. Like Islamist terrorists, self-righteous Christians, and selfish *Pagans, these anarchists are a minority who fail to understand the essential tenets of the philosophy, attacking what they feel to be wrong while communicating, in their actions, no viable alternative.

In the tidal wave of demonstrations against the invasion of Iraq, I was sad to see young Moslem fundamentalists crying out against US-led capitalism, wearing Nike trainers and drinking Coca Cola. Enraged I questioned one, but was answered with incomprehension. I began the previous chapter with the delightful concept of the contradiction in terms, but here that contradiction is writ in full neon hypocrisy. The same is true of the anarchist who, refusing to work for the capitalist system, lives on social security payments. While it might seem witty to exploit that which we don't like, such an attitude lacks integrity. It certainly is not *Pagan.

True anarchy is about self-governance. To use a Pagan term, its efficacy comes with an awareness of the web of *wyrd*. If we are to take responsibility for ourselves without our strategy being selfish, each individual must be awake to the ecosystem within which they live, that of their family and community, and of the environment both locally and globally, what *Pagans usually call their *tribe*.

The first steps of implementation are with the attitudes and actions of each individual: for unless we are awake and aware of the web, unless we are prepared to look carefully at every aspect of how we live, examining and questioning, replacing assumptions with informed decisions, our philosophy is immediately compromised by complicity. This raises another clear commonality that brings cohesion to the broad community of modern Paganism: heresy.

This is a word I love. From the Greek, *haireomai*, meaning to choose, the word *hairesis* is the choice we make in terms of beliefs, and within the word's history hums the power of autonomy. As it finds its feet in twenty first century English - heresy - that hum breaks into a hollering as it declares the critical necessity to *question*, for how else can we personally make a valid choice or decision.

Once again, a core aspect of Paganism is potentially counter-cultural. It celebrates the unorthodox. Encouraging us to question the norm, if we disagree we must not sit back, grumbling and blaming others. A story holds no audience if its tenor is complaint. Having retained responsibility for our own interaction, we must explore alternative ideas, and indeed use our wit and creativity to forge another way. If we don't understand, it is our responsibility to get off the couch and find out. To behave in a certain way simply because others do is not Pagan.

Writing in the middle of the last century, the social philosopher Karl Popper emphasized the need to question. Accepting that so much of the world exists beyond human perception, he wrote, there is no hope that we might fully comprehend it. We have theories but, developing with human ingenuity and exploration, those have been constantly updated over thousands of years. The new science of Isaac Newton brought significant breakthroughs in understanding of nature's patterns, yet Einstein proved elements of his work to be wrong. Quantum theories are now constantly shaking areas of Einstein's vision. In truth, we can only ever hope to formulate adequate hypotheses with which to explain reality. There is no certainty.

The recent philosophical trend of postmodernism extended the notion further. Questioning the binary perspectives of evidence and ignorance, of black and white, of right and wrong, of the desire for a single overarching explanation (truth), it emphasizes the necessity of always remaining open to interpretation and meaning. *How* we perceive the world is crucial, for we can have no comprehensive knowledge of *what* we see. The American thinker, Richard Rorty, expresses these ideas, exploring truth as being solely found within relationships and their language. The late Jean-François Lyotard spoke of the irrelevance of old 'narratives' of fact and truth, the 'myths' applied to define reality, emphasizing how we use language to describe and understand the flows of change and relationship that encapsulate life. Jacques Derrida goes further, deconstructing the language of written texts to uncover an infinite number of possible hidden meanings, unacknowledged by the writers.

No certainty: it is a beautifully heretical notion - and very *Pagan.

Over the centuries that monotheisms have occupied seats of government, expressing doubt about the certain existence of God has been deemed heretical. To take it further and declare that there is no certainty at all, no set of universal truths in which we can invest our sanity, is heretical to a much wider swathe of society than just the monotheistic: it questions the 'facts' held as truth and reality by the agnostic and atheist who claim to *believe* in nothing at all. Yet *Paganism looks to nature's state of perpetual change, its deep tap root reaching back to a point before science, when natural philosophy was an integral part of religious understanding. Even now, it does not reach for facts or proof with regard to the natural world. Instead it seeks clarity of patterns and purpose through observation and experiential interaction, working with full awareness of the processes of change and the limitations of perspective. Its focus is on how we coexist: on the power of relationship.

Just as we must question the generally accepted path and yet choose to walk our own, realizing that there is no certainty also requires us to live wakefully, questioning and choosing, making our own decisions. It is a reality that is reflected in the remarkable creativity of the Pagan community, with its high proportion of artists, poets, writers and musicians, its colourful society of thinkers and innovators, designers and teachers, its theatrically eccentric wardrobes. Deliciously, at the same time, this heretical foundation makes the task of finding cohesion within

Paganism even more complex, for it emphasizes the diversity of both Paganism as a whole and the individuals within specific traditions.

In the seventeenth century, John Locke spoke of tolerance. Asking, 'Where is the man that has incontestable evidence of the truth of all he holds?' he asserted that nobody could ever be sure of what is true. How do we have the right, then, to proclaim our own infallible truth or judge others' ideas as right or wrong?

Once again Locke's words support a fundamental concept within modern *Pagan thought, and one here that allows a circle of Pagans to gather together to share prayers of reverence and respect in ceremony, a Wiccan devotee of Demeter who sees her as one aspect of the Great Goddess she calls Isis, beside a Druid polytheist who lives in the service of his god Gwyn ap Nydd, a Witch who is a priestess of the horse goddess Epona, an animist honouring a power she calls Darkness, a Heathen who has struck a good deal with Odin, and a chaos magician who thinks they're all completely mad, himself honouring the power that seethes within the patterns of all life. The harmony that allows them to stand in ceremony together comes from that acknowledgement that there is no one truth that can be shared. Each individual has questioned, studied, explored, experienced life and made choices of belief that are uniquely personal.

There is no scripture in Pagan tradition. Some follow mythologies, histories, grimoires and tracts more closely than others, but all written material is perceived to be no more than ideas, another resource, pools of potential inspiration and learning. So is heresy inherent within the tradition. As each student is encouraged to question what the teacher offers them, that they discover their own truth and don't blindly take on another's vision, so does each tradition evolve, changing with the needs and realizations of the next generation.

When I first sought out the Druid community in the early 1990s, my own vision of the tradition was deemed heretical, too drenched in sensuality, too much focussed on entropy and the use of trance. I questioned the need for formal ritual in white robes and scripted words, the value of guided meditations that stressed others' imagery, the utility of working with a theology and a pantheon I didn't relate to. My unwillingness to defer to people who had not gained my respect was considered wholly unacceptable. Yet before the decade was out, as my own vision of Druidry was published, I was inundated with people who found affirmation in my vision for their own *Pagan practice: I am no longer so heretical, for I am one amidst many, and with each I laugh and challenge them, provoking further heresy, ensuring the tradition keeps growing and changing.

As a human being in a civilized, twenty first century society, I am a heretic. My body's physiology is wired in a way that provokes intense sensitivity that is both glorious - allowing exquisitely poignant sensation and perception - and at times so painful as to be literally unendurable. This vision, with which I can see the shimmering of energy, currents of electricity, residues of emotion and threads of intention, leads me to question what is assumed to be reality. Where others see nothing, I see existence. Where others see certainty, I see possibility.

In secular society, as a parent guiding my child's growing under-standing, as a patient in both allopathic and alternative medicine, as a citizen in a democratic and capitalist nation, as a human being upon this planet, I hope each day openly to express my heresy. I challenge, retaining and claiming my autonomy, asserting my need and my respon-sibility to make my own choices, making it clear that to do so I must question, unearthing assumptions, learning all I can along the way.

Most dedicated *Pagans behave the same way. Exploring the ecstasy and freedom of their own unique spiritual experience, unwilling to accept convention without question, here then is a powerfully cohesive common-ality between all Pagan traditions. The expression of perfect heresy: the art of questioning the orthodox assumptions and choosing our own way. It is a highly individual and idiosyncratic way of living, yet a beautiful reflection of the natural world, with its webs of possibilities and appar-ently chaotic patterns of erratic predictability and mutation.

Perhaps most importantly, however, that Pagan individuality so exquisitely reflects nature because it is expressed within a wakeful awareness of the web, of the ecology of the landscapes and communities within which we live.

~ ~ ~

"But it's raining ... "

At the next desk, another colleague shrugs, "I think that's the point."

And down the corridor she flies, grabbing the hand of a friend, "Come on!" Spun into the whirl of her determination, he stumbles and follows as she heads through the foyer, a whirlwind drawing towards her everybody's attention.

"She's mad," someone murmurs.

"She's Pagan," is the response.

The receptionist laughs, "If you ask her, she'd tell you it's a goddess thing."

And they all stand and watch as she skips through the doors, pushing off her shoes on the step, and runs out onto the tarmac of the car park, barefoot in the rain. And what rain! It's been three weeks since the last drops fell, and now it pours and pours, the ground beneath her teeming, instantly flooded silver-white with dancing water, alive with the storm, and with her arms open, her face lifted to the skies, she sings, whirling round and round.

Her friend stands half sheltered by the office entrance, smiling with wonder at her behaviour, barely able to hear her voice through the clamour of the rain, longing to join her, to walk through this intangible barricade that keeps him tight and upright in his guise of an ordinary sensible man, knowing how embarrassed he would be to do otherwise.

Drenched, she turns towards him, her clothes clinging, sodden, her hair plastered down, her face glowing with life. She looks so completely vibrant, shining, wet and free, and she holds out her hand to him, calling out an invitation, words he cannot hear. And in that moment, uneasy and excited, he sees her as a wild force, as Aphrodite, as temptation and delight, as complete and somehow apocalyptic freedom.

And he wonders, amazed, *Why doesn't she look foolish?*

~ ~ ~

Death and Sexuality

What we know about primitive religions of prehistory is very limited. Nonetheless, there is value and validity in considering the mindset of our ancient forebears; for although our society is radically different at the dawn of each new millennium, human nature is not so altered. Though we may express our desires in different circumstances, in different language and clothing, though our increasingly complex technology may allow us to believe our power to reason has developed, our basic human wit and passions are just the same. Our relationships are little changed.

With no illusion that they had any control over nature, four thousand years ago our ancestors would have reached to perceive nature's patterns in order to grasp some level of predictability. Life is very tiring when we are constantly trailing behind, trying to understand, accept and adjust. The same is true today: when nature's power is raw, undiluted by illusions and devices of civilization, there is seldom any attempt to hold back the flow of change. The impetus is, instead, to raft the current with dignity and ease, avoiding the alternative of being smashed upon the rocks. It is certainly a central theme in nature-based *Paganism. With a reverence for change, the teachings facilitate and celebrate the tiny shifts that happen on a day to day basis, through to the glorious processes that bring complete transformation.

Archaeology suggests that the earliest hunter-gatherer communities held death as an important focus, using energy and ingenuity to construct long barrows of massive stones and mud, such as that at West Kennet in Wiltshire. In these unlit chambers, down long narrow tunnels, the cleaned bones of the dead were kept. At times of ritual, these bones were used, perhaps to invoke the gods: powers that controlled the tides of disease, of pain and darkness, and all the mysteries of the world of the dead.

The significance accorded to death we can understand, and especially if we remove the padding of the modern world: its heating, shelter and medicine, its lack of predators and (in most Western nations) perpetual and bloody intertribal warfare. To our ancestors, death was perpetually imminent, its cause often incomprehensible, with little to ease the pain and fear. Instead of turning from this brutality, however, the barrows imply a quest to understand. The same is true of modern *Paganism. Death is a divine power of nature to be revered.

Once again, this is not about submitting to power as a governing authority. Nor do I believe it would have been for our ancestors, for to submit to any powerful force of nature is potentially suicide. This reverence is about listening, about sensitizing or opening the barriers around the soul, to experience viscerally that which we seek to understand. Allowing its current to move through our own, life force touching life force, we learn how to move together without friction.

Perhaps more poignantly than any other force, death teaches us of change. This is as true when we are losing someone we love as it is in our own journey of dying: we learn of loss and release, but also of regeneration, about accepting gracefully the scythe that brings death because of the potential (rather than the inevitability) of rebirth and renewal that it brings. Indeed, through the excruciating pain that so reeks of death, it is from that same 'otherworld' of mystery that an infant journeys to be born.

Perhaps the oldest part of the tap root of Paganism, death remains central to modern practice. The late October festival of Samhain is a celebration of the dead, a dance with the ancestors, a time to remember our own mortality, but most *Pagans will honour death each nightfall, acknowledging its presence within life. Yet because our society so obviously recoils from death, desperately stretching for immortality in creams and pills and medical technology, the *Pagan focus is perceived as morbid, or even dangerous.

It better accepts another character of that tap root: the power of fertility.

As hunter-gatherer culture declined, settled agrarian culture emerging, the focus of spiritual practice shifted, our ancestors seeking ways to understand the tides of the seasons, of sun, of light and warmth, exploring the patterns of the skies. Not only concerned with the process of seeding to harvest, the health and abundance of a tribe's children and newly domesticated animals were equally important. The magic of fertility became crucial.

This root still richly nourishes *Paganism. Although a minority are farmers, there is a consciousness in religious practice about our dependence on the mud and rain, on germination and fruition. At times the focus of fertility is about the natural conception and birth of a child. Yet all Pagans are attentive to everything that inspires and nurtures creativity, working to free the soul of all that blocks creative expression, and more often the work is upon the development of personal or tribal creativity, enabling life to be productive and rich with satisfaction.

With reverence for the power of death, here too we acknowledge another of our most primal fears and animal instincts in a context that sanctifies. For when *Pagans speak of fertility, there is no interest in forcing the magic. Fertility, flowing naturally upon the currents of the gods, is most powerfully achieved where there is pleasure. So does the spiritual focus move to sensuality, sexuality and the exquisite experience of deep relationship. As with death, *Pagans fully engage with and celebrate their sensuality and sexuality, notably at the major May festival of Beltane, but also in their daily lives. The *Pagan attitude to spiritual, emotional and physical intimacy is one of deep respect: for like death, this is a force of nature that has the power to provoke fundamental change.

The many layers of human nature are a source of fascination, the thoughtless and instinctive, the reactive and the reasoning. That we are able to feel so much and so little, to think so clearly and to complicate so utterly, inspires us to learn. We seek out the patterns, from the intricacies of mathematics and chemistry to the broader views of philosophy and psychology, exploring the currents of behaviour, of genetics and ancestry. Of course, to remain the observer in this learning is not really *Pagan: instead, at any opportunity, we slip in, swimming deep in search of profound personal experience, eager to find ways in which the soul can find its pleasure.

Society, nice and polite, once again flinches. Overt celebration of sexuality, sensuality, of pleasure derived from physicality, is uncivilized. It is tolerated as sleaze, or even as art, where a safe distance is established, for the emotional flood evoked by intimacy is hard to control; lust, hunger, need, unbridled delight are considered altogether base. Surely these things have nothing to do with religion!

Yet, as the first sunshine of early summer warms the earth, and *Pagans venture out to make love in meadows and gardens, openly and joyfully mirroring the flood of nature's dance of rising energy, the act is deepened by the knowledge that what they do is a sacred part of their religious practice. Calling to the gods of the land, the gods of their ancestors, they give and share that most powerful and divine gift of pleasure.

Indeed, it is the declared disconnection between sanctity and physicality that brings me to a point that is perhaps the most crucial in terms of a comprehensive definition of *Pagan*.

Energy and Consciousness

Thoroughly rooted in Plato's vision, Christianity in Western culture has very effectively perpetuated a dualist perspective of reality. Writing in the early fourth century before the Common Era, in his dialogue *Phaedo*, Plato determined that all physical matter was an imperfect copy of its original counterpart, its Form. Everything, from a horse to love, had its perfect original, existing in eternal purity, beyond time and space. All that exists within the manifest world, being mortal reproductions, is inherently soiled by the corruption of decay, and the most virtuous goal of any human being, trapped throughout life within the apparent chaos of nature, must be to reach for a consciousness of the Forms' perfection. For Plato, this perfection was solely to be found in the beauty of mathematics, for here he discovered patterns that he believed to be unchanging.

Plato's world view became increasingly accepted and was dominant at the time when the New Testament was written, also in Greek. Politically and philosophically, this Christian text combined the established ideas crafted by Plato with a vision for a new age. Grafted onto such a sturdy root, the Christian notion of God's perfection and the ongoing corruption of the Garden of Eden seeped into the human mind, adjusting the sands of understanding. Writing at the turn of the fifth century, in the violent maelstrom that was the collapse of the Roman Empire in the West, the intensely pessimistic Augustine further embedded these ideas into Christianity, reacting against the chaos of his era, declaring that only God could save a man from the eternal desolation of life on Earth. So did God become something distinctly separate from nature, a perfection that we cannot hope to reach until we are released from the sordid grasp of its mortality, and - if we have lived holding His perfection in our hearts and our actions - we might be accepted into paradise.

Aristotle, one of Plato's students, in part rejected this negative dualistic notion. The world, he said, was a source of inspiration and awe: the Form of something was not a separate entity but its essence, its *ousia* or core nature. He encouraged the rich exploration of life, believing experience crucial for growth, allowing each creature to find its place within the patterns of nature. To look beyond nature for perfection, he thought, was to reject life. As the empire crumbled and Plato's vision spread west, so did Aristotle's perspective find its feet to the east; it was his ideas that lay as quiet roots beneath the development of Islamic learning. It was with his inspiration that science and philosophy thrived in the Eastern Mediterranean, leaving Western Europe far behind. Not until the twelfth century did his ideas first begin to be brought back into Western thought, notably in the writings of the Spanish Jew, Moses Maimonides. Slowly they helped push forward the edges of knowledge, opening minds once again to the beauty, the inherent reason and the exquisite potential of nature.

Much ground was lost, however. The separation of spirit and matter still underlies Western thinking, where it has been further tacked down, again and again, by philosophers seeking to capture with language the universal truth of their dualistic metaphysical beliefs. Saturated with this attitude through the centuries of Christianity, the English language still conveys the gulf, not least with the common words *body* and *spirit*, which in themselves make it strangely complicated both to describe the reach of dualist assumptions and to suggest an alternative perspective. In modern secular culture, even where the notion of God is dismissed as implausible, concepts of spirit and the sacred are either thrown out as well or retained to describe the unaccountable, and all that is judged to be singular or supernatural. Spirit, in other words, whether mythic or mysterious, is still deemed to be separate from the mud and blood of real physicality; it is made of a different stuff and exists in a different reality. Perhaps most poignantly, it is somehow special.

Nature-based *Paganism is distinctly *non*-dualistic.

The forces of nature are sacred. They fill our lungs with scent, flood through our souls with emotion, wash over our skin as rain, inspiring the patterns of our thinking. They are wind and joy, moonlight, forest, rage, rain, jealousy. That is all there is: nature.

If that sounds mundane, it is simply a matter of vision. If we see a tree as nothing more than bark, sap and leaves, chemicals welded together, then why not cut it down, cut it up, *use* it. If a human is simply flesh, blood and bones, another construction of chemicals, then we can perceive individual humans as resources too, and many do. Ascribing a spirit to a human being, however, lifts him up and out of the common fray of nature. Chosen by or created by God, only he contains that exquisite God-given soul. He is special.

But there is nothing special about human beings.

At its simplest, nature is energy. Without energy, there is nothing. Still far from comprehensible to modern science, to the *Pagan mystic exploring the inner worlds, it is utterly magical. It's tempting to say it is extraordinary, but energy is entirely ubiquitous: it is thoroughly and definitively ordinary. The intrinsic wellspring of nature, it is the smallest building block of existence, of creativity.

Humming with its own being, it is just energy. In order to move, it requires direction. In *Paganism, that directive is intention. At its simplest, it is reaction. Provoked and formed by the tremors of energy around it, each intention finds its own momentum and quality, its vibration influencing all that it touches, provoking energy into action. As patterns emerge, intentions interweave and entangle with intentions, and so does the simplest whisper of energy craft itself into something more complex.

This weave and web of intentions is consciousness. Drawing energy into cohesive form, moving upon a current of intention, it allows the potential for life. At the most basic level, it is essence or spirit. Its flow can form into purpose. It offers the notion of identity. This is what I refer to as the soul, the current or song.

Consciousness: like energy, it is ubiquitous. It is inherent in nature.

It is inherent within matter, not as a ghostly form but integral to its composition at the most fundamental level. In the poetry of *Paganism, the physicality of existence is crafted as if it were the footprints of the soul. As consciousness leaves a critical point of focus, another thought rising into form, the last falls into disintegration. Though most patterns of consciousness disappear quickly, when they disintegrate slowly, the force of energy diminishing, the edges of the soul slip into matter. As the ancient Greek, Heraclitus, observed, all of nature is in the process of constant change, yet this is not all decay as Plato declared, but the power of nature's perpetually regenerating creativity.

The extent to which we, as human beings, are able to discern and comprehend consciousness through our faculties of perception and reason is limited. As it moves upon the tides of nature, emerging and dissolving, the faintest glimmers may touch our awareness as mere memories and empathies, scents, intuitions, tremors of emotion and atmosphere. Some perceive more than others, but we all perceive but a tiny fraction of what exists around and within us.

While consciousness does not need a physical reflection or manifestation, nothing in nature can exist without a song of consciousness, without the life-energy of intention. As the consciousness fades, we may feel all that is left is just the process of decay and the stories of what has been. Yet even in this quiet flow, consciousness remains, intention and purpose shifting, as those present journey through the disintegration into regeneration.

Animism is central to any nature-based *Pagan philosophy. Derived from the Latin *anima*, a richly expressive word in itself that translates as a breeze, as breath, as soul or simply life, the animist acknowledges all of nature to be alive with *soul* or song. The Oxford English Dictionary defines an animist as one who believes that 'animals and inanimate objects have souls', a remarkably judgemental statement, tripping over its self-contradiction. To the animist, all of nature is animate, for all of nature has inherent consciousness.

That internal flow of intention moves it within the patterns of its own purpose, responding to external influence and internal motivation: from the volcano's eruption to the bee's dance of discovery, the hydrogen atom's single spinning electron, the rush of the river, the crashing of thunder, the apple that falls, the seed that splits open in germination. If we are seeking a consciousness or purpose that mirrors human drives and reason, we shall find nothing; an apple is an apple, and every part of that apple is crafted with the apple's own purpose - and it is drenched in purpose.

To speak of each soul as individual, holding its own intention or consciousness, implies a separation that is not perceived by the *Pagan. Energy isn't constrained by edges. And although consciousness is drawn into cohesion by intention, there are myriad levels at which such cohesion might be acknowledged. An ocean may be regarded as a powerful goddess, a stream a sacred spirit and a part of that larger deity; but to the animist, the raindrop is no less sacred, as is each water molecule, each atom of oxygen and hydrogen, and within the atoms, the particles science can only just perceive, yet to which the priest of nature also sings. That doesn't mean the *Pagan holds any ridiculous notions about protecting raindrops; the animist perspective informs us of purpose and sanctity, of value.

There is, then, no point at which consciousness, or indeed the cohesion that allows identity, disappears or becomes irrelevant, from the subatomic to the galactic. As human beings, we communicate consciously with other human beings, but our cells communicate with each other according to their own purpose, the potassium with the calcium, and so on. On a broader level, the intention of humanity as a whole interacts with the earth, as does the forest with the skies.

Shimmering as if vibrant with curiosity, consciousness moves with nature's momentum, ever reaching out to explore the world, reacting, responding. We can acknowledge that it is possible to share an intention with another, human to human; working together, we can increase our potential and achievement. Yet this is how all nature works. Currents of energy - a song or intention, consciousness, purpose, patterns - are constantly meeting, provoking friction, finding harmony, sharing energy, breaking apart into new currents, ideas and intentions. In the poetry of *Paganism, soul meets soul. They may be humans, beetles, or atoms of nitrogen - whatever they are, in meeting there is a sharing of consciousness. It is not an infrequent and random occurrence, but happens continuously; each pattern moves within a larger pattern, each droplet of intention part of a larger stream.

When one soul's essence touches the life essence of another, it is this touch of pure energy that many in *Paganism regard as the experience of spiritual ecstasy. That moment of connection comes when intentions slide together, merging, and the soul is utterly awake and open to the experience. On a human level, this is the deep visceral craving, the ache of spiritual love, the source of religious passion, and it blows the mind apart with the pleasure of union. It is this craving, this passionate drive that is considered the source of nature's creativity. Such moments of connection happen between subatomic particles, between molecules, between snails, clouds, galaxies.

The ecstasy of connection is integral to the soul of nature, to nature's consciousness. And nature, as we can perceive or conceive it, is part of an intention or consciousness that is larger than anything we could pretend to imagine.

The Prussian Georg Hegel, writing in the early nineteenth century, proposed the idea of the universal *geist*, a word that is usually translated as spirit. Yet the German can be as accurately transcribed as *mind*, which makes the concept more comprehensible; for, although he wrote with some awe, he was certainly not reaching for a mystical concept. His notion of a universal mind was one crafted of pure reason, very much in tune with the ideas of his predecessor, Immanuel Kant. Reason, lying beyond what he perceived as the individuated force of desire, was the congruence that gave the universe cohesion. With the majority of his contemporaries, Hegel perceived reason as the quality that lifted our species above the rest of nature.

While in natural *Pagan philosophy, there is clearly a universal mind or consciousness, that *geist* is not reason. Indeed, some *Pagans might call it spirit or, more clearly, nature's soul-song. For it includes all the patterns of nature, of need and understanding, of emergence and decay, acceptance and repulsion, of direction and rejection, of passion and reason: of relationship. Perhaps most clearly distinguishing it from the Hegelian concept, it is not a force that has value solely to humanity.

Nor can this universal mind be considered to be the one God. It is not a separate entity, and certainly not outside or super-natural. It is fully integrated with all there is, down to the smallest shimmer of energy, existing in the perpetual interaction of patterns shifting within patterns. Nor does the *Pagan vision allow for a sense that superiority comes with size: though ecologically it may have a value that reaches further in scale, a forest is no more *special* than a single tree. The experience of the tree, the richness of its consciousness and the power of its soul intention is as remarkable as that of the whole forest within which it lives, albeit on a smaller scale in both time and space. The water molecule and the ocean, or the electron and the galaxy are comparable in the same way. The universal mind is simply the broadest consciousness we can begin to imagine, flowing upon its own current of intent.

~ ~ ~

Her fingers are brown from the summer's sun, wrapped around the green and red of the apple in her hands. With a thumb, she strokes it, her soul entirely focused on it, as if her skin moving over the apple's skin will deepen her perception. Maybe it does. She smiles, slowly looking up at me, "You know how when you hold a bowl of rainwater, it seems to shine, whereas tap water just sits there?" Her voice is soft with wonder.

I smile, "Yes."

She returns her gaze to the apple. "As well as the earth, mud, nutrients, the physical density ... I can feel the rain in the apple. It shines." She shines, her face glowing with the connection, her eyes sparkling, beautiful.

"And what of ancestry?"

And she speaks, softly, at times closing her eyes then, opening them, integrating the inner vision with the fruit in her hands, the meadow where we sit, blessed by the warm breeze; she speaks of the apple tree, of the orchard where it stands, wondering at the heritage of the trees, and she pauses, questioning how and where she can perceive the human input, that of our own ancestors. I offer words, and she settles on the idea that she's now sensing a broad song. Sighing deeply, smiling, she returns her focus to the one apple she holds in her hands.

"So what happens when you eat it?" I ask.

She breathes in, "Oh, I don't know how I could now! It feels so huge and important!"

And I laugh, "So it's easier to eat something when you haven't acknowledged its song?"

"But not to is dishonourable." She frowns, "We have to eat. And I think this one apple would fill me quickly, with life and nourishment. I would be much more open to receive it, to digest it, to benefit. And after all, its intention, as a fruit, is to be eaten, right?"

I smile again, "So what about a carrot?"

~ ~ ~

We began by seeking a definition of *Pagan* and, having clarified the inevitable limitations of my vision by using the asterisk, I here offer what seems to me to be the heart of it.

Perceiving all nature as sacred, retaining personal responsibility and autonomy within the community or web of nature, as *Pagans we strive to live sufficiently aware of the currents and tides of our own soul, that we might open ourselves to sharing our intention and, wakefully, respectfully, connect with another (human, blackbird, beetle, buttercup, raindrop, storm, or indeed planet: another's song of life). Nurturing relationships based on wonder and reverence, our aim is to allow our consciousness to be utterly filled with the song of life.

Here is the paradigm. Within nature there is no separation, for we are all part of the web that is crafted simply of energy and consciousness. I pose that the choices we make in life, the ethics that we live by, are defined by whether or not we accept that as reality. Our actions are symptomatic of that acceptance or lack of it.

If you, as the reader, are not prepared to open to the possibility of such a paradigm, this book could well be senseless to you. If, however, the paradigm provokes a curiosity or recognition, then I bid you continue, and be welcome, for within these pages we can celebrate the sanctity of the enormity of what we share: life.

CHAPTER THREE

DEFINING CHOICE

Three ways to justify a blow, a bite and a blessing :
a flow of water, a deep well, a cup of ale -
all of which are gifts of the rain.

Ethics and Morality

Though I have studied the theology and philosophy of Paganism for two decades and readily accept the gaps and clumsy conceptions in the scope of my understanding, enjoying each challenge that provokes me to backtrack and review, I am no academic with regard to the philosophy of ethics.

A punk through and through, my twelve years of formal education began when I refused to leave the school hallway for three full days, screaming if anyone dared approach; although I came to terms with the notion of sitting in a classroom, internally my attitude didn't change. The tedium of institutional trivia and devout pedantry destroyed for me the possibility of considering schooling beyond the minimum; instead, by the age of seventeen, I was finding my own way, using the world as a resource to sate my craving for understanding, spending my days curled up in city libraries, submerged in ideas, wading through books.

It is no doubt a side effect of my somewhat anarchic education, expressed in my life and in these pages, that allows me the audacity even to consider presenting a definition of ethics. I don't imagine that I could do so in any way that would satisfy an academic. Yet the subject is too important to be left to the ivory towers and complex wordplays of specialist professors. So is it my hope that, as a writer with rain-tangled hair and no need for tenure, I can bring simplicity to a subject that is otherwise both complicated and complicating.

In order to ensure my definition grounded, on a number of occasions throughout the past few years I have asked gatherings of Pagans to help unpack the terms that readily surround *ethics*. It is the results of these discussions that I have used as a guide here: definitions crafted by thinking people, seeking a collective clarity about how the words are used in the realities of everyday life and language in our Western culture.

Here is the first definition, derived from these gatherings. *Ethics*: the line we draw that articulates what is acceptable in terms of behaviour, and what is not, from a profoundly personal and individual standpoint.

Putting aside any notion about where that line *should* be, more basically our ethics are an expression of our needs. Bluntly, they declare what we feel the world owes us and what we feel we ought to give in return. Our ethics describe how we feel others ought to conduct their lives and how we sense we too ought to behave. Based entirely on the patterns of our own minds, they reflect how we perceive the world, both in terms of the *facts* we assume are reality, and the emotionally defended attitudes that we *believe* and often *need* to be true. Just as these beliefs shape how we respond to the world, so do they create the ethical framework of standards and expectations that we use to judge ourselves and others: the line of what is acceptable, what is forgivable. As such, our ethics provoke guilt and anger, shame, gratitude and humility, compassion and lack of mercy, a sense of injustice and righteousness. Where the line is crossed, we find fear and grief. Where we hold it inflexibly, it becomes a cloak that keeps us comforted, armour that keeps us safe, clear air that keeps us healthy. Here is the framework within which we think. As Hegel said, our ethics shape our identities.

According to the British philosopher, Simon Blackburn, human beings are 'ethical animals'. By this he doesn't mean that we have a tendency to be compassionate or behave in a way that is widely accepted as *good*. His words succinctly describe the way we are prone constantly to judge and compare, evaluating relative worth, measuring the world against our own ideas and standards. We justify our own actions, determining value and importance, criticizing and dismissing others', claiming and denying responsibility.

Naturally highly competitive, we are a tribal species. Terrified of being outcast, we do all we can to avoid rejection, perpetually seeking out ways in which we can affirm our position within a community. Just as we spend energy judging others, we also reach for affirmation that our own decisions are valid, looking for justification in others' confirmation, needing others to agree on our judgements, manoeuvring relationships to be assured of support. Consciously or subconsciously, we project our ethics onto others, and celebrate when our ethics are shared, extending them further into society.

This is where we find the edges that distinguish ethics from morality.

Recognizing the simple definition used above, the term *ethics* sits better within the anarchic community that is modern *Paganism, but equally within Western society with its individualistic and secular feel-good lifestyle. The word *morality* implies an imposed ethics, a denial of personal freedom, with ideals of duty and obligation that are somewhat out of vogue. The *moralist* is a threat to our comfortable hedonism, our self-determinism, our freedom to live well.

Yet, when I have asked gatherings to define it, although the overtones of personal threat were acknowledged, the consensus isn't all negative. *Morality*: constructed by agreement, by the community as a whole, morals are the boundary lines around a tribal unit. They both protect the tribe from the behaviour of outsiders and ensure the tribe itself maintains standards that will keep it adequately at ease. Because it is the tribe that agrees the code, it also agrees the consequences that should be meted out to those who cross the line.

Just as ethics shape our identities, so does morality serve to identify a community. It paints clearly what is acceptable and expected of those who wish to be a part of that tribe, and what is not. And I use the word *tribe* in the way it is understood within *Paganism, as any social unit within which we seek acceptance: our partner and cat, our family or cluster of friends, our neighbourhood, our religious community, the company we work for, the regulars at the pub, the local population, a nationhood of citizens. Indeed, taking it a step further, as this book will do in coming chapters, in some contexts we might consider an environment as a whole, acknowledging trees, beetles, streams and buttercups to be the members of a tribe, the 'people' who dwell within a particular ecosystem.

Crucially here, seldom does a whole community sit down in discussion to carefully create these boundaries. More often than not, it is the charismatic and the powerful within a group who present their own ethics in such a way as to persuade the rest to take them on as an agreed moral code; such people attain and protect their positions as tribal leaders. Indeed, because our desire to be a part of a tribe is so strong, often we will do anything we need to in order to belong, taking on whatever beliefs and standards are required. If someone appears happy and successful, or an organization offers an environment that appears to guarantee happiness and success (or just release from struggle and pain) as human beings we are liable to discard or compromise earlier beliefs in order to find our place within that tribe.

In George W Bush's fundamentalist American Christian morality, homosexuality is deemed a disease that can be cured, 'erototoxins' (chemicals released by sexual stimulus) are more dangerously addictive and spiritually damaging than heroin, abortion is immoral and killing animals for pleasure is thoroughly encouraged. I had imagined such ideas had disappeared from Western society twenty if not thirty years ago. Yet, with enough fear force-fed into the system, and an old myth about salvation given a new paint job, beliefs are easily turned around and what is deemed acceptable human behaviour changes accordingly. Political tribes are built around such charismatic leaders, defining the boundary fences and the threat that lies beyond, calling out their promises to keep us safe from harm.

It isn't easy to find certainty about our own personal ethics, let alone create a moral code, and most groups I spoke to were clear that their definition was in part both idealistic and semantic. In practice, there are often loyalties that hold communities together which are far stronger (such as love and family) than the shared ethics of a wider community's morality. Individual needs clash and we are forced, again and again, to prioritize and compromise. We weigh one standard of acceptable behaviour against another, continuously judging and comparing both our own actions and others', at times deciding to behave according to the standards of one group, then another.

These contradictions, inconsistencies and hypocrisies create an enduring risk to the investment we make in a community and its morality. Where we are unable to keep to the moral code, we lose faith in its validity and value; where we perceive others to be breaking it, by their actions or through our misreading of their behaviour and motivations, scepticism creeps in. With a lack of respect provoked by questioning the tribe's beliefs, when we stay within that community, morality can become the enemy, the wall by which we measure our own strength and failure.

More often, however, where we can't agree with the tribe's moral standards, and we aren't willing or able to provoke change, it helps if we don't think. Instead, with a little help from the range of distractions and drugs readily available in our society, we simply accept those boundaries determined by the tribal authority and agreed by the tribe's majority. Sometimes the consequences are beyond our ability to endure, but more often we simply lack courage: we follow the rules, pretending to be acceptable and worthy, while leaving the thinking to someone else. Most philosophers deem such action to be wholly lacking in morality. Kant put it most clearly when he stated that it is our conscious respect for the rational basis of moral action that measures our morality, not the fact that we follow the rules. It's a sentiment I feel has profound value, with its underlying *hairesis* or heresy, but sadly holds little weight in society at large.

Yet what does compel us to act in accordance with the shared morality of our tribe or to craft our own ethical code? Day by day, we are making decisions - about what and when and how much to give and to take.

~ ~ ~

The wind brushes my face, pushing a lock of hair to fall in front of my eyes, and I raise my focus from the page. Beneath the trees, a gust of cool air lifts a handful of dry leaves, allowing them to swirl and dance. In the stillness of my soul, I can feel it in my heart, the movement of freedom, like butterflies. I move a little on the bench and breathe in deeply, smoothing out the book and finding my place, and soon I am lost again in another's words.

I hear nothing of her at all until she is immediately beside me, like an imp. She shuffles her bottom up onto the seat and tidies her coat over her knees, then looks straight at me. Her face is round, her big eyes showing a depth of curiosity from other days. She must be four years old. I half smile in the English way, acknowledging her presence. She half smiles in return. And for a moment longer, we look into each other. Then she turns away to watch the leaves, the skittering sparrows, the world.

I return to my book. But my attention is distracted, my soul wakeful to the pleasure of the moment. For a while, I am curious, for I feel no need, no demand, no request from the child. She asks nothing of me, and as I realize and accept, the curiosity dissolves. I ask nothing of her. In this here and now, we are fully a part of the web, connected, nourished. We ask nothing of the moment. And it flows through us. Perfectly.

I gaze at the page of my book, reading nothing, feeling the exquisite sensation within me, and with a little sadness realize how seldom I find myself in human company when there is no choice to make, no need to sate: nothing to do. Surely this should be my wellspring, my premise, my reference, for every decision. I breathe in, aware of the stillness of the earth beneath us.

She moves, and I turn to her. Carefully slipping off the bench, smiling at me briefly as our eyes meet, she skips off, over the grass, and through the dancing leaves.

~ ~ ~

Choice. What a glorious word. It seems to me a word that is lush with the fertility of pleasure and abundance, perhaps in part due to its old French origins. For me, it is a word that evokes memories of childhood, of standing at that point where two paths meet, in the quiet of the dusty thyme-scented hills, and my father shrugging, open-hearted, "You choose, kitten, *either* way is an adventure".

Yet choice seldom retains that status of playful extravagance. As childhood slips behind us and we take on the personal responsibilities of our living, the consequences of each choice we make echo around us. The more choices we are offered, the harder it can be to decide. Indeed, the luxury of having choices is quickly lost in both complacency and the increasingly tangled threads of responsibility. In daily life, the burden of making a decision is often eased by a lack of information, followed up by a lack of research, allowing us to choose *without* knowing the full story, and thus abdicating a hefty clod of responsibility and culpability.

The last two chapters of this Part One will look at Pagan ethics, but here I shall expand upon my definition of ethics - of choice - within Western culture by casting a glance over the sands of human under-standing, observing a little of how horizons shift in the winds of time and change.

On what basis, then, do we make our decisions?

Intuition and Conscience

The first premise we use is instinct or intuition: we *sense* a course of action to be right. We may not understand or even be aware of the full circumstance or implications, but something inside draws us to behave in a certain way. Often such feelings allow us to make a decision without the inclination to explore any further. If questioned, we shrug. It isn't easy to justify: our answer is *just because*.

Intuition is an important part of human nature, but in the context of ethics it is dangerously ungrounded. Based on logical pathways that we can't access consciously, there can never be certainty that we are not simply reverting to formative or primitive fears, to prejudices and coping mechanisms. While many may claim that ethics are instinctive, that as sensible and healthy human beings on some level we *know* what is right and wrong, the gaps left in such an argument are cavernous. Even the most superficial study of human psychology convinces of the covert yet coherent influence of the subconscious.

If this were not true, philosophers and politicians would not have debated the issues for thousands of years. In human society, people constantly disagree about what is acceptable, what is right and wrong, what is owed to whom and when and where responsibilities and culpabilities lie. We might declare some choice or judgement to be *common sense*, yet within a tribe and across tribal boundaries common sense differs radically. Albert Einstein poignantly described common sense as being no more than the collection of prejudices an individual has accumulated by the age of eighteen.

Nevertheless, the notion of ethics being based upon some *natural law* has been a part of our Western philosophical tradition for a very long time. Writing in the fourth century BCE, Aristotle's argument for natural law was based on teleology. Denoting a belief that everything has its own particular purpose, teleology is used, for example, to prove the existence of a divine creator: the universe exists within certain rules that imply evidence of a carefully crafted design, any such design requiring a supernatural designer, i.e. God.

Aristotle used the Greek word *telos*, meaning an end or ultimate purpose, the telos being the natural or intended course of life that exists within the essence of every individual entity. This intention provides the place within which each entity sits most harmoniously in the patterns of the universe. The telos of an acorn is, then, its inherent goal of germination and growth into an adult acorn-producing oak.

Aristotle extended this view into his understanding of ethics. Living according to one's telos is healthy, body and soul, and what obstructs that goal is detrimental. 'Nature,' he said, 'operates for the sake of an end, and this is a good.' Because he believed reason, virtue, social interaction, balance and moderation to be integral to the human telos, it is only when we are living according to these tenets, and thus upon the path of our natural purpose, that we can achieve the fulfilment of what is ultimately *good*, and experience true well being, a state he called *eudaimonia*. He called this *entelecheia*, the state of being that wove together one's purpose with the current of natural energy, and it was, he thought, as true for each individual as it was for the groups that made up society and the state: human action is only *right* if it fits into the natural pattern, if we are following natural law. Needless to say, universal agreement as to specifically what the telos of a human being is remains open to debate.

As a system of justice, it was the Stoics that defined natural law most clearly, the Greek Zeno of Citium crafting the vision in the century following Aristotle's death, and others developing the ideas over the following four hundred years and more. Understanding the universe to be governed by distinct and unchanging laws, the Stoics' goal was to live in tune with the exquisitely rational design of nature. Because we have free will, and because reason is an inherent part of human nature and human design, it is possible to discover the patterns of natural law and choose to live within its reason. The value of studying logic and physics was purely in order to achieve this purpose. Indeed, the Stoics believed that knowledge of the natural world was necessary in order to formulate an ethical code.

Over time, thinkers have continued to explore this notion of natural law. Some assert it to be the collection of universal and unwritten laws that are relevant to all humanity, laws that don't change, for, based upon human nature and human reason, they are a reflection of nature, and not a human construct. Yet even what philosophers call the primary precepts - behaviour we are naturally inclined to consider wrong, such as intentional harm - are modified by social influences, becoming culturally specific.

If the common sense of natural law provides no certainty, what of conscience, our *moral* sense? Used to describe the part of us that observes our thoughts and actions, conscience mediates between our selfish human cravings and what we have agreed as acceptable behaviour. Shakespeare spoke of it beautifully. His Richard III, struggling out of exhausted nightmares in the early hours before his final battle, cries out, 'My conscience hath a thousand several tongues / And every tongue brings in a several tale / And every tale condemns me for a villain'.

Kant spoke of conscience as 'the moral faculty of judgement, passing judgement upon itself', 'a subjective principle of responsibility before God for our deeds'. He emphasized what he called the sovereignty of conscience, talking of our need and duty to listen to its voice, for he perceived that conscience revealed a world more profound than nature: the world of reason, immortality and freedom, the realm of God.

In the past, where theologians weren't referring to conscience as the voice of an angel or prophet, it was believed to be an innate part of the soul, a set of internal scales that guided us to avoid social rejection. Nowadays behavioural psychologists speak of conscience as an inner source of doubt that is learned, developing through the positive and negative feedback of our actions, not least those of early childhood. So is our conscience often an eerie inner echo of our parents, and the religious, school and social authorities of our earliest years. As such, we have conceived a thousand ways to suffocate that little judge inside, drowning out the quiet voice by turning up the noise of life.

Emotion and Feeling

The second basis on which we make decisions is emotion: I choose a course of action because it *feels* right. The difference between sensing and feeling may seem linguistically subtle but the distinction is clear in the experience. When we sense something, we have an inkling of its presence; when we feel something, with the information comes a measure of emotional energy. Feelings are fuelled.

One of Britain's best loved philosophers wrote of this when, in 1739-40, he published his *Treatise of Human Nature*. David Hume, in his late twenties, explained that all human behaviour derived naturally from feelings. Reason, he argued, is usually only employed in order to justify our desires and actions, either to ourselves or to others. 'Reason is, and ought only to be, the slave of the passions, and can never pretend to any other office than to serve and obey them.'

At a time when reason was a measure of virtue, Hume's ideas were seen as hedonistic. A century before, thinkers such as Thomas Hobbes and René Descartes were absorbing the Renaissance 'new science', exploring the idea of the human body being no more than a machine, as beautifully prescribed as a newly crafted clock. Isaac Newton's extraordinary revelations opened further doors to this new scientific understanding of nature. Precision was in vogue.

Yet Hume considered reason to be limited to the science of logic and mathematics. In ethics, he believed reason had no authority; human nature worked on the basis of preference, not logic. This wasn't a position in support of individual selfishness. To Hume it was not lack of reason but ignorance that generated unethical behaviour; it is our human obligation, therefore, to extend our personal knowledge and understanding of the world in which we live, and in so doing allow the heart to make decisions from a wakeful foundation.

Hume had not abandoned science. He perceived his position as firmly based on the science of human nature. With knowledge of another's position, our natural passions evoke 'sympathy' which promotes us to act in the person's favour, this virtuous action bringing with it a feeling of pleasure, which in turn affirms the value of what we have done. According to the excesses of modern philosophical language, this is a noncognitive meta-ethical empirical theory of morality. It sets rationalists on edge. Yet to Hume there were no infallible theories or causalities: our understanding of the world is solely based upon experience, observation and consequent expectation. Therefore, the most valid foundation we have upon which to craft ethical choice is that of our own natural inclinations, informed by thorough observation: common sense fuelled by emotion.

While Hume used the word *sympathy*, the eighteenth century French thinker, Jean-Jacques Rousseau chose *compassion*. A sincere Christian, albeit little understood by his contemporaries, Rousseau perceived deep sources of negativity in humanity: 'Everything is good that springs from the hands of our Creator; everything degenerates when it is shaped by the hands of man'. Human aggression and greed, he believed, could only be countered by compassion.

The German philosopher, Arthur Schopenhauer, who combined exceptionally beautiful writing with profound pessimism, also spoke of compassion. Though he felt humanity was irreparably flawed, he believed that on some level all of nature is one force of undifferentiated energy. He called this 'Will'. His vision was grounded in Kant's notion of a noumenal world. For Kant this was the immortal and unchanging world of reason, a reality that was independent of humanity and our ability to perceive it. This realm existed distinct from the world that can be experienced, the phenomenal or empirical world of time and space that can be explored and measured by science, the world as it *appeared* to be.

Schopenhauer's noumenal world was not a separate reality, but another way of perceiving this one. Most poignantly, it did not contain individuated entities; in a world outside time and space, nothing exists in a distinct time or place. Therefore, in the noumenal world, there is no differentiation: all is one. This was the basis of his understanding of ethics. It is because in the noumenal world we are actually one, existing as a single seething mass of energy, yet in the empirical world we appear to be separate beings, that we feel such powerful compassion towards others. So are we drawn to act with ethical integrity, feeling empathy as we identify with another's suffering and joy. Further, if we hurt another, we are in reality also damaging our noumenal self, our essence.

Although through his pessimism he advocated a path of rejecting life, in the arts he found spiritual value, and particularly in music. Here was an expression of the noumenal oneness, revealing to us the nature of reality, for the power of music removes us from time and space, lifting us out of the prison of separation.

Rational Sense

When asked what is the most valid basis for decision-making, the most common answer I have been given is *reason*. I make a decision because it *makes sense*.

When we make decisions based on feelings, we bank on others' empathy for agreement and acceptance. Reason, however, can be more convincing, whether our actions were sound or not. With reason, we can more easily account for our behaviour, claiming it to be ethical, with all manner of logical explanatory threads. Arguing our case, step by step, we are more likely to feel that our choice was not only ethical but morally acceptable as well.

That singular old Prussian, Kant, declared true morality to be sourced solely in reason. This, he believed, is because human desires are always coercive, persuasive, distracting and ultimately selfish; it is only by detaching ourselves from desire that we are able to find reason. Indeed, it is when we are able to achieve independence from desire that we find freedom from individuation, from the loneliness of separation; for here we share in the universal and eternal perfection of reason, which he related to God.

In part his argument is hard to counter: our reasoning is perpetually saturated with underlying agendas based on emotion desires to have this or to avoid that. And stepping beyond desire is far from easy to achieve. Kant himself lived his life alone, with the reputation of being a cold and grumpy man. However, if we are to reach for that point beyond separation, to the universality of perfect reason, the quest for the affirmation a universal moral code provides becomes tantalizing.

This Kant laid out as the root of his Categorical Imperative, the first part of which states, 'I ought never to act except in such a way that I could also will that my maxim should become a universal law'. In other words, in making a decision about my behaviour, whatever I decide I must be willing for that decision to be true for everyone.

Philosophers have for millennia dedicated their lives to creating unassailable proof of a universal morality; the monotheistic religions have been the most committed of these but not the only ones questing. Indeed, the notion that a patchwork of different moral codes might be valid was barely contemplated until the end of the nineteenth century, for consideration of anything other than a universal Oneness was beheld as either sacrilegious or illogical, simply lacking in the necessary processes of thought.

It is easy to suppose there are rules of social behaviour that are globally relevant. Paedophilia, murder, mutilation, torture, slavery, incest and lying commonly occur all over the world, and most presume they are judged immoral throughout human society. However, the acceptance in some nations of child brides and female circumcision wipe out two of the above. There are moves in the USA to make judicial torture legal, justifying extreme intentional harm to one individual for the sake of others.

Morality, by definition, is culturally specific. Deriving from the Latin word *mos* (plural, *mores*), in its simplest meaning it translates as a custom. In the richer use of the language, the definition includes tradition and law, but the word also speaks of a person's nature, his humour or inclination, his mood, or indeed that of a people, a community or tribe.

Understanding that morality can at times be valid only within the relevance of one context in time and space is called relativism; it is a notion that is traditionally unpopular with philosophers, perhaps because the motivation of the thinker is so often to solve the untidy problems of nature's diversity. The English moral philosopher Mary Midgley, for example, argues that values such as justice, integrity and compassion, are universal, but variously expressed in different cultures. Yet relativism inspires tolerance, and indeed the attitude that steps beyond toleration into the celebration of pluralism. The ethical relativist is awake to the intricacies of difference, fully exploring circumstances in order to find understanding about a choice or action.

Humanity craves the calm certainty and cohesion that comes with order, though, and uses meticulously reasoned arguments to substantiate every notion that may provide it. Throughout the twentieth century it was political ideologies that, *if only everyone would agree*, would bring about salvation from hardship and conflict - from communism to fascism. Some modern cynics, like the British thinker John Gray, perceive Western free-trade democratic liberalism to be yet another monist construct whose proponents simply require everyone to submit to the philosophy in order to save the world, once and for all! While there is a growing awareness that no single idea is acceptable or appropriate *globally*, it is easy to understand why monist ideologies are again gaining ground, now most poignantly in religious fanaticism.

Of the world's 193 nations (acknowledging the independence of Taiwan), the majority are in a state of war or internal crisis, ruled by a Gordian mix of global corporations, macho tyrants and endemic corruption. With biotechnology and weapons of mass destruction, the mess of trade restrictions, oil wars and the illegal drugs industry people are increasingly confused and scared. The effects of pollution and environmental devastation pay no attention to national boundaries. Refugees from hunger, civil war, natural catastrophes and tyrannies are surging across borders. If many in the comfort of Western society really knew who was in control and how little control there is, the levels of fear would only rise. Amidst the chaos, if it were ever a possibility, now would be a good time for a transcultural morality.

Balancing Pleasure and Pain

Another tack we use to clarify how we make our choices is a blend of both reason and emotion: I choose my course of action knowing that it will affect others, perhaps negatively, but *overall* it seems to be the best thing to do.

Mary Midgley confronts the issue from this standpoint. Choice, she perceives, is not about the rationality of logical deductions. Instead, our capacity to reason must be employed to arbitrate between priorities, appreciating and considering the interests of all involved. In some ways, she is drawing reason and emotion together: I choose a course of action because it offers a reasoned balance between benefit and pain.

Her words are softly reflected in Hume's who, writing two and half centuries earlier, addresses the difficulty of finding a broadly acceptable set of behavioural standards. Bringing it back to the personal in his inimitable style, the genial thinker shrugged: 'I offer assistance to those in need because it makes me feel good to do so, and I am fair in my dealings with others because it would make me feel bad if I were not. All of morality rests firmly upon the natural human inclination to seek pleasure and avoid pain.'

It was this notion that Jeremy Bentham developed, laying out his moral philosophy of utilitarianism. Born in England in the mid eighteenth century, he was a social reformer who condemned the idea of natural rights as a provocation and justification for violence. Instead, he believed that improved education and extending the franchise would lead the people to vote for policies that would be in their own best interest, collectively improving social wellbeing. In simple terms, what he thought natural was a collective sense of care based on what felt good: an action is justifiable only if it generates an equal or higher level of happiness or pleasure in all who are affected by that action. If it does not, the action is judged to be wrong.

How it is possible to measure pleasure is debatable. Bentham spoke of keys such as the intensity of the sensation, how long it lasts, whether it is anticipated or we can anticipate it happening again, how close we are in time and space to that which provoked it, what effect it has on the rest of our life (accepting that some moments of profound pleasure have miserable consequences). Understanding pleasure in this way, it is deemed possible to make choices that will result in 'the greatest happiness of the greatest number'. He used a term which I love: the felicific calculus.

Utilitarians have developed these ideas since Bentham, not least one of his students, John Stuart Mill, whose own writings on justice and liberty were extremely controversial in his time. The Australian Peter Singer, a penetrating utilitarian thinker who originated the ideas of the animal liberation movement in the 1970s, continues to rock the boat of any ethically complacent society.

The understanding that pleasure is also derived from the *absence* of pain is important; after all, our drive to avoid pain is almost always greater than our drive for pleasure. This was explored by Richard Ryder who stepped aside from utilitarianism to present his own vision of morality called painism in 1990. 'Pain,' he said, 'is the only evil'; acting morally, then, is solely about reducing the pains of others. Nor can the pain or happiness of a number of individuals be accumulated, creating a greater pain or happiness. This is poignant in practice, and where Ryder diverges most from utilitarianism; in any situation, it must always be the condition of the one in most pain that is addressed first.

This is a very different morality from one based on law, for there are times when it would seem ethical to ignore a state's legislation or social laws of a culture, if circumstances mean that to abide by them would create more suffering than happiness. Killing a rabbit with miximatosis, blinded and deranged, would without doubt reduce its confusion and suffering; to end the suffering of a human being, living in a conscious nightmare of pain, is illegal within most societies. The utilitarian would consider euthanasia to be the ethical option.

Of course, if we are to base our morality on avoiding causing pain, we have to consider a definition of pain. Many Utilitarians include suffering, distress, fear and boredom as pain. GE Moore adjusted the utilitarian notion by saying that beauty and friendship had inherent good, even when they didn't give pleasure.

The early twentieth century British philosopher, Richard Hare, shifted the focus, saying that any decision should maximize the satisfaction of the preferences or desires of the most people. Yet many Western philosophers are increasingly acknowledging what has always been a key notion in spiritual mysticism and Eastern thought: absence of pain comes with the absence of desire or drives.

Whatever our definitions, poignantly problematic to this balance of pleasure and pain is the inability to predict all that will happen as a result of an action, weighing up every social and ecological thread pulled within the web. In 1958, Elizabeth Anscombe coined the term consequentialism to deal with this issue, declaring that an action can only be judged by its consequences.

Yet many Utilitarians don't view the world in black and white, as good or bad, but acknowledge the process of gradually shifting values and effects. A zygote becomes an embryo, a foetus, an unborn child, until at birth it becomes an infant, to grow slowly into a self-aware human being: instead of debating at what point it becomes a human or a *person*, the utilitarian considers the potential for suffering in every aspect of the situation, within each entity and individual involved. Where laws draw clear lines, nature is not so specific. Life is a spectrum between the horrific and the wonderful.

Adding to the brew, many of the cravings that provoke happiness are not intelligent, reasonable or tenable. Living in a stupor of drugs might make us happier in the short term than the higher seas of emotionally wakeful living. Denial, ignorance and passivity can be constructed by an authority to ensure a populace lives in 'happiness'.

Religious Law

The next basis for choice is religion: God says what I may and may not do.

For a prodigious number of human beings, God (with a capital G) is the true source of morality. Indeed, the notion of personal ethics is redundant, for God provides the code for the whole community: its morality. Thomas Aquinas declared that seeking God is tantamount to studying natural law which was, effectively, the 'reason of divine wisdom'.

Different monotheisms work in different ways: Judaic Halakha is made up of well over 600 laws, its authority coming not from any rational understanding but in the devotional practice of obeying it. It covers every aspect of life: when to wake up, what one can eat, how one can marry, business practice, holidays and religious festivals, how to treat others. In effect, following Halakha saturates even the simplest act with religious significance.

Based upon the Decalogue of the Old Testament, Exodus (34), Christian strictures don't appear as prescriptive as Judaic law, yet fundamentalists seek out any notion of Biblical guidance and declare it a mandate, establishing and maintaining as close to certainty as is possible. For most, however, Christianity works with just the twofold commandment found in the common era's Gospels: love God and love your neighbour. In John (4:12), the Bible reads, 'For anyone who does not love his brother, whom he has seen, cannot love God, whom he has not seen'. In Romans (13:8), 'Love worketh no ill to his neighbour. Therefore love is the fulfilling of the law'. Love here is *agape*, the willingness to care for another human as much as (or more than) oneself.

With the sands of Western culture shifting over the last few centuries away from a religious to a secular mindset, the ideas of most religious thinkers have been held within their own tribes. However, a good example of a modern philosopher whose writings are drenched in religious understanding, yet who has been profoundly influential, is the Lithuanian-born French Jew, Emmanuel Lévinas. A man who devotedly followed Halakha in his daily life, he said that all philosophy should be more about 'the knowledge of love' than the love of knowledge; this love was an *agape* which he described as an 'infinite' requirement to care, at least in terms of other human beings. Ethics must be based upon placing the concerns of others before one's own in every choice we make. While he seldom reminds his reader of the religious undercurrent of his thought, the limitless nature of this *agape* is clearly based upon a devotion to God.

From the outside, Islamic laws appear stringent, however for the most part this is simply the more rigourous implementation of tribal ethics. Moslem religious ethics make it clear that mankind was given a moral sense by its creator. The Qur'an seldom explains good and evil, but reminds the reader that he already knows which is which, and that his behaviour will be judged on that basis. Surah Al-Shams (91:7-10) reads, 'The human soul - the way He moulded it and inspired it with knowledge of its evil and its good - bears witness to the fact that he who cleanses it of impiety shall be successful, while he who corrupts it shall face doom'. Where the scripture does lay down a universal ethical principle, it is because too much ambiguity or temptation is likely, such as in *hayaa* (issues of sexuality) and *riba* (the use of money).

That God's law does not suffer from the vagaries of relativism or historicism allows this divine morality to be proclaimed stable, remaining valid in every land and era. It is this that has made such religions so aggressive a force of cultural and moral imperialism.

Yet the belief that a rational God created the world on principles we may not grasp but must accept indicates, to the non-believer, a conservative human authority that seeks simply to retain the *status quo*. Over three hundred years before the birth of Christ, Plato posed the idea that religion is too often used to give validity for ideas which have no validity otherwise. No politically religious or monotheistic society permits critical scrutiny; we may imagine a few scriptural or philosophical inconsistencies would topple the house of cards, but faith needs no evidence. It doesn't require a foundation of human reason.

Religious laws are always strongest during times of crisis. The Judaic God was a harsh father caring for his 'children' through struggle and upheaval. Christianity found its form as the Roman Empire was collapsing, its strict morality casting a net of control where the old empire had lost it. Islam was born within a time of social chaos, Muhammad laying down tenets by which the people could rise out of conflict. Catholicism was the bedrock of opposition to the authorities in Communist Poland, eventually generating from the ranks of its priests the most conservative pope in recent history. Under Bush, the US has been creeping towards a Christian theocracy as Islamic fundamentalisms call for a global Moslem *khalifate*.

Writing in the turbulence of the mid nineteenth century, Karl Marx called religion 'the opium of the masses': it eases the soul and means we ourselves don't need to think. A sufficient breadth of beliefs lays a foundation of assumptions that cannot be questioned, so providing a clear code of moral conduct. Should we fail to live within this code, punishment is damnation, an eternity of suffering, a penalty far greater than any that could be crafted by mere humans. Yet if we do manage to behave, the rewards are far greater than human creation: an eternity of bliss is the child's fairytale ending.

Marx lived in poverty, his atheism disallowing him an academic post, but Kant remained as Christian as he needed to be in order to keep on the right side of both the law and the emperor of his beloved Prussia. He despaired, nonetheless, that people should live within the guidelines of Christian morality only because of the repercussions. Such behaviour lacked respect and responsibility for what he saw as those laws' divinely rational foundation.

Schopenhauer, born in what is now Poland in 1788, was the first to be overtly atheist within the Western tradition. He considered the notion of God to be an anthropomorphized projection of human need and meaningless as a result. A century later, Friedrich Nietzsche, inspired by Schopenhauer, was criticizing Christianity freely as, 'all hatred of the intellect, of pride, of courage, of freedom ... of joy in the senses, of joy in general'. Yet his best known phrase, 'God is dead', was not a celebratory stamp on the grave of outdated religious beliefs, but a rallying cry of protest: he saw society no longer chained by Christian dogma, yet still living within its value system, and thus its morality. Christianity, he perceived, promoted weakness, self-denial, self-sacrifice and submission, a life of self-negation in the service of others. This slave mentality and its morality, he declared, was entirely worthless. All that is best in humanity, its courage, progress, literature and art, were produced through strength and self-determinism, freeing each individual to develop his full potential unfettered by a morality of weakness.

In response, the Russian writer Fyodor Dostoevsky wrote, 'If God is dead, everything is permitted'.

The Greek thinker, Epicurus, living in the third century BCE, didn't dismiss the idea of the gods completely, but his claim was that the gods no longer had any interest in human affairs. His vision was that human life is made unbearable through fear of divine intervention and fear of death. The focus of his work was, therefore, to eradicate both; with regard to the gods, his solution was simply to ignore them, and thus to enjoy a life of freedom, the freedom to indulge in a life of pleasure. Needless to say, when the French philosopher Pierre Gassendi revived Epicureanism in the mid seventeenth century, a good deal of attention was brought to its apparent lack of morality.

Social and Political Law

Another basis for choice is, of course, the secular authority: I choose to act a certain way because it is legally or socially acceptable.

In one of the gatherings I mustered to discuss Pagan ethics, the source of a nation's laws was raised as an indicator of social morality. The formal legal framework of a society is known as its positive law and, since Aristotle, it has been considered desirable for natural law to form the foundation of positive law, establishing a social structure based on what is termed the *common good*.

Yet, how much a nation's laws are based on social morality is debatable. Pierre Joseph Proudhon, the nineteenth century French philosopher, is attributed as having said that laws were 'spider webs for the rich and mighty, steel chains for the poor and weak, fishing nets in the hands of the government'. Over a hundred and fifty years later, the same opinion is common. In most Western nations, positive law is created through the judicial system and parliament, both motivated by the criminalizing of behaviour, by negative judgement. That judgement can only be biased: courts and government buildings are populated by the upper tiers of society. Living in a world of new cars and restaurants, clean warm secluded houses, private health care and private education, it isn't possible to grasp or remember the realities of lives lived in poverty, insecurity and ignorance. Furthermore, those whose status is based upon the democratic vote focus their attention on what one of a discussion group termed the 'wittering' classes: people with time enough to stop and complain.

Whether or not we accept a legislature depends on where we source our own sense of ethics and with whom we share those through a tribal or community morality. Rousseau wrote that the first notion of society that we encounter, both individually and evolutionarily, is the family, and it is within this unit that we first learn of morality. But the family is no longer such a powerful force; most children in Western culture spend their first four years babysat by the cartoons and commercials of TV or within the clamour of a busy crèche. At around four, TV time is diluted by attendance at an under-funded and overcrowded school, where the culture of competitive bullying, trivial rules and inane systems of reward and punishment add to their developing ideas of *right* and *wrong*. Everywhere we turn, we absorb critical judgement.

It used to be said that the morality of democratic secular nations was balanced by three anchors of society: the government, the judicial system and the free press. Asking my gatherings which of the three they would trust, the consensus is always 'none of the above'. The reality of politicians and judges being in each other's pockets is regularly demonstrated; the US Supreme Court's ruling to put Bush in the White House when he clearly lost the 2000 election is an example *ad absurdum*.

There is, however, an uncomfortable awareness of the media's omnipresent messages. In the words of British philosopher, Richard Ryder, the media, once the guardians of freedom, 'have also become the great destroyers. They are the most serious sickness of our free and democratic society'. Far from wellsprings of ethical behaviour, the media are nonetheless an important guide in terms of tribal morality of Western culture. The bias of each story told expresses what is acceptable and what is not. That they tend to redraw the lines according to the pressures of the moment makes them a wholly unstable guide; the cynic might call them absurdly relativist. Of course, however, the continuous adjustment means they must be continuously referred to.

That these tides of social narrative influence the codifying of law into legislation is poignantly indicative of how something familiar becomes acceptable, then normal, then required by convention, expectation or law - and how, eventually, to act otherwise becomes categorized as deviant, criminal or just insane.

Rights

Nature is not fair. Human self-awareness and reason, however, offer us the chance to create fairness within society. Where laws, whether social, religious or statutory, are not providing that fairness we seek out for our decision-making a basis of justice. Here we find a much overused term: I choose to do something because I have the *right* to.

It is a much debated concept, and my gatherings of Pagans crafted this definition: a *right* is a claim to belong to a tribe and so be treated according to its moral code.

As such, rights are a complicated notion, for the edges of tribes are not always clear. Do chimpanzees sit within the tribe of sentient and self-aware animals who can feel pain and so can justifiably claim the right to be treated as other animals within that tribe, such as human beings? What about other intelligent creatures, such as pigs or parrots or political criminals? The morality of an African society that practises female circumcision delineates the edges of specific tribe, within which different rights are claimed and expected; but the girls who undergo the ritual are still a part of the wider tribe of humankind. The authority we reach to for defence of rights is clearly dependent upon how we identify the individual (or ourselves) in terms of tribe. If we are not able to claim that right for ourselves, who will make the claim on our behalf? In other words, where do they or we *belong*?

Our rights give us permission as to what we are free to do, what we are free not to do, and what we are free to receive or possess within the tribe. Existing some way between laws and morality, these claims both pull at the less clearly defined codes of behaviour and push at the framework of positive law, demanding the justice of acceptance. For if a claim is backed, that individual's place within the tribe is acknowledged. No wonder rights are so contentious. They speak to every member of the tribe about how they not only should treat their fellow tribes folk, but how they *must* and *who* they must treat according to the agreed morality they themselves have subscribed to. We face issues here about what an individual is judged to deserve. Rights express clearly the extent of tolerance and flexibility within a society, therefore, revealing truths about social bonds, empathy, generosity and loyalty; they delineate the boundaries of equal consideration.

In other words, rights define the *moral status* an entity is accorded.

Most thinkers agree that the most fundamental is the right to be treated with respect. Yet conflicts arise. One person's claim of liberty may suppress another's claim for equality. Do we vote for the drug addicts who need a rehab or the residents of the quiet suburb where it is to be located? Do we care for the thousands of primates tortured in pharmaceutical testing or the few dying children? In any situation of conflict, natural instinct guides us to cling to the safety of our own tribe. The greater that threat, the smaller the notion of our tribe becomes, from that of our species, to our nation, our community, family, or household. Alone, however, alienated, outcast, we have no rights: the freak has no tribe with its morality to protect him.

The issues have a long history within the heritage of our people. Amidst the violent social upheaval of post-civil war England, John Locke developed the notion of natural rights. Locke believed that human beings, in a natural state, are free and equal. When they come together, however, creating social groups, their instinct is to protect themselves from others, ensuring their own safety and the integrity of their property. To Locke these instincts were drawn from natural law and its foundation of human reason, and any governing authority that secured those prerogatives was protecting natural rights.

Writing in 1776, a century later, in his booklet, *Common Sense*, Thomas Paine wrote that 'society is produced by our wants and government by our wickedness', for 'were the impulses of conscience clear, uniform and irresistibly obeyed, man would need no other lawgiver; but that not being the case, he finds it necessary to surrender up a part of his property to furnish means for the protection of the rest'.

Thomas Jefferson, drafting the American *Declaration of Independence* in 1776, was not proposing original ideas. What he did do, however, was to summarize the ideas of liberal European philosophers such as Locke and Paine, and present them as 'self-evident truths', implying that they are so natural, and so thoroughly based upon reason, that none could argue against them: 'that all men are created equal, that they are endowed by their Creator with certain unalienable Rights, that among these are Life, Liberty and the pursuit of Happiness'. The Constitution, with its Bill of Rights, was founded on those ideals.

Two years later, as envoy to France, Jefferson guided the Marquis de Lafayette in the writing of the French *Declaration of the Rights of Man and Citizen*. In seventeen simple points, accessible and concise, Lafayette expounded his vision: the aim of government is solely and fundamentally 'the preservation of the natural and imprescriptible rights of man. These rights are liberty, property, security, and resistance to oppression'.

Defending the ideals of the French Revolution, Paine wrote in *The Rights of Man,* 'Every history of the creation, and every traditionary account, whether from the lettered or unlettered world, however they may vary in their opinion or belief of certain particulars, all agree in establishing one point, the unity of man; by which I mean that all men are born equal, and with equal natural right'.

Yet rights are fought over as much as they are fought for, each proponent quite sure their position is one of self-evident truth. The United Nations' *Declaration of Human Rights* is as vague a document as could be agreed upon by such a wide range of human cultures, of tribes. As such, what it declares to be the right of any human being gives opportunity for behaviour that others would never condone as morally acceptable.

Indeed, on a personal level it is easy enough to find justification in terms of rights for decisions: our right to liberty allows us not to work for a living, but instead to paint or ponder, supported by government benefits or begging. Comparably, our right to equality backs up the petty pilfering or stealing that many feel acceptable if the victim is wealthier than themselves. Our right to pursue happiness justifies the use of Ecstasy or sex with underage boys.

In a society that reaches for its rights, people feel they are *owed* something: usually an easier life, more attention, love, money. Certainly in our capitalist culture there is a sense that we each have a right to a bite of the cookie of progress, to get a little richer, happier, freer, as if the simple act of living brings with it an increase in terms of what we deserve. Rising claims and expectations generate inflation in a tribe's currency of rights.

Marx criticized any morality that he perceived to be based upon rights, for he perceived such a system served the individual instead of the people as a whole. Yet liberal thinkers speak of rights protecting the individual *from* society and the state; for a true democracy is a tyranny of the majority within which minorities need protection.

From within the chaos that followed the English civil war, another thinker was also writing, whose ideas appear more popular in the US government now than those of Locke or Paine. In his key work, *Leviathan*, Thomas Hobbes described what he considered to be the true 'state of nature'. Humanity, he said, is driven by only two natural impulses: the fear of death and the desire of power. Believing all social structures could and should be created using laws of geometry, he saw human beings as mechanistic, fuelled by subjective preferences founded upon those two base instincts. Without the necessary controls, he said, human lives would be 'solitary, poor, nasty, brutish and short', for as each individual seeks out satisfaction for his own needs, naturally he will come into conflict with others.

The focus of his vision is still nature, albeit a long way from Aristotle's *eudaimonia* or the Stoic harmony of natural law. His vision offers another base of ethical justice, the social contract: you treat me well, I'll treat you well. As a philosophical concept, Hobbes believed human society had to be based upon spoken and unspoken rules that kept our violent impulses in check.

The basis of the contract was about abdication of personal power. In exchange for security, the majority ceded authority to a single person (or body) who had claimed the right to the position through demonstration of dominance. This ruler suppressed the violence and self-serving impulses of the people by using whatever force was required. He maintained peace, albeit through fear and obedience; the people lived in peace, albeit without freedom. It is not entirely dissimilar to Plato's vision of a perfect republic, ruled by the educated and selfless elite. Plato too acknowledged no personal liberty; the masses have no right of self-determination, but live in the freedom of peace created by the government's power. Like Hobbes, he too was writing at a time of devastating social upheaval.

Hobbes acknowledged that this was not ideal, but felt it not only the best option and preferable to the natural brutality he called the 'state of nature', but also one that society leaned towards of its own volition.

Established at some point in the distant past, it was a contract made that could not be revised, for society had evolved no other way of working. His contract was, therefore, or so he believed, a clarification of human nature. As a political philosophy and a moral justification, the notion has been used for centuries.

The classic tension between autocratic government and natural impulses is poignantly expressed in the tragedy *Antigone*, an extraordinarily powerful play written in the fifth century BCE by the dramatist Sophocles. The tyrant Creon refuses to allow Antigone to bury her brother on the grounds that he was a traitor. Antigone, moved by love for her brother, by family duty, and convinced of the injustice of the command, buries him secretly, for which Creon immures her in a cave, where she hangs herself. Her lover, Creon's son, commits suicide. Not only does such autocracy come about within individual states, but it is the morality claimed to back up imperial ambition. One superpower, using brute force, holds the world acquiescent: currently it is *pax americana*.

Rousseau's account of the social contract fully revised Hobbes' conclusions. Writing in a period of European history when the revolutionary thinkers held notions of individuality and freedom as vital, he saw that Hobbes' concept allowed and supported inequality and servitude. Rousseau acknowledged that people would cede authority in return for the benefits of security, but that inequality can only be justified by agreement. In his *Social Contract*, he wrote, 'the social order is a sacred right which is the basis of all other rights. Nevertheless, this right does not come from nature, and must therefore be founded on conventions'. If the one holding power did not provide that security, the people were then free to disobey the laws, rising up in revolution in order to craft a new contract.

Hobbes believed conflict was both natural and necessary to find the most capable (read: dominant) ruler. Two hundred years on, Darwin's work on evolution suggested that natural selection through 'survival of the fittest' (a phrase originally coined by the English sociologist and philosopher Herbert Spencer) is not a merciful process. Writing a few decades later, Nietzsche's vision of human potential and satisfaction supported the notion that the strongest would and should dominate society. What makes humans better than animals, he said, was their courage and strength of will. They are innovative and creative, nature's leaders, born with a 'will to power', to dominate through natural superiority. Conflict is natural, and must be acknowledged as acceptable, because through conflict the weak will be defeated and the strong will rule.

Yet not all people are sufficiently awake, intelligent or able to play an active part in forging the contract that justifies the morality of a society. When the needs of a select few individuals overwhelm the rest, individual investment in that contract deteriorates. This is not simply because people crave liberty more acutely when they are oppressed; the more people are controlled, their willingness to retain personal responsibility slips away. If the authority controls everything, it can also be blamed for everything.

The late John Rawls, a twentieth century American philosopher, addressed these issues in what is called contractarian liberalism. Although many different philosophies can be glimpsed in Western governments, Rawls' influence has been significant in modern political thought. His vision of 'fair equality of opportunity' with regard to education and the free market looks at where there are conflicting interests; using his 'difference principle', decisions are made to benefit the least advantaged social group in any situation. Rawls asks the question: what kind of society would you choose to live in if you didn't know the position you would occupy within it? He stated that, where contracts are crafted, they should be done behind a 'veil of ignorance'; in other words, the person cutting the cake should do so without knowing which piece he himself will be getting. Individual responsibility is shuffled back into the deck, not only for oneself but for one's community.

Personal Freedom

The final basis for choice is freedom: I choose to do this because I *want* to. Freedom, though, has two layers. There is the ability within our own soul to experience and express ourselves without the restraints of conditioned conscience, inhibitions and fears of social or divine rejection. Then there is the freedom that allows autonomy from and freedom within the state. That balance between liberty and security has always generated fervent debate.

During the ten years through which I home-educated my son, the most common anxiety thrust at me, like the dog-eared Bible of the evangelist, was summed up in one word: *socialization*. Needless to say, my household was ever full of interesting and interested people of all ages, and my son learned how to interact with the intelligence and enthusiasm of any child who is listened to, but still I faced the concern of those who felt a school environment essential to the development of a human being. Yet, it was specifically the moral culture of institutionalized competition and consumerism, so prevalent in schools, that I did not want my child socialized *to*. At the age of fourteen, comfortable in the idiosyncrasies of his individuality, he headed off to school, continuing to question, happy not to conform.

Where any tribe - whether a family, a school or workplace, a local community or an interest group - encourages exploration and discussion, instead of passive acceptance based on collective fears, the cohesion that crafts its morality is more compassionate, more flexible, and more willing to embrace both diversity and change.

As a nineteen year old in the harsh recession of the early 1980s, fervently backing the strikers out on the picket lines of Thatcher's England, I watched society around me losing itself. Later in the decade, Thatcher's words summed up her vision: 'There is no such thing as society. There are individual men and women ... There's no such thing as entitlement, unless someone has first met an obligation'. From where I stood, in an era when a school leaver getting work was little more than a vague possibility, the vision of Karl Marx and Friedrich Engels seemed the only solution. From the industrially voracious mid nineteenth century, they considered it to be not only possible but inevitable that the evolution of society would bring a time when the political 'state' was no longer necessary. Inspired by the French count, Henri de Saint-Simon, who gave up his title, wealth and property to live in poverty in support of the Revolution's ideals, Engels spoke of a time when the people would overthrow the ruling classes and, through their co-operative self-governance, 'the government of men will be replaced by the administration of things'.

While my own revolutionary socialism faded with a few more years and books behind me, Engels' certainty was rooted more deeply. Based on Hegel's understanding, he saw the entirely natural and rational process of a primary concept being opposed by its countering balance, that conflict creating a third reality based on aspects of the first two: thesis, antithesis and synthesis. It lay as a foundation to the view that socialism was a scientific inevitability, a part of nature's patterns.

Anarchists, even Emma Goldman who was actively fighting tyranny at the turn of the twentieth century, have shared Engels' vision of the dissolution of the state, though not as a scientific inevitability. To the anarchist it is an ethical necessity: while one might view the state as a construct crafted by civilization to ensure a balance between equality and liberty, some see it instead as the structure that maintains the problem. Without social rules codified into positive law imposed by a hierarchy, however, most doubt that rights would be respected. Is it too optimistic to imagine that humanity could behave morally without coercion or threat of retribution?

Human beings are driven by passion and selfish desire. Beyond those few who dedicate themselves to its study, there is very little understanding of the complexity of our own human nature. We do tend to be easily persuaded, emotionally unstable, ambitious, insecure. Larger forces - and they get larger with globalization and the information revolution - push us in directions that we are not aware of. However much we hate it, advertising works. How can we make our own decisions when we are so ignorant and weak? Should we not acknowledge and submit to the care of those who appear strong and wise, as Plato and Hobbes advised?

To most philosophers, the notion of anarchy is idealized nonsense. To the anarchist, the notion of a wise elite is mythic and dangerous, not least because human beings will all too often grasp an opportunity to follow a leader, one who allows them the relief of not having to think or take responsibility for themselves. And not many are wise.

The Austrian-born Karl Popper, writing in the antipodes in the 1940s, thoroughly criticized both Plato, connoting in his attack on *The Republic* the fascist Nazism of his era, and the Marxism that had led to the twentieth century's communist revolutions and tyrannies. Popper declared that a society must be *open* enough to allow critical discussion, regardless of all moral considerations. Only then did he believe there was hope of continuous progress.

Emma Goldman's critical stance on an unthinking society is just as sharp. '*What I believe* is a process rather than a finality,' she stated. 'Finalities are for gods and governments, not for the human intellect.' When we believe we've found the answer, we tend to sit in satisfaction and close our minds. So is the continuing process of questioning crucial if we are to accept our responsibility and find integrity in our heresy, our *haireomai*, in that process of choosing.

This has echoes in the now unfashionable existentialism of Jean-Paul Sartre, which was so much a declaration and celebration of human freedom. Inspired and frustrated by the rate of change in post-war France, for Sartre, there was no pre-existing blueprint of humanity to which we must conform. In a world brimming with possibilities, individuals are not constrained by either society or their own past choices, needing only to overcome their own self-deception or 'bad faith'. Instead, by taking responsibility for what we are, we cast off the burden of all those excuses we have carried for failing to achieve what we want from our lives.

This is the essence of freedom: we choose what we become.

In this chapter, I have covered a vast area of ground, skimming over the surface, taking a biplane over those ancient plains of human thinking, crafting brief pen and ink sketches along the way, the shifting dunes and horizons, always created of the same sand.

I have divided the bases on which we make decisions into various contours: intuition, compassion, reason, the prioritising of need, divine law, a state's legislation and community's social laws of acceptability, our rights and the deals we make to claim a place in a community, and lastly our own freedom and desires. Even if simplistic, the overview is important. For in the next two chapters, I shall lay out the tenets of *Pagan* ethics: their source, rationale and the currents of nature upon which they flow. From this place, it will be easier to perceive the forms and colours that make *Pagan ethics distinct, and to see how their roots reach back through the history of Western thought.

CHAPTER FOUR

DEFINING PAGAN ETHICS

A young man learns three lessons before he understands love :
immorality, mortality and mystery.

The Moral High Ground

A few years ago, a young Australian was staying with me. A philosophy graduate working on his doctorate while studying Druidry, he spent the afternoons sitting on the lawn in the summer sunshine talking through key philosophical issues with my son, then fourteen years old and not yet at school. It was a delight to witness the easy intensity of their conversations, ideas mostly still wrapped in the softness of abstraction. When, now and then, their words touched reality, I saw moments of quiet, as if both were feeling the edges of the space in their lives that was yet to be filled with experience.

One day, meandering through the landscape, the young fellow turned to me and said, "You know, sometimes I wish I were a Christian. Wouldn't it be great to be able to *believe* in all that stuff: just one god, one church, one priest, giving you all the answers. You wouldn't have to think about anything at all". He gazed over the meadows, imagining the peace and ease, and I laughed. But later, sitting on the grass, watching the bumble bees in the clover, I wondered: *what answers?*

Feeling a wash of relief, I thought it was age allowing me the serenity of no longer needing to know 'the answers'. Yet, as I have been gathering together words for this book, it has dawned on me how little *Paganism is based on the quest for answers. An old teacher of mine laughed as I pulled out my hair, unsure of a decision I felt desperately needed to be made: 'If you feel you have to choose,' he said, 'you don't yet have the necessary information. When you do, there is seldom a choice to be made.' As a Druid now myself, I take that thought a little further, for it is not about finding the information, but about creating the relationships through which life naturally flows.

This is the heart of *Pagan ethics.

~ ~ ~

"Where do they kill them?"

I open my eyes and breathe in. The question was like a splash of cold water on warm skin.

And I lift myself from where I've been lying in the grass to sit up beside him. We've been challenging each other with increasingly complicated algebraic equations, a maths class in the late afternoon sunshine of the meadows, and my head is a tangle of $a^2 + 3b$, the sky larks rising in the clear blue sky, spiders moving through the long grass.

I watch his face, but his gaze doesn't shift. For a moment I realize how well I know every curve of his face, the long fair eyelashes, nine years old, and I know too that he needs an answer to his question. Beyond the stream, about a quarter of a mile away, the old herdsman is pushing and prodding the lumbering cows along the track. But they are slow, meandering, tired after a long hot day, with milk-heavy udders and flies constantly irritating, and the fellow brings his stick down on the soft brown flanks as he yells, in his broad dialect, "Cam on, ca-am on, fockin coos, gertcha!", loud enough for his voice to reach us across the valley. My son half-smiles at the old man's cursing, but the thoughtful sadness returns.

"There are regulations," I say. "You can't kill animals on the farm. I think you need a special licence or to be registered as a slaughterhouse, so that inspections can be made, standards of health and safety have to be met." I'm aware of not knowing enough.

He frowns, "So they don't kill them in the barns down there?"

"No," I say softly. One of the paths that brings us out here onto the meadows takes us through the farm, and at this time the yard will be heaving with the cows. So many times we've perched on those slippery muddy gates and chatted to them, squealing with horror at the long drools of mucus, stroking the softness of slightly drier noses, discovering their names printed on their ear tags, feeling the great weight of their bodies pushing against each other, drinking from the old trough.

"The milkers aren't slaughtered, though, darling, not for human beings to eat ... " I'm not sure what to say, unsure as to the thought processes that brought him to the question, feeling wonder again at how a child learns about the world.

"No," he says, still staring at the slowly shifting line of cows along the track, the old man yelling, "Cam on, fa fock's sake, gertcha!" He turns to me, tender and serious, looking into my eyes. "I think perhaps we'll go home along the forest paths today."

~ ~ ~

Throughout Western society, ethics are tattered and crumbling, agreed moralities pushing into friction, leaving many without a clear sense of social acceptability and cohesion. Tribal groups based on religious beliefs, claiming a moral high ground, are asserting their morality more strongly as a result. Secular groups, declaring an advantage through an intellectual or rational high ground, consistently fail to clarify a moral code, squabbling instead about rights in political bantering.

It is not my intention here to claim any high ground from or for a Pagan or *Pagan religious perspective. After all, if the ethics of the modern Pagan community were more widely practised, it is likely I wouldn't be writing this book. Although I write thoughtfully, weaving others' ideas together with my own, my words are essentially an expression of observation and experience, not a declaration of knowledge. I've no doubt that they will be provocative, perceived as contentious; it is in my nature to explore areas where the challenge is greatest, rather than simply to celebrate achievement and accord. However, as the Pagan community continues to grow in numbers, exploring, crafting and sharing clarity is critical.

Before I speak of the deeper undercurrents of natural *Paganism, I shall offer an overview of Pagan ethics as they are usually thought through and presented, together with my thoughts as to why these are not adequately effective as moral or ethical guides.

Wiccan Ethics

Asking Pagans during my research about the basis of their ethical code, a great many referred to a single phrase. It comes in slightly differing variations, the most common being: 'An it harm none, do what thou wilt.' It's a beautiful expression, one that younger folk coming into the tradition no doubt believe holds an ancient and magical heritage.

As with much of Wiccan ritual, its history is not altogether clear. In Gerald Gardner's 1959 book, *The Meaning of Witchcraft*, he states that Witches 'are inclined to the morality of the legendary Good King Pausol, "Do what you like so long as you harm no one"'. Typical of the easy blending of fiction, mythology and history in most Pagan traditions, Pausol is a utopian monarch in an early twentieth century novel by Pierre Louys.

Rejecting social convention, reaching for a new utopia was a fundamental motivation for Gardner as he forged ideas for his new religion. This was emphasized by Gardner's interaction with Aleister Crowley, the reckless spiritual explorer, opium addict and poet considered by many to be wholly amoral. Inspired by his work, Gardner refers to Crowley's *Book of the Law*, written in 1904, in which Crowley wrote, 'Do what thou wilt shall be the whole of the Law'. Certainly, in the early days of Wicca, there was far more focus on the structure of ritual, and the form and practices of the faith community, than on any moral code. Within a movement fuelled by counter-culturalism, the lack of extensive rules was a crucial element of Gardner's Wicca, as it continues to be within most Western

Pagan traditions. However, as the tabloid press tore into the group, relationships becoming fraught, Gardner's key priestess, Doreen Valiente, did what she could to address their reputation of apparent hedonism. It was she who, using her own enchanting poetic ability, crafted Gardner's notes into the long dedicatory prayer called the Wiccan Rede. Her two line summation of the full text, usually dated to 1964, is most commonly recited as, 'Eight words the Witches' Creed fulfil / If it harms none, do what you will'. When people speak of the Rede, they are usually referring to those final eight words.

The simplicity and brevity of the summation is exquisite, and probably explains why it has been adopted by so many Pagans, even those with no training in or inclination towards Wicca.

When, as a teenager hurling myself through life's opportunities, I first came across the Rede, I loved the challenge of its apparent balance. For, then, the advice against harm seemed not as relevant to my journey as the encouragement to explore. *Do what you want* was a feast of possibilities, enticing the seeker to venture by emphasizing each word differently: *do* faced up to apathy and indecision, *what* spun out the dark threads of potentiality, *you* deconstructed identity, autonomy and society, *want* disentangled desire from need.

If it harms none, to my young mind, was less intriguing and more complex. My options were limited to trying my best not to be thoughtless. Believing my youth was to blame, putting any depth of question now to those who hold to the Rede, however, brings little in terms of satisfactory answers: on examination, these four words are close to meaningless. What does *harm* mean? This is a far broader word than the pain or suffering considered by the utilitarian philosophers like Bentham and Mills.

Furthermore, who or what is covered by *none*? The difference between *none* and *no one* is also potentially significant: like the sixth commandment of the Biblical decalogue, 'Thou shalt not kill', does this only refer to human beings? If it refers to other animals, there is no line clearly drawn where the guidance stops: are we allowed to harm the slugs eating our lettuces, the greenfly on the roses, the bacteria making us sick, the ash tree whose roots are breaking up the plumbing? Surely *harm none* includes the pig slaughtered for a bacon sandwich, the child slapped out of its sugar-hyped screaming, the ants squashed on the kitchen floor. Emerging out of the Second World War, there was certainly no notion of pacifism or veganism in early Wicca.

Frederic Lamond, a Wiccan high priest whose initiation in the 1950s was into Gardner's own coven, is known for speaking out about his disappointment in Wiccan ethics. In his books and at conferences he regularly refers to the problems of evident stress, obesity and cigarette addiction seen in Wiccan circles: 'surprisingly not all Pagans regard their own bodies as part of the *none* that should not be harmed'.

Another high priest, John MacIntyre, however, points to the final word of the Rede as 'no mere whim or impulse', but 'the True Will, the expression of spirit that is both our inmost self and a tiny spark of the Divine fire that flows through every part of this living universe'. His words beautifully and articulately describe a foundational tenet of mystical Paganism, reflecting in many ways the vision of thinkers like Schopenhauer. Aleister Crowley believed that if one acted according to our True Will, we can only do good; yet, as MacIntyre concedes, distinguishing just what that True Will is amidst the passions of the human soul leaves the Rede with 'some flaws as a practical guide to conduct'. Furthermore, most Wiccans are not mystics, but ordinary folk seeking easy guidance.

Some Wiccans point to another source for their ethics: the Charge of the Goddess. This invocatory prayer was also written by Doreen Valiente; interestingly, though they are held as profoundly sacred, there is no requirement for the words to be of an apparently divine source, the poetic creativity and insight of the high priestess being sufficient. The key words, in the ethical debate, relate back to Crowley. They are spoken as if by a specific goddess: 'for my law is love unto all beings'. Yet what is *love* in this context? For the average clumsy human being, love is most often a transitory and painfully confusing rush of blind passion and need. Its use here is as meaningless as the edict never to cause harm.

To the initiate, of course, like the Rede, the Charge is a powerful reminder, always spoken as if by the goddess. In prayers, it is an invocation of those divine forces that years of religious training have brought him to understand. To the Wiccan with access to this mystical resource, those simple English words - love and harm - shine with depth and meaning, drawn from his own visceral experience of spiritual love. As a law for the uninitiated (which presumably it was not supposed to be, but is now assumed to be), for many it is just too vague to be practicably useful.

The other prominent law given to Paganism from Wicca has no clear base in the history of the tradition at all. This is the Law of Threefold Return. Later in her life, long after Gardner's death, Valiente implied that he'd made it up. He believed in - no doubt, a Westernized view of - the Hindu notion of *karma*, yet in Wicca the consequences of one's actions are more often meted out in this life, not (necessarily) the next. This is demonstrated in the Wiccan second degree initiation rite, dated to around 1949; the initiate is scourged by the high priest, but is then required to scourge the priest in return, three times as hard and as long. Some, either with distaste or with affection, remark that Gardner simply liked a little naked, sexually-charged flogging - in traditional Wicca, the initiate and initiator are always of opposite genders; however, many speak of the scourging as a powerful lesson. In the published version of the rite, the high priest states, 'Thou hast obeyed the Law. But mark well, when thou receivest good, so equally art bound to return good threefold'.

The threefold return of negativity is equally emphasized in the way Wicca is taught. In 1971, in his book *What Witches Do*, Stewart Farrar talks of this as the Law of Return or the 'boomerang effect', saying that all working 'carries the seeds of its own retribution'. He states, 'It is a well-established occult principle that psychic attack which comes up against a stronger defence rebounds threefold upon the attacker'.

In the 1980s, another Wiccan author and high priestess, Patricia Crowther, spoke of this law in terms of divine justice, saying that, 'if a witch did intentionally set out to harm anyone, he (or she) would not only be breaking a very strict law, thus incurring the wrath of the Goddess, but would also be putting himself (or herself) in jeopardy, as the magic performed would rebound on them threefold'. Both she and Farrar seem to be falling back on superstition and notions of authority in order to instil an ethics that is fuelled by fear of judgement and consequences.

As a modern voice in Wicca, writing in the journal *Pagan Dawn*, MacIntyre speaks of this law in more fluent terms, explaining how his tradition's practice of magic is effected from the practitioner's innermost being. So does 'the accumulated record of all that a magician wishes and works for [become] a part of their magical identity and influences every-thing that they do. And everything that happens to them in consequence'. While crucially emphasizing the significance of personal responsibility within Pagan ethics, he is also pointing to the way in which the Pagan strives to perceive all nature as inherently connected. However, like the Rede, it is 'not an ethic for people who don't think, or seek easy rules to follow'.

Often referring to the tradition's poor interaction with nature, Lamond blames what he calls the Wiccan ritual 'language of command and aggression', still thick with the energy of Freemasonry and the Greater Key of Solomon, and thus the patriarchal and dualistic sentiments of Renaissance magic with its focus on dominating nature. To Lamond, too much focus has been spent in Wicca on increasing confidence in our Will, and not enough on our relationship with nonhuman nature.

The Witchcraft I myself was taught proclaimed a slightly different tack: 'perfect love and perfect trust'. Beautiful words, but what did they mean? Observing the normal if wearing human squabbles and tensions that were prominent within the faith community around me, I asked after teachings that could provide the necessary deeper understanding of these concepts, but was offered nothing other than the promise that I would come to understand in time. With high priestesses perpetually bitching, the promise sounded patronizing: I was far from convinced. It seemed that the majority were holding to a foundational law that, without significant committed study and sufficient independent wit, meant little in practice. Were stricter commandments and layers of superstition necessary to instil a sense of ethical behaviour in those who would not do the deep study or could never understand?

Druidic Ethics

Within the second largest Pagan community, Druidry, there is perhaps even less clear ethical guidance. Because Druids don't tend to practise magic through ritual and spellwork, instead seeking inspiration in order to answer doubts and crises, the immediate need for ethical consideration is deemed to be less. Furthermore, of all Pagans, Druids are especially focused on the autonomy of the individual and their own small tribe, being principally informed by locality in terms of landscape, ancestry, heritage and personal sources of inspiration. As a result, there have been even fewer Druids than Wiccans willing to speak out about ethics.

The largest Druid Order worldwide, the Order of Bards, Ovates and Druids, expresses its standpoint on ethics in its own gentle and philosophically inclusive way, through five key tenets: (1) taking responsibility and feeling empowered, (2) engaging with the world at large and valuing community, (3) trusting that life is fundamentally good and holds an inherent meaning and purpose, (4) appreciating the contrasts and polarities of life, (5) being of value to others and the world. Just to emphasize the issue of diversity, as a Druid myself I can't comprehend the notion that life may be fundamentally good; the sentence is incomprehensible to me. Yet, furthermore, the tenets express values that could have emerged from any spiritual tradition. For many that perennial generality is affirming, but for others the lack of distinctive Druidic quality diminishes the value: where the tribe is smaller, its character unambiguous, the desire to belong creates a tighter cohesion, the motivation to hold to its morality becoming more acute.

So, while many in the Druid tradition have a vague sense of Druid morality, accepting the need to source their own ethics, a good many seek the identity and certainty provided within the histories of their heritage: what in Scots Gaelic is called the *Sinnsreached*, the customs and mores of the ancestors.

Canadian author Brendan Myers, a respected student of the old texts and mythologies of Druidry, suggests the principal value within pre-Christian British and Irish society was truth. Particularly referring to the seventh century Irish text, *The Testament of Morann*, Myers talks of truth being a spiritual force within nature, one that must be adhered to if we are to be assured of justice. As the key moral tenet, a Druid must 'always choose Truth, in the expansion and enrichment of human knowledge, in ourselves and others, and at all levels of our being'. In a culture where art, poetry and music were given such high status, the context of Morann and other medieval writings doesn't imply truth as a court of law would understand it today: this is not about absolute facts. *Truth* is a way of being.

From a perspective of natural interconnectedness, and where that perspective is fuelled by the mystical *experience* that is a complete lack of separation, this understanding of truth can be an extremely potent premise of morality. The same is true of love, as I have mentioned above, and both these words I will talk of later in greater depth. However, where the understanding of nature's web is still theoretical, holding to a notion of truth for morality brings a catalogue of problems, individual truths and needs rising like an autumn mist. To clarify what is acceptable within a tribe, Druids, like Wiccans, tend to resort to the pedantry of asserted inter-pretation, creating lists of how an individual should behave or believe if they want to belong to a particular group or tribe. Such exclusivities in Wicca are usually based on personalities, creating exclusivities of covens and teaching lines; in Druidry, such dogma and insularities can touch on the far more dangerous racism of blood, most particularly within the modern Celtic nations and their diasporas.

In the search for certainty, some in the tradition still turn to the Brehon Laws. Now compiled as six thick volumes, these outline a judicial system written in early medieval Ireland, undoubtedly reflecting pre-Christian society, a system which was in use until the Norman invasion in the 1170s. Far from what some Pagans may perceive as respecting autonomy or personal ethics, these laws craft in minute detail the regulation of human behaviour, duty and social order, relationships, contracts, industry and trade, property and ownership: they lay out a clear and comprehensive morality. Yet they are still well regarded for the simple reason that, as a civil code, judgement is based within the local community. Every deed considered harmful, whether malicious or accidental, has its compensation clearly specified, the amount varying according to the degree of harm and the social status of both victim and wrongdoer.

Such a system wasn't only found in Ireland, of course. These kinds of legal frameworks stretch back to humanity's first attempts to codify laws, punishment and compensation. The best known example is in Mesopotamia: the law code of Hammurabi, king of Babylon, date to the eighteenth century BCE, almost four thousand years ago. While the context and relevance may now be lost, to some Druids the system of direct recompense is profoundly inspiring and thought-provoking.

A more poetic source of ethics much loved by Druids are the triads. These Irish and Welsh sayings were essentially mnemonics used by storytellers, holding within them, say, the names of the key characters, their social status or the gist of a plot; for example, 'Three unfortunate things for the son of a peasant: marrying into the family of a franklin, attaching himself to the retinue of a king, consorting with thieves'. Gathered into collections from various manuscripts, many feel they contain an invaluable insight into the world of the medieval (or even the ancient) Druids, and as a result many have been adapted, softened, broadened for the modern ear. They appear to express a beautifully poetic ethics.

Holding to Myers' focus on truth, a well known example is: 'Three things which strengthen a person to stand against the whole world: Seeing the quality and beauty of truth; seeing beneath the cloak of falsehood; and seeing to what ends truth and falsehood come'. Though probably Irish, it is a triad often seen as connected to the Welsh Gorsedd's rallying cry, *Y Gwir yn Erbyn Y Byd* (translated as: the truth against the world), taken from Iolo Morgannwg's memorial plaque in Bont-Faen and, if not written by Iolo himself, probably crafted by his son, Taliesin. It is a declaration now often used as a justifying banner of obstructiveness, heavy with a weight of rejection not sufficiently balanced by creativity, but to some the underlying meaning shines through.

Playing with the old British love of threes, many triads come in multiples, such as this, another well known Irish one: 'Three things from which never to be moved: one's Oaths, one's Gods, and the Truth. / The three highest causes of the true human are: Truth, Honour, and Duty. / Three candles that illuminate every darkness: Truth, Nature, and Knowledge. And Honour above all!' The last of the three triads, in Irish Gaelic, *Trí caindle forosnat cach ndorcha: fír, aicned, ecna*, is probably genuinely old. If the first two are more modern additions, they are written in the same spirit - the same flow of tribal identity - and thus equally accepted.

As one who walks the Druid's path myself, it is through the medium of triads that I have scattered ideas though this book. Like the Japanese haiku, they require a visionary poetic and mental discipline that hones our thinking in a way that I greatly appreciate.

Heathen Ethics

In Heathenism, ethics are seldom laid out with the complexities and analysis of either Wiccan or Druidic thinkers. Throughout the spread of Heathenism, there is a most distinct importance placed on being self-sufficient, self-contained, whether as individuals, ritual groups or hearths, or in the wider tribes of community. Indeed, that quality is one of the Nine

Noble Virtues most often quoted by Heathens. Codified by John Yeowell and John Gibbs-Bailey of the Odinic Rite in the 1970s, the full list is usually courage, truth, honour, fidelity, discipline, hospitality, industriousness, self-reliance, perseverance, and though some hold to the words as if they were liturgy, many acknowledge the importance of referring to the whole texts that are their sources: notably the Hávamál of the Poetic Edda, the Icelandic Sagas and Germanic folklore.

Quoted by Robert Wallis in his book on experiential British Heathenism, *Galdrbok*, author Tony Linsell describes a more concise Heathen Code: '1) the keeping of oaths, 2) loyalty, 3) courage, 4) hospitality, 5) boldness - in thought and action'. Conveying beautifully the Heathen priority of holistic strength in an uncertain world, as opposed to the Wiccan focus on spiritual power, Wallis writes about the nature of humanity in his exploration of ethics: 'Everything is struggling, all of the time. This is not a pessimistic view. Rather it leads to a clearer understanding of life, and gives rise to an *enlightened self interest*, tempered by the virtues of the Heathen code'.

His words bring to my mind the British philosopher, Mary Midgley, who writes, 'War and vengeance are primitive human institutions'. As such, human morality is often overtly and primarily based on the simple need to avoid potentially violent conflict. Through its origins in the cold northern European climate (both Nordic and Germanic), and its history of tribal disputes, migration and invasion, the Heathen pantheons, mythologies and peoples have never shied away from facing the issues of difference and strife. Heathens still don't.

The pre-Roman British were the same, much of their pride lying in the sharpness of the blade, an attitude still celebrated in swathes of modern Celtic culture. The tribe is a powerful cohesion of community and belonging, pacifying and directing inherent forces of violence; as such, the tribe creates the parameters of behaviour and metes out the punishment to those who breach its edges. In Irish heritage, the word often used is *tuath*: the notion of a tribe bound together by the blood of a common ancestor, one that can still be recalled.

Reflecting the Heathen vision, another well used triad states: 'The three manifestations of the true human are: civility, generosity and compassion'. Generosity or hospitality, *aíocht* in Irish Gaelic, not only establishes a tighter boundary around the tribe, but eases pressure when it comes to the potential threat of others. The American Celtic Reconstructionist and Druid, Erynn Rowan Laurie writes, referring to medieval Irish culture, 'Poets, druids, smiths and artisans were treated with reverence and courtesy, for one of these might create good fortune for a family, or curse it to oblivion with a deadly satire or a raw bolt of magical power'.

Loyalty to the tribe is even more powerfully crafted when, as was often the case in our pre-Christian heritage, it was believed that when you died, after a period of healing and feasting with the gods, you were reborn into the same tribe, the same bloodline. Consequently, your descendants were considered fully responsible for repaying your debts and making recompense for your mistakes if you yourself were for some reason unable to.

~ ~ ~

The moors are humming, the wind skimming the heather, as if bringing with it a darkness and rage. Yet in the circle around the black iron firedish, flames flickering in the wind, there is no sense of being out of place. Every soul here, wrapped in coats with collars high, smiles with a strength and warmth that comes from the confidence of their connection with the land: the dark mud and prickly heather shine in their eyes, the rage is no destructive force but a firmness of step in the face of nature, up here in the high hills. I feel honoured to be among them, a guest in the tribe.

His strong mouth smiles broadly as he places a silent kiss on the forehead of his baby son, and hands him with absolute care to his wife.

Then striding to the altar stone, in heavy boots and kilt, he kneels and breathes deeply before lifting his hands and his eyes to the skies. "Father," he whispers, then clears his throat and speaks again, loudly enough this time for the whole circle to hear, for his words to be taken by the wind still whole and true, "Father!" He brings his fist to his heart. "You of my blood, you who gave me life and the pride and love I feel for this land. You who gave me strength, through your memories of war, your memories of poverty, through your bitterness and disappointment, through your fear. You who gave me strength with the kick of your boot, with each bruise you left me, with each wound inflicted by your rage - "

Beside me, his wife rocks the tiny child in her arms, settling her own soul.

" - through the hunger in my belly and the shame in my heart, with each drunken blow you left on my mother's body and on my own." He pauses, seeking the stillness of truth through the emotion and determination. "Father, now as a grown man, I walk with my head high through the town here, amidst the people of our community, through each day, not because I deny you, but because I have paid for your violence and paid the debt well."

There is a murmur around the circle, an acknowledgement both of the cost and that the deed is done. One old man, his face crumpled with age beneath his flat cap, nods with a surety that brings tears to my eyes. At the altar there is no sign that he has heard the circle's affirmation; again he pauses for a moment, then taps his fist firmly against his heart.

"On this day, with the moon full and the summer before us, I bring my firstborn to this sacred place, my own son, to be honoured and welcomed into the tribe, and I speak these words to you. May they be witnessed by your father, his father, and all our grandfathers before them. May they be witnessed by the gods I swear by and by those you swore by." He drops his eyes, closes them, and breathes for a moment through his bond with the land.

Softly stepping over the heather, his wife comes to his side, touching his shoulder.

~ ~ ~

Secrecy and Persecution

While here I have presented some of the ways in which Western Pagans have sought out intellectually constructed forms and content for ethical or moral guidance, my limitations of space are increased by the limits of what I have access to. Through my experience of the Pagan community over some twenty years, I feel my overview has validity. However, there are many Pagan groups, families and small communities that have tight moral codes, usually based on similar lines to the principles listed by Linsell or Laurie, yet who hold their tribe hidden in the shadows of secrecy.

This separation through secrecy has - inevitably - significant influence on the codes of acceptable behaviour. The edges of a tribe tighten under threat, whether imagined or real: as the West responds to radical Islamist terror, we have all around us clear examples of morality shifting, priorities and values adjusting to allow for different choices. When contemplating the state of a Pagan morality or ethics, it is important to take into consideration the effects of long-term prejudice and persecution, both on individuals and on the tradition as a whole.

Although in Britain the laws against practising Witchcraft were finally repealed in 1951, of all Pagans, Witches and Wiccans have suffered and continue to suffer the worst prejudice. Still carrying the suspicion and mistrust borne by the cunning folk of healers, midwives and seers, it is not surprising that they have struggled; throughout its history, the word *witch* has been synonymous with the selfish and destructive power of sorcery. Fairytales explain the wicked inclinations and supernatural powers of the witch to the children of our society from the earliest age. In one village where I lived, the wife of the local Church of England vicar came over to discuss a charity event I was helping with: I offered her a mug of hot nettle tea and the fear it evoked was tangible, for the witch in one of her young daughter's story books had done just the same.

In a culture where the authorities have claimed Christianity their rule of law for over a thousand years, problems are inevitable. Although the correct translation of the Biblical Hebrew, *m'khashepah,* is a sorceress, the English word used in the King James and later versions is *witch*. The Torah and Bible both make clear that being a witch, using magic and the worship of other gods is grounds for violence, from ostracization to murder: 'Thou shalt not suffer a witch to live' (Exodus 22:18). I have stood in ritual, in a circle of Pagans, celebrating the beauty of the harvest, with evangelical Christians shouting such words through the safety of the hawthorn hedgerow.

Witchcraft hasn't been helped by the media, who throughout the 1960s to the turn of the millennium used imagery, symbols and ritual taken from Wicca and Druidry in order to present Satanic, demonic and psychopathic behaviour. Though portrayed in fiction, such images and stories sink into society, creating powerful attitudes. Chair of PEBBLE (the Public Bodies Liaison for British Paganism), Steve Wilson, commenting after a recent survey on Pagan discrimination, spoke of a case where 'someone attempting to have Paganism included in their council office's faith diversity day was first accused of "bringing the devil into the workplace", and then, after Union intervention on her behalf, was told "we'll do it after 5, when any kids have gone home".'

In schools, problems are common. I was recently told the story of a young son of a Druid who had returned from school in confusion, desolate with tears. Each child had been asked what they had done at the weekend, and this gentle six year old had happily spoken of his trip to Stonehenge where he and his parents, with a big circle of Druids, had watched the sun rise and sung to the gods. Reminded that he must always tell the truth, he'd been asked again, this time to tell the class about his weekend, not an elaborate story. Accused of lying, he'd spent the day in the 'naughty corner', teased and prodded by his classmates, chastised by his teacher. His story was all true. His parents were livid.

Amongst ill-informed Christians, the mere sign of a five-pointed star, particularly if worn by someone clothed in black, is still believed to be the sure sign of a Satanist. If it hasn't happened to them themselves, almost every Pagan knows of someone whose workplace boss has asked them to remove their pentagram in order not to upset the customers, clients or patients. The Thor's hammer often crafted in silver and worn by Heathens, although usually forged as a replica of a specific archaeological find, can appear to the paranoid Christian as an upside-down cross.

Most persecution nowadays, according to Steve Wilson, is 'teasing that becomes ridicule'. For some it is worse: from Pagan funeral services disrupted by the singing of hymns, to stones being thrown and windows broken, or threats about job security or a parent's rights to keep their children. When a society pushes you away, unwilling to listen, the basis on which you make your choices naturally changes.

Yet when a tribe begins to identify itself as persecuted, it can only make the problems worse.

Victim consciousness in the Pagan community has been nauseatingly exacerbated by a persistent belief in what is dubbed the Burning Times. In the late 1890s, American feminist and political activist, Matilda Gage, rewrote history in order to support her campaign for women's rights, stating that nine million women had been burned alive in the European witch trials. This apparent war of terror waged by a patriarchal Christian authority had identified women as the enemy; in the feminism of the 1970s and 80s an increasingly liberal interpretation augmented that attack into a hatred of all that women somehow represented: nature, community, midwifery, natural healing. To some contemporary Pagans, it was their principal deity, the Goddess, under fire, and thus it became a war on women and Paganism.

Closer to the truth is the horror of a violent, superstitious and xenophobic society - our Western heritage - where up to fifty thousand men and women were killed between 1400 - 1800, the concentration being through the inquisitions of 1560 - 1630. It is a significant number, but a long way from nine million. Through the writings and music of Celtophiles, feminists and environmentalists, however, all too many Pagans took the Burning Times into their hearts, creating a barricade of defensive self-righteousness that is only now being deconstructed.

Paganism bore another blow, its persecution complex fuelled, when scandals of 'Satanic abuse' broke in both America and Britain in the 1980s and early 90s, children taken from their parents in night raids to be interrogated for long and terrifying hours by panicking social workers. Nothing was revealed but atrociously poor levels of government-funded social care and negligible information about both Paganism and Satanism. Fraudulent and constructed 'recovered memories', together with the influence of television shows, were primarily to blame, but Pagans suffered as a result. Where normal human insecurities were making life hard, particularly in the workplace, with doctors and social security, and amongst those struggling to care for children on low incomes, paranoia crept in.

Moralities and ethics built on foundations of persecution are always twisted by defensive priorities. Voodoo and Santeria, evolving out of African American slave culture, are two traditions of many only recently finding a strength of beautiful positivity, after centuries during which their values were skewed by self-protection. In some threads of Yoruba, and other tribal religions, all that survived intact after generations of persecution were the skills of cursing, of defensive magic, and the rites that dealt with the dying and the dead.

As we clamber through the first decade of this new millennium, times are changing. The term *white witch*, originally used in the seventeenth century to denounce the cunning folk as simply whitewashed sorcerers (still black as sin underneath), was used liberally not so long ago to assert the distinction from sorcery, but is now heard less often. The tabloid media, no longer convinced Paganism is a dark well of scandal and misdemeanours, seldom get in touch.

Yet some of the ethics still remain: both personal and tribal behaviour can be closed, insular and untrusting. An emotionally secure person may not mind being teased, but persistent ribbing can wear down the strongest individual. The constant need to breathe in and find strength before explaining one's religion to an enquirer is exhausting. Working, as I do, on a daily basis, talking to people about the Pagan community's needs and sensitivities, can still be a very steep climb.

The Occult and Privacy

The process of opening mainstream Paganism into something that is integrated, familiar to and accepted by conventional society (if heretical), particularly in the work of presenting a clear moral code, is at times stalled by the issue of occultism.

Many occultists would not identify themselves as part of the Pagan faith community, or indeed of any religion at all; their ritual focus is on raising power in order to control nature, not on reverence. Furthermore, a significant number of occultists over the past few hundred years have based their work on the belief that humanity was inherently special and had the right to be dominant: an attitude very much out of synch with modern Pagan views. However, just as Gardner used the work of occultists like Aleister Crowley in his creation of Wicca, others continue to do so. The study of nature's patterns and forces holds a prominent place within Paganism, notably in the Druid tradition. As a result, the edges between the occult and Paganism continue to be blurred.

In 1660, when what had been the Invisible College became the Royal Society in London, it was still not as a centre of rationalism, but a gathering of mystics, alchemists and utopians, like the Freemason Robert Moray, the chemist Robert Boyle, the extraordinary reformer Samuel Hartlib, and even Isaac Newton. A century or so later, their 'new philosophy' was finding acceptance; during the eighteenth and nineteenth centuries, the radical thinkers questioning the accepted truth and norms were a new generation of heretics, the occultists whose position was

clearly in between the established Christian perspectives and the rationalism of the Enlightenment's new science that was now rapidly deconstructing sanctity. The occult became, according to historian Ronald
Hutton, 'the language of radical counterculture in late nineteenth century
France, just as Paganism did in Britain during the same period'.

At the turn of the twentieth century, Samuel MacGregor Mathers,
living in Paris, was developing his occult system of the Golden Dawn,
blending his own visions with those of his wife Moina, languaged through
Egyptian hermeticism, Classical Greek and Roman theology, Hebrew
Kabbala, Freemasonic and Rosicrucian traditions, forging the foundations
of what are now most Western occult practices. Crowley, ever the liber-
tarian, at first involved with the Golden Dawn, then inevitably and
inimitably the alienated troublemaker, took what he knew and began his
own chaotic, inspired and warped mystical exploration; in many ways, he
was simply continuing in the old tradition of secret societies through the
ages, from the crafts guilds to men's drinking clubs, the ethics of which
have always been primarily loyalty, courage and brotherhood.

~ ~ ~

Yesterday, putting on my robes for ritual, I was acutely aware of the shift
in my soul song. Perhaps it was because it had been such a hard morning,
so fraught with distractions, that the easy action of taking off my clothes
and feeling the soft simplicity of the black linen on my bare skin so
utterly altered the focus - the purpose - of my soul.

Turning off the engine, the headlights, I feel washed with the
darkness, the stillness and quiet of empty countryside, and I remember
that feeling. Stepping out of the car, it is as if a layer of clothes is
removed. As I walk towards the old buildings, another slips from me.

I feel the buzz: nobody but the few inside have the slightest idea
where I am or what I am doing tonight. I lift my hand to lay the prayer on
the door and a few minutes later it is opened. He smiles a smile that

doesn't touch his mouth, inviting me in.

Leaving my boots in the cupboard by the door, we walk together, barefoot and silent, through the darkness of the corridor, and with each step I feel myself increasingly naked, layer by layer falling away. At the door, he makes the prayer, and it opens before us. As I slip past the curtain, into the twilight of flickering candles, I feel the purpose of my being completely. Instead of my ritual garb of linen, I am robed in the exquisitely soft and fitted gown of darkness and secrecy, held by the wordless land and the night all around.

Kneeling by the altar, I listen to the whispers of my ancestors in my breathing.

~ ~ ~

Within most secret societies or closed groups, the morality is very clearly defined. It may resemble that of the wider community, or it may be quite different, the acceptable freedoms being particular to that small tribe. In closed Pagan groups, those differences are often to do with intimacy. Committed seekers and priests of many Paganisms will reach to understand and experience deeper levels of nature, through the intellectual, emotional, spiritual and physical, the creative and the sexual; seeking the exquisite creative flow and visceral rush of inspiration and connection with nature, with deity, with life itself, it is necessary to craft sufficient trust, honesty and openness to allow for exploration, levels that are not easily achieved outside the cohesion of a particular circle of people. Setting a group or ritual aside into the holistic privacy of secrecy perspicuously delineates what is effectively another tribal boundary, providing the opportunity for a very specific morality.

In Paganism generally, having an isolated morality is not always helpful. Fifty years ago, most of the Pagan community was made up of closed and hidden groups, but today, the Pagan population growing quickly, individuals and groups are integrating better into society, albeit with a counter-cultural edge that questions the conventional. The separateness that allows for differing moral codes has become less inevitable. However, there are still reflections from the centuries of isolation, flagging up another problematic issue in terms of ethics: relativism.

Relativism

Many Pagans would call themselves relativists. Not subscribing to any notion of universal truth, most would agree with Hume's perspective, that value is more important in ethical choice than apparent fact. Value is subjective; it is also an important element in the agreements that make up the shared ethics of a tribal morality.

Pagans, whose religious practice is designed to draw them into a closer bond with the landscape within which they live, with their ancestry and heritage, accept wholeheartedly that such interaction creates differing perspectives: a Pagan priest of the Cornish coast will have overtly different values from a priest of the Derbyshire moors or the poverty of inner city Glasgow, let alone one from a Brisbane suburb, the Alaskan forest or downtown São Paolo.

However, localism can create blinkers. My relativist perspective was judged by a Christian who, although in dialogue with other established religions, didn't extend his interfaith work to shamanic, indigenous or Pagan traditions. He justified his position by speaking of a Japanese Shinto group that, while being fiercely protective of its own ancestral lands, expressed no empathy or environmental care for islands that were beyond the spiritual reach of its people. I was sceptical about his ability to understand the Shinto vision, but willing to be saddened too if his words expressed even a glimmer of truth.

In his book, *Druids, Witches and King Arthur,* documenting the history of Western Paganism, Ronald Hutton wrote of Wiccans he knew: 'all believed in a tolerant and pluralist society with maximum potential for individual choice and self-expression'. They shared 'a concern for environmental issues, and especially those which directly affected their own home districts'. However, 'none actually joined protest camps formed to halt the latter - in sharp contrast with Pagan Druids and non-initiatory Pagans with whom I was also acquainted'.

The unwillingness of Wiccans, and indeed many Pagans, to get involved at the muddy edge of interaction is not always due to the general apathy of Pagan ethics, but at times can also be attributed to their relativist perspectives. The current pope, Benedict XVI, rails against what he perceives as the 'dictatorship of relativism' in modern culture. His words are poignant: 'a particularly insidious obstacle to the task of education is the massive presence in our society and culture of that relativism which, recognizing nothing as definitive, leaves as the ultimate criterion only the self with its desires'. While I would not agree with his solution (his concept of a single divine truth), nor his dismissal of relativism as a whole, his words are poignant: relativism can too often allow inaction, and inaction based on selfishly blinkered attitudes.

In our comfortable yet spiritually impoverished Western culture, the generic depression creates an apathy that wholly lacks both courage and inspiration. Individuals cower before any notion of authority, justifying their inaction with a shrug of impotence. Worse still is the *I'm alright, Jack* attitude that protects familiarity and comfort, dissuading us from stepping forward to confront injustice. When we feel as if we are living on the edge of sanity or survival, our world shrinks to the near horizons that encompass only what we can just about cope with; we look after our local patch, our home, our family, but anything beyond is different and must look after itself. After all, how can *we* know what *others* might want?

Where interest groups create communities with no local geographic commonality, the issues have added complications. These are not only evident in Paganism, but throughout Western society; however, because Pagans may live in areas where there are few or no others who share their beliefs, the internet has allowed for a rapid growth in web-based Pagan communities. Yet, without the subtleties and scents of face to face human contact, the moralities of these small tribes are inevitably weak, lacking roots in which to ground. They often maintain strength while sharing little honesty in terms of members' identities. Allegiances are created without true loyalties. Furthermore, internet communities gather in the ethereal space of shared ideas but, as a result of the hours spent away, the individuals return to physical tribes of their geographic neighbourhood (culture and society) in which their soul investment is often significantly diminished.

Pagans will vigorously defend the pluralist perspective, celebrating diversity within their own faith community and within all human cultures. They will wholly defend the celebration of individuality, which actively encourages a fullness of personal creativity, the exploration of personal truth and freedom, and happily acknowledge the eccentricities and idiosyncrasies that inevitably emerge. Pagans are proud of the unwritten elements of their traditions, the teachings passed down through the stories of their heritage, and eagerly justify the way in which the oral tradition allows for change, encouraging individual input and insight, always requiring a situation to be addressed in its own unique circumstances. Yet, with a community that is definitively so diverse, where do individuals find their ethics, and how does the community cohere those into a shared morality? Further, where a tribe supports anarchy, as Paganism clearly does, the few written sources of ethics - such as the Wiccan Rede, the Heathen Code, old collections of triads and the Brehon laws - are inevitably going to be deconstructed by many in the community, very often to the point of being useless.

In every group I have assembled to talk of Pagan ethics, after the main sources have been unravelled, the answer becomes clear. It is simple: relationship. Pagans find and craft their ethics through the experience of relationships. It may sound obvious - like love and truth are obvious. As an ethical foundation, why then does it so often fail to work? And when does it not?

In the following chapter I shall explore the ethics of Paganism that are not so much crafted or constructed as emerge more naturally through our heritage, through human nature and our bond with the land. I shall look at natural *Pagan ethics.

CHAPTER FIVE

NATURAL PAGAN ETHICS

Before honour sits in the belly :
we face our community, we face ourselves,
and with pride in our hearts, we face those who have lived before.

The rain is so fine, though I can barely feel the tiny drops landing on my skin, I am vaguely aware that we are slowly being drenched. The couple are holding hands, tight, gazing down over the valley. The view from here on the ridge is beautiful, even on such a damp and misty day. And we wait, knowing that anything might happen, knowing that all we can do is wait, as they hold hands and gaze: I can feel the emptiness that fills their minds. The world must look strangely new.

One of the lads behind us, one of his friends, shuffles his feet; I turn to see him trying hard to suppress a sneeze. He fails, instead breaking the quiet with the sudden tumultuous noise. The couple turn, and gentle smiles are exchanged, full of tenderness and apologies. But the moment is ended, perhaps not inappropriately. They look into each other's faces, and I am painfully aware of the weight inside each one, the weight that makes each breath so heavy to take.

Stepping forward, I wait again, this time for the moment to speak, when I can feel they both have their feet on the ground, fully present, knowing what I am about to say. Most of the small gathering of witnesses have less idea of the course of the rite, but they watch: his father in a dark blue donkey jacket, shimmering with the tiny droplets of rain, her sister in an old wax coat, an Indian scarf of pink and green loose around her neck, the handful of friends easily identifiable as his or hers.

"You have offered your thanks to each other," I say softly, "for all that has been learned, all that has been given and received. You have exchanged gifts in recognition of all that you have shared. You have honoured the gods of this land and the gods you swear by: the vows that tied your souls in your handfasting rite have been acknowledged and set aside. In the eyes of the gods, the land and the ancestors, you are no longer bound as husband and wife." I pause as their eyes meet, and between them comes another flood of confusion and grief, of all that is now accepted but may never be understood.

When I speak again, my words reach for the end. "Beyond the edges of this circle are the paths of the future. Are you ready to walk them?"

A blackbird sings in the hedgerow that edges the meadow and for a second she turns to find it, with gratitude, her face wet with rain and tears. He closes his eyes, allowed a moment in which to frown away another muddy surge of anger and grief. The love that lingers is calling for comfort, for care, for an embrace that will ease the pain, but instead there is an expanse of space between them. And she nods, as does he, and they both whisper, "Yes".

"Then let it be done, with honour."

They lower their heads, half a bow of acknowledgement, half a brief nod. And turn away from each other. And walk away.

When everyone has left, I find her sitting beneath the shelter of an old oak some way from the path. I crouch beside her, asking if anyone is with her, if anyone is taking her home. She looks up and shakes her head. "I'm ok. I really wanted to be alone, to feel this moment. It's been so much about ending, and now I have this tiny glimpse of beginning. I didn't want to disappear into all the distractions my sister is so sure I need."

She opens her hand to show me the silver wedding ring: his ring. Hers, I imagine, is now in the darkness of the inside pocket of his coat. "I've been thinking. I reckon I'll get it re-forged, into an oak leaf, a pendant I can wear on appropriate occasions ... like when I'm really sad or feel angry at him, forget to honour it all. He was so tall, and sturdy, so resilient, like a bloody great beautiful angry oak tree."

~ ~ ~

To begin with a divorce rite may seem peculiar, yet such times are often when ethics are least evident. In a *Pagan rite, where the couple are required to have carefully considered all that they have gained from their marriage, and sufficiently to allow them to exchange gifts of thanks, it is a time that most poignantly describes both a need for and an expression of honour. It is one of those crucial events where our ethics are all too clearly revealed.

Honour and Order

Honour: it is such a mysterious word, almost hung about with cobwebs and the rough weight of chainmail, the rustle of skirts on stone floors and the scent of grease candles, thick smoke from the hearthfire and that sense of indisputable feudal order. Yet, presented in the mix of modern cultures and tribes, it conveys a spectrum of definitions that differ, just enough to provoke confusion. Furthermore, because it always embraces significant issues, weighting the word in one or another direction can lead to catastrophic misunderstandings. Altered little from Samuel Johnson's 1755 definition, the Oxford English Dictionary uses words such as 'high respect, esteem, deferential admiration'. It talks of 'glory, credit, reputation, good name'.

Etymology takes the word back to the Norman French, *anur*, its English spelling referring to the Latin, *honor*, which also conveys a sense of the dignity and grace that comes with a certain position within a society or situation. If a person is deemed to be truly honourable, it is because they appear gracefully and fully to abide by the rules of the tribe. Their reputation is held up as a shining example of how that tribe would like to perceive itself. Honour is an expression, then, of moral identity.

It is the unwritten rules that matter here. A nation's codes of law, or indeed that of any tribe or community, are a written legislature implemented by the ruling authority. However, where a people are beyond the reach of the law - for example, being nomadic, geographically isolated, claiming a social status that is above that of the ruling authority, or of a criminal underworld that slips beneath it - a tribe relies purely on its own codes of honour. The same is true in lands before laws were crafted, or where the governing authority is unable or unwilling to impose the rule of law. Within the moral framework of the tribe, individuals are allowed to respond to injustice for themselves.

Of course, when a legislative system is established, or re-established after a period of civil war or some other disruption, it can be enormously difficult to convince a populace to give up their autonomy of retaliation, and to be confident that the authority will respond adequately on their behalf. Having the freedom to execute revenge is a powerful way of life. The homicide rate is far higher in countries where individuals have (or feel they have) no access to a judicial system, and so still retain a respon-sibility for meting out justice themselves. Those figures change very slowly. Access to legal help in England and Wales is far older than in Scotland, where the honour codes persisted as a source of justice; the rate of male-victim homicide in Scotland is still over double that in England and Wales (according to the Scottish Executive, in 1999 it was annually 28.84 per million population, compared with 13.40 in England and Wales). In countries such as Columbia and Papua New Guinea, where the state legal system has little influence, the homicide rate is thirty to forty times higher.

In communities where tribal warfare and blood feuds continue, honour killings are often of women who have acted in a way considered immoral by the tribe, whether that is marrying or sleeping with, or being seen with the wrong person, or even as a victim of rape. Such attitudes may seem outrageous to a society that lives within the comfort of a working judicial system, but female honour has for a very long time been related to sexuality. A woman's honour is equated to her virginity or her monogamous loyalty to one man. In societies with any measure of a patri-archal and chauvinistic attitude to status, a man's position is made vulnerable through his attachment to a woman, by blood or marriage: she is a liability to his honour and that of the tribe, so must be controlled.

In modern Britain and Ireland, though there are still lapses in justice, the majority have reasonable access to the law. However, preserving the dignity of the tribe - whether that be the family, a community or the nation - and ensuring its status is held above criticism, saving face, have been fundamental elements of our culture as far back as we can know.

The Power of Face

American Druid, Erynn Rowan Laurie has written extensively about her vision of an ethical code based on early Irish and Welsh law. Working from a realistic perspective about pre-Christian British and Irish culture, she writes of the prevalence of violence provoked by tribal blood feuds and the like. 'Honor and *face* or social perception were very important to the Celtic peoples. Honor consists largely of the [people's] perception of each individual's level of truthfulness, right action and loyalty.' In a culture where boastfulness was a virtue, and the community of the tribe (or *tuath*) was everything, social standing had to be upheld at any cost and, whether in a brawl at a feasting hall or out on the wild moors, it was often defended to the death.

The word used in the Gaelic is often *enech*, which, from a shared Indo-European root, provides *enep* in Cornish and Breton, and *vynep* in Middle Welsh, softening over time to the word now used: *wyneb*. In the old tales, we find the words *anryded* and *glot* (*anrhydedd* and *clod* in modern Welsh), sometimes translated as honour, yet these speak of a rather more superficial sense of personal status, of fortune and fame respectively. *Wyneb* is poignant: the action of being face to face with another, *vyneb yn vyneb*, implies that it is the individuals' (and usually their tribe's) honour that is being weighed.

That in our old British culture, the human head is given such significance in terms of identity goes to intensify the importance of face. As is clear in the old tale of Bran, even after a person has died, his head retains both the essence of his own soul or identity and his soul's connection with the tribe: his honour. One of the lasting images in my own mind is of a picture I saw as a child, of Guy Fawkes and his band of rebels who, in the early seventeenth century, having failed to blow up the Houses of Parliament and been executed brutally and slowly in the contemporary style (hanged, drawn and quartered), made a grisly line of bloody decapitated heads. To see these faces stuck on pikes was particularly powerful to me, having been told by my father that the lads were really heroes. When Charles I was beheaded in the mess of the Civil War, forty three years later, contemporary writers describe the nation at a loss, for the first time without a monarch, having lost its head of state, its *head*.

The human head, and face, hold more meaning for us than we can clearly express. The clown distorts his in order to show how we live with both the painted mask and naked vulnerability: his role is to be the fallen, the one without dignity, unsupported and alone. As he plays the man dishonoured, he provokes in us the anxiety of empathy and yet, like the thriller or horror film, eases our soul with relief that it isn't us, with 'egg on our face'.

Courage, Generosity and Loyalty

When I am asked about the basis of my *Pagan ethics, invariably I use that one word: honour. Yet, with its historic connotations of pride and vanity, its provocation of irrational violence, how can the word have any ethical value in twenty-first century spirituality?

It is important not to project a modern mindset onto older contours of human culture and understanding, and judge our ancestors' behaviour as ethically lacking. Equally, I see no point in dismissing the value of codes of law that, crafted so early in our heritage, have allowed these islands a wealth of peace and creativity compared with so many other nations of the world. Further, in order to consider the validity of honour in the context of our modern Western society, I do so by seeking out the undercurrents of the word that have carried it through so many centuries.

Because *Paganism is based upon reverence for nature, its religious practice is all about our each and every interaction. Pagans don't reach for a supernatural deity, a god that exists outside of nature. Pagans have no belief in a heavenly paradise, nor some infernal penitentiary; the focus of their living is this planet, its environment, its ecologies and tribes. How we perceive and treat another - whether that *other* is a human being, a cat, a beetle, tree or stream - is the foundation of *Pagan theology. It is in this crafting of relationship, as a spiritual act, that I place the word honour in order to find its essence. Delving through the myths of human culture over millennia, distilling definitions of duty and virtue, from Aristotle and Kant to Pagan theologians and thinkers of today, at the risk of creating a triad, I place carefully upon the table three words that for me sum it up: courage, generosity and loyalty.

In every tale from Homer's *Iliad*, through the stories of Lleu Llaw Gyffes, in the sagas of Tolkien, to the *Wizard of Oz*, the characters journey through crises, facing fear, meanness and betrayal - both in themselves and in those they encounter - as they learn how to interact with honour. Crafting relationships with landscapes and those who live within them, ordinary folk become heroes as they find dignity, peace and perhaps abundance, through courage, generosity and loyalty.

We find the same themes in the comic books of our childhood, in films and novels, in holy scriptures and legends of religions across the world. And when folk sit on my couch and talk through the turbulence of their own lives, their stories hold the same crises: of debilitating fears and reckless courage, of dreadful betrayals and loyalties blindly clung to, of miserly tightness and energy given to the point of depletion. I can imagine our distant ancestors at the openings to caves and hide benders, around the fire, gossiping and grumbling about the same issues and, now and then, over-dramatising the tales and times of those who broke through the fears to claim their freedom, and bring honour to the tribe.

For when someone does find the courage to step through fear, sharing their resources with ease and holding the bonds of relationship with trust, the tribe celebrates that individual's action. He or she shines with all that the tribe reaches for in terms of its self-image, its own moral identity.

Courage, generosity and loyalty: exploring honour with students and fellow *Pagans, it is clear that the three words need to be held in balance. We may be fearless, seldom lacking in courage, with a zealous devotion that is our loyalty to those of our community, but suffer from an insecurity that doesn't allow us to give of ourselves freely. We may, on the other hand, be effusively generous, daring and spirited, but in our search for love or affirmation lack sufficient loyalty, compromising our relationships within our community. Or, despite our unquestioning bond to the tribe, and our willingness to give and share all that we are, all that we have, we may have not enough courage to step forward and do anything.

When we lack one quality of honour, we often try to compensate by being especially strong in another of the three, holding this virtue up as a badge of justification: *but I am ...* Our honour, nonetheless, is flawed.

I love the words. They feel rich with our heritage, each one finding its modern form upon a journey from the Old French, through the chivalric days of medieval Britain. Courage is rooted in the Latin, *cor*, meaning heart, which speaks for itself. Generosity comes from the Latin, *generosus*, meaning of noble birth. The verb *generare* means to produce or beget, *gens* is a tribe, *genus* our descent, race or nation. Knowing the root gives the word breadth, ensuring we hear in it the full reach of connections that make up the tribe. Loyalty comes from *legalis*, the Latin word meaning legal, suggesting the necessary actions that provide acceptance within a tribe.

They may not have the clobber of old Saxon in their etymology, from which most of our four-letter words are derived, or the poetic older history of Welsh or Gaelic, but they are blunt words, nonetheless, with the earthy qualities of a less civilized era. Because of this, some find them hard to deconstruct sufficiently in order to use them to clarify the ethics of our choices and behaviour. There are three words, then, that I use which extend the old words into a modern context, this triad being honesty, respect and responsibility.

These three don't have the same raw kick of the old words, the thump of a fist on the feasting table, the *schlice* of a blade drawn from its sheath. Yet, they effectively hold within their subtleties the essence of our twenty first century culture, here and now. If we listen to the gossip, the chattering of soap operas, it is these three qualities that folk are now always complaining are lacking.

The correlations aren't exact, for the two triads interweave more holistically as six words, yet to marry them up can be useful. For without courage, honesty is often too heavy and sharp a blade to manage. Further, remembering the Latin *cor*, if we are to live with honesty, we must work to balance our reason and passion.

And if we are to find within us the willingness to give with generosity, we can look to the need for personal responsibility to guide us: as an integral part of nature, we must retain conscious responsibility for our every action and inaction, understanding the impact our living has upon both humanity and the environment within which we live. We are responsible, in part, after all, for the honour of our race, our species, our nation: for the face of our tribe.

So too does loyalty work in conjunction with respect. Without respect, our loyalty is little more than constructed duty, lacking that fully positive motivation Kant felt to be crucial. There are times in life when we are struck with an awe that is respect for an individual; however, such times are for most of us infrequent. Respect is an attitude that requires a little work, the time, perception and receptivity, the willingness to hear the story and understand the effort that has been made. Equally, earning respect goes hand in hand with earning the gift of another's loyalty.

~ ~ ~

Her eyelids flicker. Something had broken his concentration and, for a short while, he's been looking at her face, and now he wishes the seer was with him, wishing she could tell him how much that flicker meant. Can she hear him? *Mama?*

He sits forward on the uncomfortable hospital chair that he's already pulled to the side of the bed, and very carefully, nervously, puts his fingers onto the pale and mottled skin of her hand, every knobbled bone evident, the veins blue and swollen, tired. And he searches her face, *are you there, mama? Are you aware that I'm here?*

"Mama?" The word comes out croaky. He clears his throat and looks down, suddenly strangely conscious of himself, 57 years old, always so down-to-earth and yet, here, so completely at sea. The words of the seer move through his mind, and he finds himself breathing in deeply, seeking the calm again, the calm of not expecting, of not hoping, of not clinging on, and more importantly, of not asking her to.

Without looking up, he begins to speak.

"One of the things ... I remember most is our house on Sycamore Road, you know? I can't have been ten then. The big garden, with the lawn that Dad used to complain about mowing, but we all figured he loved it really, with his portable radio, the chattering of cricket on that little radio every summer weekend. And the roses, your roses ... I know we didn't pay much attention, Jack and me, and Dad, but," he frowns, "there was something so precious about that, something I've never quite been able to find again. In fact, I didn't realize I was trying, until now. Your care, for those roses, was ... " His voice drifts into thoughts.

A nurse shuffles in, busy but smiling. Her youthfulness is like sunshine and noise in the quiet, soft light of the room. "Ok?" she says to him, with an easy gentleness and distance. Checking the charts at the end of the bed, she makes a note, then shuffles out. The door slides to, then closes. Her momentary presence leaves a sudden ache of feeling alone.

"Mum?"

He turns to look out the window, then returns his gaze to the patterns on her hand, "I know you are tired. I just want to say that it's ok. If you want to go, it's ok. And ... I know that you love me, and you always have," he sighs heavily, "even through the bloody awful times when Dad was dying, and then when Kate left me. I think you know that ... that I love you. I love you, Mum. We're just bloody daft human beings, all flawed and ... stupid, trying our best and ... " *always bloody fucking it up.*

Aware of not saying the last words aloud, he is reminded of the seer's advice: don't talk to yourself, talk to her. He squeezes her hand, very gently, and nods, "It's just ... you've lived it, and it's ok. So ... if you want to go now, you do that. You do that."

He brushes the tears that are trickling into the evening stubble of his cheek, and opens the dog-eared old paperback again, sniffing, finding the page. "I love you, Mum," he whispers, and breathes in. "I'll, um, I'll go from the beginning of the chapter again ... " and he starts to read. " 'I had been at Camusfèarna for eight years before I piped water to the house; before that it came from the burn in buckets ... ' "

~ ~ ~

Evil and Disconnection

If we are seeking out ethics, and how and why we choose to behave as we do, it is important to clarify the definition of another key word used in the study of both ethics and religion. As ever within this book, my definitions are crafted from ideas shared by my teachers, forged from my own experience as a student, teacher and priest, together with input from the various Pagan gatherings I have brought together specifically to talk such issues through.

The word is *evil*; it is not one that sits easily within *Paganism. To the *Pagan, the initial problem is the perception that evil is an untouchable force: in order to retain our ethical integrity, we are supposed to stay away from it.

Needless to say, to the person intent on finding Paganism amoral, the above sentence will be a rich source, and as such makes me smile. Yet how can we address a problem if we judge it too abhorrent to face?

Inevitably it remains too mysterious to solve or ease. It becomes fascinating, frightening yet compelling.

Such attitudes are only concreted by theologies that hold belief in an embodiment of evil: a big bad fella whose primary purpose is to tempt the susceptible human into breaking the rules. He clearly needs to be avoided. However, he's also a necessary scapegoat, a person (sentient, conscious and present, albeit supernatural) who can take the blame.

Western culture, at least in Europe, may now be primarily secular, but these ideas linger in the broadest swathe of society amongst those agnostics who, while not subscribing to any clear religious tradition, are still prone to belief in some incomprehensible creative force, polarized by a power of chaos and destruction, somehow even harder to understand or explain. Such beliefs have roots within the soul of humanity reaching back very many thousands of years. Because so often we feel the fear of having no control, from all-out panic to instinctive unease, the suspicion that there is some sentience directing the course of nature is hard to purge, however much we hold to the rational and dismiss the myths and superstitions of religion. As my young Australian student expressed, there is a longing for explanation, a God who created everything and understands the reason why.

In *Paganism, however, there is no directing or controlling deity, no creator or creatrix, no all-powerful force of good that cares about humanity, or judges its behaviour. Similarly, there is no divine or spiritual embodiment of evil. The *Pagan doesn't claim his place of honour through his fight with some satanic überbeing or supernatural demon: nothing exists beyond nature.

Nor is evil a part of nature; it is a human judgement. There is no force of nature that is evil. The tsunami that caused such devastation in December 2004 was not evil. A *Pagan who perceives such an event as a gathering of gods would not judge their intention as malevolent. The gods, as powers of nature, are simply following the flow of their own purpose.

Nor is there within human nature a current of evil that needs to be managed or assuaged, in the way that is true of love and jealousy, hunger, lust or rage. Like a tsunami or quake, these natural drives may come together within us, creating chaos and devastation. That is nature. It is not a sign of evil.

If a man behaves in a way that is generally considered abhorrent, such as beating a child unconscious, we judge whether or not the fellow planned the action in advance. If he didn't, the *Pagan response is that his motives must be acknowledged, his story understood: what white-water currents were flowing through him at the time? They were, no doubt, the simple emotions of fear and anger, rising up in some soul-storm, creating a hurricane of human emotional expression, a mudslide of devastation. Emotions so easily flood the human soul to the point of rational disfunction. That's nature. It is not ethical or acceptable, but neither is it evil. Easy comfort may provide us with the slack to cope with bouts of tension, but not all humans live with the privilege of ease.

If the fellow did plan the attack to beat the child, a culture may judge him to be evil. Premeditation has allowed him the time to ponder upon the possibility and its consequences, to empathize and realize that the action would cause profound harm. Yet his story still needs to be fully heard. Even the complex motivations we call competition, possessiveness, the quest for power, the need for attention or consideration, to reek vengeance, or just to feel, can all be deconstructed into the simple drives of fear, rage and hunger, most often further complicated by ignorance and curiosity, variously entangled and encrusted over time. That too is nature. At times a fuse blows, and at times the pressure builds within, seeping from our soul in a constant expression of caustic tension, provoking choices that are wholly misguided. As is taught in Stoicism, so much destructive behaviour is simply human expression when natural reason has been corrupted by nature's surging tides of emotion: self-awareness drowned in self-delusion.

It is considered modern compassion to say that such behaviour is human sickness, a soul wound: the man needs help. However, when a person's behaviour is regarded as worse than wrong or harmful, perhaps because the perceived or imagined (potential or actual) impact on the tribe is considerable, our cultural instinct is not to help. The call is for revenge, and the removal - through banishment or death - of the culprit.

Christianity, like many other governing authorities, as the ruling morality for many centuries, extended the notion of evil into a catchall called *sin*, which cleverly taps into this human desire. In the concept of sin, any number of laws of conduct can be imposed based upon the authority's own definition of good and evil, each one aggrandised by the threat of divine retribution. The ultimate revenge: banishment becomes the eternal suffering of life in a subterranean inferno.

Though so important through the long years of our Christian heritage, sin is not a term used in modern Paganism. One of the boisterous four-letter words of our Saxon linguistic inheritance, a *synn* was an infringement of God's law. The Biblical Greek, *hamartia,* from which it is translated, and the Hebrew *khate,* both more or less mean an action that fails to hit the mark. In a religious context, the words describe a discon-nection or estrangement from God, a failure to choose or act in a way that hits the mark that is his law.

If we remove God and his nemesis, though, the problem of evil becomes altogether human. Without a single creator and judge, there is no sin. It is our human fault. To the *Pagan, it is not fear of disobeying God's (or any deity's) command that inspires his ethics; it is the fear of shame that comes when we behave in a way that is deemed dishonourable. If we misuse a relationship, we lose face and our position in the tribe. Indeed, in the language of literature and theatre, hamartia is now an English term used to describe the fatal error of judgement made by a hero, a decision or action which provokes his tragic downfall. It is only when we are disconnected from the web of wyrd, from the wholeness of a moment within the cycles of nature and each soul present, that we risk making choices that miss the mark.

Yet each relationship is unique; universal laws are often irrelevant. Once again, we return to the issue of relativity. In *Paganism, it is accepted that behaviour is integral to local and personal relationships: there is no one 'mark' to hit. What is considered immoral to the point of a dangerous evil in one tribe or era may be celebrated as a freedom in another. A feminist may declare female genital mutilation to be an indubitable evil, while local tribeswomen will talk of their puberty circumcision rites with evident pride. Because tribal values differ as remarkably as the contours and ecosystems of this planet's landscapes, there can be no assumptions that every human community would live by the same moral code. The notion of evil is wholly a social construct, as Nietzsche said, crafted by the ruling morality in order to accentuate the accepted *good*.

Taking no more than a few hundred years, the ruling morality of Western culture has at various times excluded from its care Jews, gypsies, women, Moslems, the physically and mentally disabled, the aboriginal peoples of every continent, non-Caucasians, nonhuman animals and indeed every other part of nature: the losers. The dominant or winning tribe doesn't perceive its actions as immoral, even though retrospective perception may judge them to have been evil.

Further, when Peter Singer states that nonhuman primates should be given membership of the human moral community hands are flung up in horror. Yet he isn't calling for apes to be treated like humans: many of our needs and desires are very different. He is pointing out the problems of relativity that allow us such effective blinkers and prejudices, questioning the validity of setting other primates so determinedly beyond the pale.

Beyond the pale: it is an idiom often used but seldom fully understood. Derived from the Latin *palus,* a pale is a stake, sharing the root with words such as impale and pole. These are the fence posts that historically, and now more often metaphorically, we use to create the defensive boundary of our community, our tribe and its morality. What exists outside the boundary is foreign, dangerous. Those who are driven beyond the fences are outcast, stripped of belonging, no longer protected by the tribe's moral code.

The idiom also reminds me of the stakes onto which the decapitated heads of enemies and traitors were impaled, taking us back to the importance of pride, dignity and *face* that allows honour within a tribe. When an individual's behaviour implied an evil, an absence of morality that is psychopathic or contagious, whose nature, whose soul or identity, seemed to remain actively dangerous, at death our ancestors would dispose of the body in ways that didn't allow their songs to dissolve back into the mud, nor their soul to journey to the lands of the dead: burial face down, in marshes or at crossroads ensured the person had no link to any tribe, living or dead. While the heads of vanquished enemies and revered leaders may be displayed, these faces were not.

Freedom

At the beginning of this strand I said that the problem with evil, to the *Pagan mind, is the perception of it as untouchable. Seldom is a human being so dangerous they must be outcast completely, but even within our post-Enlightenment culture, complex superstitions actively fed by emotion play a large part in our unwillingness to consider circumstances fully. Not hearing a person's story means their motivations remain a mystery: so do we call them evil.

With no concept of evil to fall back on, the *Pagan seeks the story. Ancestry, history, landscape, all weave together to create moments that are sometimes too hard to bare. Very often we can with validity say that the wrongdoer is mentally ill, yet the statistics of those in Western culture taking mental health drugs are rising so steeply the diagnosis becomes blurred. In a tribe where alcohol, diet and illegal drugs all compromise clarity, the edges of agreed morality are already confused.

Blaming sickness is not enough. The task is to accept that bad behaviour is natural, forces of nature colliding into situations that are destructive. This is the *Pagan perspective. Nature as a whole is an exquisite force of creativity, within us and around us, mostly beyond control: our task is not to attempt to tame, but to learn to work with it. To work with harmful behaviour? How can we not? It surrounds us, in almost every corporation that provides the stuff that fills our homes, that insures the bricks and mortar, that plays through the TV and radio. *Pagan ethics require us not to avoid the chaos of immoral and unethical actions, but to hear the story, to *face* the truth with courage, to express the generosity of listening, to respect how people stumble through life's difficult crises, humiliation and terror, and then to act.

And as we act, if we are to be honourable in our response, we must take responsibility for our complicity in the circumstances that lead some into harmful behaviour, understanding that each and every one of us contributes to the song of humanity. If someone's behaviour is beyond the pale, culpability is never theirs alone.

Christianity has a tendency to explain evil through the idea that the omnipotent creator gave human beings free will: providing individuals with the option to choose ensures a sense of freedom in a world that has otherwise, they believe, been specifically designed. In modern Paganism, where the universe is perceived to be a marginally viable moment of cohesion within the tumbling of nature's self-creativity, there is no great debate on the issue of whether or not we have free will. If the idea requires complete freedom, then it does not accept the power of nature: we are clearly limited by the resources available to us, through ancestral inheritance - from economic to genetic - and the circumstances of our tribe, all of which provoke tides of emotion that we have varying abilities to manage and ride.

However, as the existentialist Sartre says in his rather tediously verbose prose, in essence, if we don't make the most of what we have, even within those natural limitations, we ourselves are to blame. Too often we don't realize (literally) what freedoms are available to us, allowing fears to provoke apathy and habituated reactions, turning from opportunities in what Sartre calls 'bad faith', lying to oneself.

If we are to live with honour, and indeed to honour the gift of life given by our ancestors, we must grasp our free will, as the Wiccan Rede states. Reverence for nature's forces is not expressed by submission: the rush of craving that is lust doesn't *require* us to sleep with our neighbour's husband - we can choose not to. We have self-awareness and reason.

And most often it is not an emotional tsunami that floods the soul, disabling our ability to think. It is far worse than that. To the *Pagan's view, most of what the world calls *evil* is done, or allowed to be done, through careless and deliberate evasion of personal responsibility, through the determined yet offhand denial of involvement, through the simplicity of what is the most human brutal act: thoughtlessness.

At the heart of *Pagan ethics, honour is achieved when we acknowledge our free will, with the courage to be honest, with responsibility for our actions, with the respect that allows loyalty and generosity, knowing we are all utterly and irrevocably connected.

Awareness of Death

Another influence on our ethics is our understanding of death. If we are convinced that beyond death lies a paradise offered only to those who die fighting for the 'one true' deity, our behaviour will reflect that, not least because our investment in that world and its tribe will compromise our care for this one. If, as some Christian fundamentalists believe, global warming and international conflict are sure signs of an apocalypse that will bring the return of Christ, driving an SUV that does twelve miles to the gallon is an overt religious statement, declaring a very specific morality.

Although he may well be reflecting earlier thinking, it is once again Plato's overwhelming pessimism that is brought to mind, for its influence has lasted so long. Writing in an era when the ruling nobility was collapsing and a new democracy emerging, one that had sentenced to death his mentor, Socrates, and killed members of his own aristocratic family, his attitude towards the world was no doubt tinged with bitterness. Within this upheaval of change, Plato perceived little but decline, a force of decay he believed would only continue: viewing the powers of change as a corruption, he wrote in *The Republic* of a state that reflected its original Form, a perfect homeland, existing before and after the decaying currents of nature took a hold. Clearly the dream of a bitter if extraordinary thinker, such an image becomes dangerous when it is cast as a heaven to polarize the evil chaos of the world we live in.

That sense of collapse into decay saturates so much unthinking human perception. In the grumpy old man's mumbling complaints, in letters written to the BBC, in the indignation of the middle-aged mother watching her teenagers' behaviour, there are the same assumptions: it wasn't like this in the old days, when we were young ... *year by year, it's getting worse and worse*. With the apparently irreversible environmental damage perpetuated by civilized humanity, coupled with an untenably expanding human population, it isn't hard to believe that we are destroying our world, striding with blind arrogance down an evolutionary dead end.

However, such attitudes tend to inspire dreams of paradise, polarizing once again in order to ease the fear within. In secular culture, where heaven is not something offered at death, these dreams are expressed in any number of equally futile and destructive ways: the required holiday in the Gambia or the Maldives, entirely protected from the surrounding poverty and any personal responsibility, is a neat example, for advertising both perpetuates the illusion and its validity, while creating resentment, compounding the polarity, for those who don't have access to such ease, money, time off, heaven. Yet equally dangerous is the polarity of death as annihilation: the total release from responsibility and any ongoing knowledge of what devastation we have wrought: if one day, we won't know about it, it isn't really our problem.

Within the theologies of modern Paganism, there is no single understanding about death, at least not in specific terms. The theological freedom of understanding, interpretation and exploration means there is no need for any individual to try to, or have to, believe in anything at all. However, what is not a part of the *Pagan attitude to death is the notion of this life being an audition for the tribe of heaven. Life on Earth, right here, right now, with its every interaction and relationship, is what matters, not a holiday in the midst of it or at the very end of it.

Indeed, for what appear to be an increasing number of Pagans, there is no sense of an afterlife in the sense of another world. For those who do talk of the summerlands and feasting halls of the gods, there is very seldom any sense of these worlds offering a life of perfect ease. Those for whom the lands of the dead are literal tend to be the polytheists whose gods are often in conflict! More often, such talk is poetic, acknowledging a lack of knowing and without a striving to know any more until the time comes.

What is more important is the feeling that we not only continue to exist in some form, but that this form is integral to the cycles of rebirth that nature teaches us usually follow death. While some Pagans hold to a conviction that an aspect of our soul or consciousness has lived many lives and will be reborn again and again, others perceive this rebirth as the flow of stories, of creativity inherited and left behind, as genetics and consciousness. Both death and rebirth aren't wholly about the self, but about the river of life. When we die, a part of our song dissolves into the mud of the grave or the dance of the flames; a part continues to be sung by our tribe, by those with whom we've shared love and food, sweat and blood; a part disperses in the wind with our breath, our words, the stories folk will tell of us in the years to come; and possibly, if we wish it or cannot let go enough to avoid it, a part of our consciousness will remain coherent enough to coalesce once again into the intention and creativity of another material form, perhaps another human being, maybe even as a descendent of a tribe we have been a member of before.

Death, then, to the *Pagan, is a gateway of release, exquisitely trans-formative, yet also simply just another step or two along a much longer road. It is not untouchable. Death is a part of the journey that needs to be *faced*, not just our own but within our tribe, not just at the moment of release but as a part of life. The German thinker, Martin Heidegger writes about this in a way that attunes perfectly with *Paganism: the phrase he uses is 'being-toward-death'. Instead of exploring ethics, which he felt had to be subjective, Heidegger focused on the nature of identity and integrity, on how clarity of awareness of self and nature allows an 'authenticity', and particularly when we accept that death is a constant companion. 'Only being free *for* death gives *Dasein* [my translation: the human soul] its goal outright and pushes existence into its finitude [or finiteness]. Once one has grasped the finitude of one's existence,' he wrote, 'it snatches one back from the endless multiplicity of possibilities which offer themselves as closest to one - those of comfortableness, shirking and taking things lightly - and brings *Dasein* [the human soul] into the simplicity of its fate.'

That simplicity is a key within *Pagan philosophy. The tangled complications of life come from over-analysis, from failing to walk in rhythm with nature's currents, and tying ourselves up in human constructs and illusions about that other potent force of nature and ally of death: time. It is another issue that forms our ethics. For within our culture that reaches and clings with its fear of scarcity, time is the resource that is painted as the scarcest, slipping away into the void, pulling us towards its compatriot, death. Encouraged to deny death, our language equally expresses no honour for time. If we fail to save it, we waste it, lose it, at best managing just to *use* it. Yet in *Paganism, time is acknowledged as a wise if often harsh teacher, a god who is ever present and watchful.

So we honour death's presence as we ride the flows of time, with respect for the brutal power they both hold, with enough courage to grow from the lessons offered and to hold our responsibilities upon their tides. *Pagan ethics require us to walk with death, wakeful to the currents of time, through every fall of autumn leaves, as we drop the carrot tops and cabbage leaves into the compost, with each dead pheasant we lift from the road to place with gentleness into the hedgerow, as we sit in the silence with another dying friend or relative. Death, no longer unfamiliar, guides us in our generosity and the immediacy of our honesty. Time, no longer an adversary, becomes a volume of experience and potential that guides us to understand who we are with honour. As Heidegger says, time is the context of our existence, the 'horizon' of our being human.

The Integrated Being

Nature's simplicity is the point I return to in order to close this chapter, and nature is simple, even human nature: it need not be any other way. For in our quest to avoid the tangled complications of human perception, to see the world as simple, I return to the problem of dualism (see Chapter Two). In nature-based *Paganism, at death the spirit does not lift off to leave behind the inert physical residue of flesh and blood. There is no such divide. There is no complexity of separation. There is just nature: being.

Indeed, it is this *Pagan lack of dualism that is, in many ways, the defining element of *Pagan ethics. In Chapter Two, I outlined the paradigm: nature is a beautifully self-crafted and ever-changing web of simple energy and consciousness. There is no dualistic separation. The choices we make are defined by whether or not we accept that vision of a *wholeness of being*.

At first perhaps disseminated by thinkers such as Plato, then taken up by the early Christians, it was the rationalists like the early seventeenth century Frenchman, René Descartes, who flooded our cultural mindset with the ideas of dualism, cleaving nature in two. On one side is the base stuff of mud and blood, of emotion and passion, of feelings and intuition, and on the other are the bleached notions of reason, intelligence and thought, of the mind and spirit - what the British philosopher Gilbert Ryle derogatorily referred to as 'the ghost in the machine'.

That the sides are so radically different - and determinedly so in order to assert clarity of distinction - creates a dynamic of opposition. As a result, what Mary Midgley calls the model of binary logic encourages us to separate aspects of nature by deconstructing each element into its apparent components and playing them off against each other. So do we struggle to reconcile our heart and mind, our feelings and reason, our intellect and physicality, when none of these are isolated in nature.

Declaring that only (Caucasian male) humankind had been blessed with divine reason, and therefore had a soul, Descartes confirmed what was implicit in the Bible: that nature's purpose was as a resource for humanity's use. He glorified an attitude that made humans heroes and the rest of nature into slaves. Every other element or creature within the natural world, from the nonhuman animals to the mud of the land, could be perceived as unaware, impersonal and mechanical. Although some reaches of Western society concede that other animals can suffer, science was created and is still wholly dependent on that radical dualist separation between the human mind which observes, measures, reasons and experiences, and matter, the rest, the *other*: that which is assessed, deconstructed and utilized.

Exploring the fallacy of this reductionism, Midgley writes scathingly of the rational scientific attitudes that declare 'the way to understand anything is to break it down into its constituent parts, identify their individual properties, and then deduce from these the properties of the whole. The source of this reductionist bias in philosophy is of course the pervasive tendency to regard science, and in particular mathematical physics, as the model for all rational thought'. However, this is not the way human beings think, nor is it how nature functions. Nature, fully integrated, is far simpler.

Dualism as such is now an unpopular stand in modern philosophy, yet from the *Pagan perspective little has been gained, for the separation between mind and body has not been healed. It saturates our society. American philosopher, Christian de Quincey refers to it as a cultural pathology. 'This fragmentation runs right through our science, our medicine, our education, our social and legal systems, our interpersonal relationships, and our relationships with our own selves, splitting body from mind. It is deeply ingrained in the way we think, and in what and how we know anything.' That it is so profoundly embedded means it is hard to extricate, or even perceive just how far it seeps into our cultural thinking.

The key objection to dualism has always been the gap in reason that queries how a non-material mind can interact with a physical body or brain: the only solution has been the medium of God. Because the problem can't be solved, as religious beliefs recede, arguments arise to counter the dualist ontology, hoping to vindicate the approach of modern science. The idea of *mind* or soul is relegated to being a fiction, leaving us with the soulless mechanics of materialism. De Quincey, courageously writing on the controversial edge of his field, says in *Radical Nature*, 'Science has exorcised the ghost from the machine and left us with a desacralized and despirited world'. The American philosopher, David Chalmers is one of the few who still hold to the notion of a separate mind capable of the subjective mental experience not yet understood by biology. The tide of philosophy, however, still moves with materialism, using scientific rationalism to explore the edges of our comprehension.

For de Quincey, as materialism reduces 'feelings' to neural electro-chemicals, hormones and nerve cells, it only goes to compound Descartes' brutal split, allowing the pathology that divides the human ego - as individuals, as nations and corporations - from the rest of the natural world. 'All values, meanings, goals and purposes are created by and lie within these collective egos. Nature's only value is how it can serve them; it has no inherent sacredness or meaning.'

The *Pagan's perspective and *Pagan ethics are rooted in a landscape not rent apart by the dualist's scalpel. However, neither is it dulled by the despirited perception of the materialist. Energy and consciousness, poetically termed in *Paganism the soul, spirit or song, the essence of being, are inherent in all of nature.

The renowned thinker, Daniel Dennett, states that where there is an internal natural language controlling our use of neural resources there is consciousness. It holds within it glimpses of what the German philosopher Franz Brentano called 'aboutness', the notion that consciousness is defined by its intentionality, its reaching out for an object with which it interacts; however, Brentano used this idea to distinguish the mental from physical, mind from matter, the latter he perceived as having no intention.

Consciousness: it is an important term. In nature-based *Paganism, it is inherent within every aspect of nature. It hums through the quarks and, no doubt, the threads of connection just beginning to be explored by quantum physicists. It hums through the macrocosmic orbit of galaxies. It is in this sense that British philosopher and psychologist Max Velmans sees continuity, matter and consciousness co-emerging at the birth of the universe, and co-evolving. As matter became more differentiated and complex, so did consciousness become more differentiated and complex, each biological form having a unique, associated consciousness. This is no new perspective; it has been described by panpsychists for centuries, and has been integral to the worldview of tribal, shamanistic and animistic people for very many millennia. Consciousness is nature's own narrative: it is the intention that brings into coherence and directs nature's energy.

There is consciousness in the cells of my fingers, and consciousness within myself as an individual person, yet I am also a part of the consciousness of woman, of humanity, of the web of this valley that is my home, of this planet, of all nature. When I die, elements of that consciousness disseminate and cohere in different ways: a part may survive as the individual human soul, a part survives within the soul of my tribe, a part dissolves into the mud of the valley, and so on. I am connected. Those connections extend beyond myself into the broader songs of humanity, of animal, of ecology.

Yet in my living too I am equally connected. Through an awareness of this wholeness of being, I have the option to relate only through the identity of my human self, yet to do is isolating and inevitably dishonourable. If I allow myself to be awake, to empathies and influences, feeling the threads of the web, the resources for my life exquisitely extend: not as access to a world that I can use, but as a wealth of relationships that can inspire, invigorate, heal, teach, guide and share.

When I say that *Pagan ethics are based upon relationship, it is with this perception of nature's consciousness and energy as the essence that both underlies and connects all of life. As the rain is intrinsically connected to the stream and the sea, so is every human connected to the mud and the wheat, to the water they drink, to the dead and to the children yet to be born. And through every gust of wind into which my breath disappears, I breathe the breath that has been breathed by each fox and roe and mouse in the forest, air that has moved through the leaves of the trees, that spills out into the stillness of dusk in the song of the wren and the call of the buzzard who rides the thermals above us all.

The connections are not linear, like food chains that can be sketched on a page to be learned by a schoolboy. They are the fabric of nature, crafted through every level of intention, through each soul's inherent purpose, from mayfly to granite boulder, moving within and around the currents of time.

To live with honour is to face each one of those connections, as awake to the relationship as we can possibly be, engaging with courage in honesty, with generosity and responsibility, with the respect that comes of loyalty. Doing so because we choose to, having questioned, and where necessary challenged, explored and found a path of integrity, in each action we represent our tribe - of family, community, humanity - and thus the moral identity of that tribe. To do so without shame or ignorance allows a deep and vital pride that comes from knowing that we have shared well, in truth and in freedom.

PART TWO

THE PATHWAYS OF
OUR CHOICES

For a moment, take into your hands an imaginary bar of your favourite chocolate. Break the seal on the paper wrapper and undo the crumpled foil to reveal the rich brown and aromatic sweetness. Lift it to your nose and breathe in that distinctive scent. Take a bite. Take your time. Let it melt in your mouth.

There is so much about chocolate that perfectly triggers the most primitive cravings within our physiology, those designed to encourage our ancestors to seek out each infrequent opportunity for high calorie food, the foods that would help build the fat layers necessary to get through times of famine and cold. Most people love it, whether the milkiest sugary version with less than twenty per cent chocolate and plenty of cow's milk and butter to make it sweet and creamy, or the connoisseur's dark and bitter alternative with eighty eight per cent cocoa solids and nothing but a little sugar to dilute. If you can't abide it, bear with me.

In a book on ethics, it is a wonderful subject to raise. At each of my gatherings, as discussion moved from talk about definitions and theories to the practical application of our ethical principles and moralities, I posed a range of examples we might use to guide the flow, such as abortion, battery-farmed eggs, euthanasia, animal testing, each one a glorious web of emotive complications. Yet each is also patently problematic. Having made the suggestions, the example I always took was chocolate, for it perfectly illustrates what must be a crucially fundamental issue in Western ethics: the *luxury* of choice.

One of the world's major cash crops, cacao is native to the Orinoco and Andean regions of south America, where the best quality beans were grown until the tides of the international commodities market, plummeting in the 1980s, threw huge numbers of farmers out of business. The very best cacao used to be grown in Venezuela; by the turn of the millennium, that country grew virtually none. The majority is now grown in west Africa, notably Cote d'Ivoire where it is only the use of child and slave labour that keeps many farms viable. While farmers continue to use dangerous pesticides such as the carcinogenic lindane, and irreplaceably clear tracts of old rainforest for short-term use, the handful of enormous global companies deny any responsibility, buying indirectly through world markets, and continuing to make vast profits for the highest strata of their management and directors.

The cacao beans provide the cocoa, but what else is in your chocolate bar? Many of the same globalization problems are equally prevalent in the sugar market, which is notoriously protectionist and poor in environmental considerations. Adding to the ethics to be discussed are the bovine milk products found in most chocolates, which raise the issues of the use and abuse of animals, and the pharmaceuticals which keep the majority of dairy cows alive and profitably productive. Most of the cheaper and sweeter chocolates contain hydrogenated vegetable oils, such as genetically modified soya and corn. Many contain palm oil, another increasingly environmentally dirty, ethically dubious and exploitative industry.

Then there are the problems of chocolate being irresponsibly marketed in countries where obesity is a rapidly increasing health crisis, particularly for cheaper chocolate containing saturated and hydrogenated fats, where children are targeted. Further, most of the major chocolate manufacturers are companies with ethically poor records, not least Nestlé whose behaviour in developing countries has provoked boycott calls for many years, and Kraft which is owned by Altria, formerly Philip Morris, the cigarette manufacturer.

That some or all of these issues may be deemed ethically pertinent or irrelevant is a personal decision, yet one further emphasized by the fact that, for the majority in Western culture, there are alternatives that address almost every ethical problem linked with the product. In terms of ethics, little can be challenged about fair trade, organic, vegan chocolate, except where the manufacturer is owned by an unethical giant: Green and Blacks was recently bought out by - or sold out to - Cadbury Schweppes, a reasonable company compared with many, but still one that continues to evade taking responsibility for its contribution to the problems of obesity and hyperactivity (and the catalogue of disorders these provoke) in Western children. Further, although some would want actively to support organic cacao growers in the hungry majority world, particularly through companies that use fair trade standards, others question the validity of buying any food that is grown or produced overseas, the transport industry being one of the most seriously polluting of our age.

Of course, many will raise the issue of cost: organic and fairly traded chocolate is a good deal more expensive than that produced with slave labour and given its solidifying bulk with hydrogenated vegetable oils. Yet these complaints only go to underscore more heavily the ethical deficiency, for chocolate is always completely unnecessary. We have a choice as to whether or not to buy it because we live in sufficient luxury.

The reality in our Western culture, however, is that the foremost dilemma for most people in their consumption of chocolate is based entirely on whether or not it is fattening.

In Part One of this book I laid out definitions and theories, describing the context of my perception through the traditions of both Paganism and Western philosophy. The latter, I suggested, has debated for millennia the validity of decision-making based on a number of clear parameters: intuition and common sense, compassion or reason, the prioritizing of needs, the strictures of divine law, a state's legislation and a community's social laws, the rights and deals we make to claim a place in a particular moral community, and lastly our own freedom to satisfy our desires. Individuals, tribes, politicians, continue to play these off against each other, using whichever tack seems more likely to succeed in any given situation.

Yet morality and ethics are not simply about the actions that make up our behaviour; if we are to craft an ethics that is relevant, usable and tenable, it is crucial to explore the motives that underlie our decisions. Those motives emerge out of what we understand to be the complete context of each situation. To the *Pagan, that context is always going to be flawed if existence is perceived through the filters of dualism. In a world still saturated by its notions of separation, humanity fights through polarized beliefs. All the standard ways in which we evaluate ethics and make our choices are disabled by this binary compulsion. Stuck in the mindset of a black-and-white world, believing there will always be one right and one wrong choice to every question, we hold righteously to one idea, remonstrating against another, ignoring the possibility of a spectrum of alternative solutions.

In *Postmodern Ethics*, sociologist Zygmunt Bauman writes, 'The majority of moral choices are made between contradictory impulses'. Acknowledging that almost every action we take will create immoral consequences in the spread of its effects, 'The moral self moves, feels and acts in the context of ambivalence and is shot through with uncertainty'. As a philosophical attitude, the postmodern acceptance of the problem is pertinent, but too often that uncertainty leads to catatonia or apathy. We cannot be passive.

The search for the story is the current that guides the *Pagan through to action. We may never have all the information, the knowledge or the understanding that we require, but the story provides the context of a moment, in time and space, in nature's web of life. And what provides the strength and momentum for that search is that ancestral staff of honour.

As the core moral code of Paganism, I defined honour through three chivalric words: courage, generosity and loyalty. Beside these I placed three that sit more articulately in modern Western thinking: honesty, responsibility and respect. However, these can as easily as reason or legality be implemented through a dualistic mindset, perceiving the world as torn into two opposing forces, the good and evil, the human and the nonhuman, the divine spirit and the vulgarity of flesh and mud.

While I maintain that honour is an essential measure of Pagan ethics, what makes the difference in *Paganism is the non-dualism: the understanding and experience of nature as *whole*. Living within a world where consciousness is inherent within the fabric of all existence, ethics are crafted through an awareness of integral connection.

Just what choices based upon this perspective look like is the journey of Part Two: practical ethics. Guided by the traditions of Western philosophy, I shall address a number of the key issues of our contemporary world, the decisions we make as members of the growing and yet defensive tribe that is Western culture in the first decade of the twenty first century.

Starting with the nature of human relationships allows me to explore further the fundamental issues, while the following chapter focuses on the value we give to human life, looking at birth, illness and dying. In Chapter Eight, it is the lives of nonhuman animals that I consider, and in Nine the world around us, our environment and climate. The final chapter in the section is about distribution of wealth, globalization and other world issues based on resources, greed and need. None of these are problems that we can leave to governments. We make a difference, each and every one of us, with every penny that we spend, with each newspaper, television show and internet site that we support, implicitly condoning its take on the world.

Moving from principles to practice, the philosopher has always faced a dilemma: does he give an opinion? Some have held determinedly to a notion of their own objectivity, preferring to explore many sides, even the wholly theoretical, artificial and constructed or the ethically dubious, rather than reveal any allegiance, as if to do so would dilute the quality of their words: daring to reveal even a glimmer of subjectivity, they lose their place in the forum of academic validity. However, this is an option only really available to the philosopher whose stand is apparently wholly rational and objective, claiming to express some perfect universal

Reason. Needless to say, this is not my stand. As Mary Midgley says, 'feelings, to be effective, must take shape as thoughts, and thoughts, to be effective, must be powered by suitable feelings'. Though we may play with emphases and relevance, nature does not separate the emotional from the intellectual. In this book, then, I shall risk the indignation of your disagreement; exploring what I feel to be based on *Pagan principles, I shall not unduly avoid expressing my own view.

So do I return to chocolate - take another bite - for this extraordinary blend of plant life and human ingenuity prods unrelentingly at our culture's morality and our own ethics. Encompassing issues of human rights, the rights and welfare of nonhuman animals, the way in which we interact with the environment and inequalities between the West and the majority world, it also addresses the issue of human relationships: that pervasive and highly exploited confusion between our craving for love and security and a desire for animal fats and instant sweet calories.

I begin, then, by looking at human relationship.

CHAPTER SIX

HUMAN RELATIONSHIP

Three foundations of good relationship :
hearing the other's story,
knowing our own story is heard, and
walking the road of a story together that will be told by those
yet to be born.

Facing an Other

So much of philosophy is ontology, the metaphysical study of the nature
of being. Indeed, in Part One my own exploration of ethics led to an
ontological conclusion: that of the inherence of consciousness within
nature. However, where a philosophical system focuses entirely on the
problem of ontology, there is a real risk that everything becomes confined
to what is happening within the mind. Blinkered by the craving to grasp
a comprehensive meaning, philosophers reduce nature to just one
conceptual 'being', perceiving the world through the single if multi-
faceted prism of the self. It can be argued that this is necessary in order
to craft philosophical sense; in some arenas of thinking that may well be
true. Ethics, however, quickly lose their value if they fail to clamber out
of the tidy boxes of theory, and walk.

Emmanuel Lévinas, tired of the self focus of Western philosophy,
terms this ontological reduction as 'egology'. Believing ethics to be the
only valid occupation of philosophy, the core of his work lay in the way
that we perceive and treat other people, and for this he employed the
philosophical notion of the 'Other'. Although the term had been used by
John Stuart Mill and others before him, in general it had meant simply the
other human being, in all their differences, with whom we interact.
Lévinas refined its meaning: pointing out the fundamentally limiting

problem with perceiving that other person simply as an *object* of consciousness, Lévinas emphasized the need to recognize the Other as a *subject* in its own right. Writing in agreement, Zygmunt Bauman describes it as a 'moral travesty' to use the word *we* as the plural of *I* in the context of ethics: by projecting myself onto another, I completely negate their individuality and thus their needs.

As a Jew in occupied France during the Second World War, Lévinas spent time in a German concentration camp, and his inspiration is as clearly informed and fuelled by that experience as it is by his Judaism. Our obligation to the Other, he writes, is absolute. In our search for meaning we seek our humanity, and to do that we must turn towards the Other, addressing its fears and needs before looking to our own.

Heidegger used the term 'Mitsein' to present the sense of *being-with* another, but Lévinas criticized the implication in this that both parties were apparently the same, allowing the moral obligation to be equal. Instead, he used the French term 'être pour l'autre' (*being-for* the Other) in order to express the naturally evident difference, and to emphasize the priority we must give to the other person's needs.

*Paganism, based upon the experience of relationship, does not require us always to prioritize the Other above ourselves, nor indeed is the Other only given full consideration if it is a human being. Nonetheless, placing interaction as the key ethical focus, there is a great deal in Lévinas' postmodern perspective that sits well within a *Pagan philosophy, not least the importance he places upon the word *face*. Using it particularly to describe the extraordinary yet ordinary process of encountering another human being, he speaks of its intrinsic power. We are constantly 'being faced' by Others, an experience that shines a defined spotlight on our responsibilities and obligations, for as faces we are clearly distinct individuals, never the same; there is instantly a recognition of our difference, our separateness. Indeed, as Bauman says, this is exactly what makes every human encounter a moral event.

Whether consciously or not every time we come into contact with another human being, we are not only acutely aware of the Other's proximity, but also aware of the distance between us, created by the individuality of our distinct identities. Furthermore, even as we experience the separateness of our identities, we can't help but communicate across that gap. In *Entre Nous*, Lévinas writes, 'Man is the only being I cannot meet without my expressing this meeting itself to him'. Whether we are willing to greet the person or in refusing to do so we turn away, there is communication. This only increases our moral obligation.

From a *Pagan perspective, communication is not only inevitable but perpetually flowing. Even if we place the idea purely within the context of human interaction, we can't help but be connected. Each individual is not crafted as a defined physical object somehow magically informed by its own isolated and ethereal mind: in nature, that level of separation is not recognizable. Although *Pagans commonly refer to this spiritual or ecological connection as a *web*, this can imply single threads that connect separate beings and nature simply isn't that tidy or specific.

As cohesion of intentional consciousness and fuelling energy, each human being is a living entity without clearly delineated edges. The energy of our life force, the effect of our thoughts, of our memories and feelings, extends out around us as if it were a light. That light may shine like a beacon or glow gently, but even blindfolded and deafened by white noise, the majority of us can feel another's presence, at times across some considerable distance. We are affected by another's emotional energy simply passing them in the street.

In Druidic philosophy, what we are perceiving is termed the song: the natural and ongoing expression of an individual's essence, the journey they have walked and the current of their intention. Our song is about who and how we are, *here and now*. It is rooted in our own story and all the stories we carry of our ancestors and our heritage, each one contributing to our sense of identity. It is that identity which gives us a face.

Of course, faces can provoke us to forget that the separation we feel, particularly when we are close to others, is an ethical not an ontological issue. The distance that shimmers across the gap of proximity is no more than uncertainty: the other person's song is not our own. Yet it is the humming of others' songs that creates the distinct quality of our family units, our communities, our tribes, and - together - the song of humanity.

However much we may now and then crave the peace of solitude, longing to be released from the burden of the moral obligation created by facing another, and however well we do cope if we find ourselves alone for long periods of time, as human beings we are naturally tribal creatures: we crave the communal song. A tribe provides a bank of certainties about what we can and can't do in order to avoid the horror of rejection, of being cast out beyond the pale. Indeed, because of that inevitable and constant flow of human communication, the presence and acceptance of the tribe offers an assurance of our very existence, a simple reality that extended time alone can strangely throw into doubt.

All these happen even if we live with a general passivity, meandering along the wide verges of a tribe's morality, doing as little as we can. When we consider those around us as Others with faces, each one becomes a person, alive with their own emotions and sensitivities. Our well of empathy deepens and our priorities change. Just as Lévinas spoke from his experience of human brutality, the writings of Archbishop Desmund Tutu come through the sadness of South Africa's violent history. Basing his understanding on Christian love and compassion, yet acknowledging his heritage through the African concept of *ubuntu*, Tutu's words are poignant: 'a person is a person through other persons'.

The Tribe

Tribe: for someone who loves words as I do, this is one that I hold to despite its dearth of etymological richness. The closest alternative, clan, from the Gaelic *clann* (and the Latin *planta*, a sprout) too strongly implies a restriction to blood kinship. From the Middle English and French, *tribu*, the word comes from the Latin *tribus*, mean a tribe, the *tri* referring to the three distinct peoples of the ancient state of Rome. Once used for the human grouping between a family or band and the larger chieftainship or state, the definition has become more complex; wanting to move away from the imperialist notion of tribes being primitive societies from the darker reaches of the majority or 'less economically developed' world, some anthropologists now refer to kinship or ethnic groups, or even 'small scale, semi-sedentary, trans-egalitarian societies'. Without the confusions of political correctness, in archaeology the definition is simpler: a significantly extended family or group of families held together by common threads of blood, language, culture and ideology, a tribe shares some focus of occupation, employment and ceremonial tradition, and is governed by a recognized authority that stands above the level of family.

It is a term much used in modern *Paganism, and most of the above definition still applies. Yet, compared with today, in the distant past the tribe was a simple unit. A few centuries ago, it was still relatively easy. Now, however, those parameters that hold a group together are not only more extensive, but the vast majority of individuals are bound into more than half a dozen different tribal groups, each of which may have its own moral code.

There is the tribe at our place of work, those with whom we share employment, with perhaps its layers of authority and a collective need for the company to survive and thrive. There are the tribes of people with whom we share an interest, a hobby or pastime, with whom we drink in the pub or club, and the tribe of our religious affiliations. All of the above have their own various traditions, rituals and ceremonies. We may share a tribal bond with the broader community of our geographic neigh-bourhood, albeit one that may only arise when some aspect of the landscape is under threat. Then there is our ancestral or parental tribe, and the tribes of relationships forged by blood, marriage, love and children; as Western adults we may not live with or near other members of those tribes, and the extent to which we share interests, occupations or even culture may be limited, but often there are still strong common moralities and traditions. And when the World Cup is on, our whole nation becomes a tribe, glued by a handful of football songs and a common desire to *win*.

Every day, most of us travel from one tribe into others, knowing exactly where the boundary markers are, the fences that delineate each territory, the gates we must walk through, acutely aware of the differing moralities of each one, making adjustments in our identity as we do so, becoming the person we need to be accordingly. And though at times we may resent it deeply, that wish to be a part of the tribe is profoundly natural, even in an environment that we detest where we are horribly conscious of any necessary lack of honesty or authenticity in our being. A tribe provides safety. It gives us the space we need to breathe and the food we eat. Whether we are awake to it or not, a tribe provides a powerful incentive to survive.

According to Zygmunt Bauman, a tribe may need to fight for cultural sovereignty in order to establish its place of strength, and as such it is often crafted on a strong sense of *us* and *them*. Sometimes barely perceptible tests, sometimes outright challenges, are employed to prove whether or not a person is a member (or potential member), for a tribe needs to be secure. While our British or 'Celtic' ancestors were seldom reticent about declaring enemies and fighting them back to the point of submission or annihilation, in our twenty first century Western culture our battlefields are generally a little less bloody; they are often no less determined or well defended.

A tribe's cohesion comes with a bond of trust. When we trust another person, that Other becomes special to us: we have received sufficient assurance that we can safely invest in them, offering an openness of honesty. If our gift of trust is not to a fellow tribal member, it is often given as an invitation to join the tribe, but this is not always the case. At times it is necessary to trust an outsider. Although it may take a great deal of courage, loyalty and generosity, this is crucial to *Pagan ethics: when we trust with honour, we can't demand that this gift of trust be reciprocated.

Honour and the Stranger

How we treat those from other tribes, enemies or not, defines the tribe, identifying the nature and location of its edges. Objecting to the ontological inference of 'sameness' when an Other is seen as an object, Christian theologian Hans Boersma writes about how this attitude has poignantly 'suppressed hospitality toward the stranger'. They are two powerful words: hospitality and stranger. The former, much used by Lévinas, reflects the chivalric generosity so meaningful in our heritage. Hospitality, like trust, as a gift of oneself, does not *require* reciprocity. It is an integral part of *Pagan honour.

And how little both trust and hospitality are shown in our Western culture. For on the whole, individuals not in our immediate tribe are strangers. With strangers, we have no agreed moral codes, no assurance of trust. Strangers have no faces. Bauman describes strangers as '[i]nhabitants of no-man's land - a space either normless or marked with too few rules to make orientation possible'. He uses Martin Buber's term, 'mismeeting', to describe the way in which we avoid engaging, attentively ignoring and making it clear that we are ignoring the stranger, to avoid both sympathy and hostility: 'no rights and duties are presumed'.

Buber was an Austrian Jewish philosopher who, escaping Nazi anti-Semitism, settled in Israel in the late 1930s, and his dedication to that tangled landscape, and a binational (Arab-Jewish) state, is reflected in his thinking. As early as the 1920s, however, his writings were defining two kinds of human encounter, the first being *Ich und Du*. The English translation, 'I-Thou', reflects what were almost certainly sources of Buber's inspiration: the enormously influential American thinker William James, writing of his mystical experience and philosophical exploration of consciousness, was overtly reaching for relationship that adequately expressed spiritual connection and respect. In *The Will to Believe* in 1897, he wrote of the universe as 'no longer a mere It to us, but a Thou, if we are religious; and any relation that may be possible from person to person might be possible here'.

My sense is that the words work better within a modern context as the more colloquial *me and you*. It is perfectly expressed in Chapter Three, in the little girl who comes to sit on the bench. *Me and you* is the meeting of two individuals without the distractions of expectation, connotations, associations and demand. In *Pagan terms, this is the soul to soul connection, each person wholly present and awake to the song of the Other.

As a monotheist, Buber extended this notion into his religious understanding: when you truly face another person, you are perceiving the divinity within them. Indeed, because God has no perceptible face, the only meaningful relationship we can forge with God is through the true meeting with another human being, face to face. This isn't far from *Pagan ethics. Because the *Pagan's gods are nature - human and nonhuman - the *Pagan acknowledges his gods in his recognition of nature's inherent value. He responds to that sanctity in his relationships with all of nature, in the way that he *meets* Others, not least other human beings. And, as Buber would agree, it is in this state of presence, soul to soul, awake and untethered, that we can access true freedom.

The second of Buber's human encounters is the *Ich und Es*, and here I accept the usual translation of 'I-it'. In my own previous writings, before reading Buber, I called this, perhaps too simplistically, the political relationship. It is barely a relationship, for the subject is not meeting another individual but an object onto which he projects his own desires and expectations. Indeed, there is no person to communicate with, for the object is no more than an idea, an abstract concept, constructed of what he believes to be a perceived threat (an authority) or something that can be used (the inferior being). It is an entirely utilitarian relationship. One of the most beautiful formulations of Kant's Categorical Imperative speaks directly of this situation, and has continuing echoes in *Pagan ethics: 'Act so as to treat others and yourself always as ends, never simply as means to ends'. The *I-it* encounter treats the Other as nothing more than a help or hindrance to the aim of achieving an objective.

This is the 'mismeeting' Bauman refers to, for the object is faceless, a stranger who remains a stranger: without a face there is no moral obligation, no responsibility. Though a human being may stand before us, this physical manifestation is nothing more than the abstract represented. Though we may yell at this stranger's face, it is not a real face but a human mask worn by the true object beneath, the faceless concept.

This objectifying of the Other is a perfect summation of all that is *not* *Pagan, for by not acknowledging the inherent value of the other person, there is no relationship - and every aspect of *Pagan ethics is founded upon relationship, honourable relationship. Seeking a position of honour, *Paganism teaches us instead to meet the Other always as an individual, listening to the stories of their tribe(s) and their own life's journey with sufficient receptivity to accept the moment. We don't need to like it or them, nor to throw down flowers and declare peace. We need simply to be fully present, and that requires honour.

How then do these ideas play into action?

I shall divide the rest of the chapter into three. The penultimate section will look at how we relate to children, the last delving into how we craft intimate relationships. Firstly, though, I shall explore the currents of our attitudes and the *Pagan ethical perspective towards the broadest of human relationships, those of our social and working lives. As a human being with a significant measure of feline in my soul ever urging me find solitude, this is an important area. For there are people we fully choose to be with and there are strangers we walk right past, but in our modern world most of us have to engage with very many who fall into neither category.

Being with Other People
Having ordered a new telephone line on the internet and heard nothing from the company, I try to call them to arrange a time for the engineer to install the necessaries. It takes some searching of the complex website before I find a telephone number, and when I dial I am connected to a

machine: the self-assured female voice gives me a couple of options. I choose one and wait, listening to the ringing. The same voice answers and offers me half a dozen more choices. We've all been there ... half an hour later it is hard to differentiate between the machines and the people: each and every voice has become an embodiment of the entire corrupt and unreliable telecommunications industry, and as such must be made to accept responsibility for its every failing before being torn repeatedly limb from limb. Yet not only am I responding badly, but each of the five people I talk to express no desire to hear me. The customer, complaining and demanding, is a stranger, the medium of the phone allowing a faceless encounter. We are each, idiotically, in dialogue with (yelling at) the representation of an idea.

I sit in the garden, meditate with the butterflies, and dial again, knowing now how to navigate through the labyrinth to find a human being, and with unwavering determination I start to talk, *me and you*: "Hi, did you say your name was Sally? Hi, Sally. Hey, I'm having a hard day, I think we need a thunder storm, what do you think? How's your day? Do you have kids? They are so wild when the weather's like this! Anyway, what I'm calling about is ... " Needless to say, it wasn't her job to book an engineer, but after a brief chat about the high energy of a primary school playground and the problem of children's lunches, she transferred me to the right office and it was arranged within minutes.

Becoming flooded with emotion, spilling rage blindly at anyone within reach is normal human behaviour, albeit lacking in emotional intelligence, and honour. Yet even when the tides are not so immediately overwhelming, and indeed the system not so obviously geared towards the impersonal, we are still prone to lock onto faceless targets. The media perfectly express this, as if employed to caricature the human flaw in exaggerated detail; and as a powerful guide within any society (albeit *mis*guiding), its effect is to glorify and encourage such behaviour.

Politics does the same. Enormous institutions addressing the needs of the masses, our governments and political parties respond to the Other as a faceless concept, prioritizing ideas based entirely on collectives and assumptions. Unseen as individuals, we protest and react with an equivalent disregard, and though many of us may now recognize the faces of a number of politicians, seldom are they acknowledged as human individuals. In collusion with the media, nor do we wish them to be, for ordinary folk are prone to ordinary failings of selective hearing, misjudgement and misunderstanding, character clashes and inappropriate empathies, untimely lust or love: the normal flaws of being human. In order to ensure that they take all the blame, leaving us free from responsibility, we are happy for the media to raise these people onto pedestals of power and importance, and kick them off. Buying into the process, reading the magazines and newspapers, watching the television shows, our culture revels in how a hero can be dragged through the mud, believing in some way that as a result the superhuman has been brought back down to earth, made human again; yet there is no *me and you* in this attitude.

That our culture does the same with any fool willing to take the burden of celebrity shows how much we crave the heroes: individuals whose true faces we hide with masks of glamour and power, that they might be used by the tribe as objects to play with, as dolls to paint and crush. Just as the thrill of a horror film is made enjoyable by the knowledge that the horror is happening to someone else, so do we take our seats at the gladiatorial Circus to watch celebrities fight their insignificance, their shame and mortality.

The *I-it* encounter is also endemic in relationships based upon need, such as with the medical profession. The doctor isn't a person: people are too fallible, after all, and generally incapable of miracles. Instead they are strangers who represent the authority of the entire medical profession, incomprehensible in its mysteries and thus capable of providing any and all necessary supernatural deeds. To many doctors, that their encounter with another patient is a mismeeting, is professionally hidden by a smile of apparently caring concern. Patients represent the interminably and tediously sick population, objects to be prodded, poked and prescribed for. Though this may compromise their ability to listen adequately, more important is the flow-through of strangers to be seen.

Indeed, wherever an authority is perceived or assumed, human beings are liable to treat each other as objects, as *means to ends*. It is the foundation of business - and though no doubt it has been for millennia, it doesn't only apply to the slaves and those on minimum wage. Except in a tiny minority of work environments, when we agree to take on a job, we are agreeing to abide by the rules of that organization and commit to its aims. We put aside a part of our individuality to be a part of a production line, knowing that the product will take precedence.

The larger the company or organization, the more prevalent the attitude, and the easier it is for a *person* to be lost. With a hierarchy of authority fully embedded, a hierarchy of value is usually as evident. Those on the lowest rungs are too often unrecognized, not only as individual human beings but also in terms of what they individually give to the whole. Though she may be the face at reception, management don't see her; though he may be the voice who answers the phones, management doesn't hear him. As a result, millions of human beings go to work each day to struggle, faceless, with environments, colleagues and chains of responsibility and authority that they detest. The notion of respect is severely limited.

The problems are not restricted to the established hierarchies. Within a tribe, we shuffle and manoeuvre, aware of power-plays, threats and opportunities, carefully securing the limits of our obligations and duties of care. In every story told, we don't hear another's soul expressed: the gossip allows us to find our place in a tribe, placing others, checking and adjusting our own position. With trust so uncommon, it is hard to interact with honour.

Our human ability to adapt is unquestionably a key factor in what has allowed us, as a species, to become this dangerously successful. In order to earn the necessary income, many of us leave the tribal bounds of our home community to enter the tribe of a company with a very different morality. For some that means a deeply wearing compromise, requiring us to hide our soul's needs, our ethical sense and creativity. Yet the need to adapt continues. Each day, we move between tribes: leaving work for the pub, back home to a partner, out with friends, on the phone to mum. Most of us become thoroughly proficient at shifting how we behave according to the sometimes subtle differences in agreed morality.

After years of moving between significantly distinct moral communities (groups that judge in very different ways), it can be hard to remember what our own opinions are. Any clarity as to where our compromises begin and end is eroded by how we are faring according to each tribe's differing measures of success and failure. Inevitably, such an attitude to honesty affects our relationships. Our ability to trust crumbles. So does our willingness to listen dissolve, as we hold firmly to any constructed narrative that offers a handhold of certainty.

When I shop, I go to stores where the person behind the counter knows me, knows what I might want and will help me get it, where he will carry my purchases out to the car or arrange delivery without a fuss. When I take someone on to do a job, I choose someone who will look up from his tools so that, face to face, trust is established at the outset. Both as an individual and through the voluntary organizations and the commercial business that I run, I don't want to engage with a company that doesn't engage with me as a person. Good business, whatever the aim, must be based on *me and you* relationships. Only when we value the Other, and express that openly, do we discover what he can truly offer - and in most cases that is a good deal more than was evident at first.

That is also fundamental when we are employed by another. If a company makes us faceless, never hearing our story, there is no relationship for us to invest in. We hold on to the job because of our own need, not through the honour of loyalty, respect or responsibility. Yet where there are true relationships, where value is acknowledged, that honour becomes integral. And the amount we are willing to give expands accordingly.

Perhaps it is because so many Pagans have experienced overt discrimination that the emphasis of subject to subject meeting has continued to be so crucial a part of *Pagan honour. Prejudice is the action of judging (coming to a conclusion about an Other's behaviour based on our own ethical or moral code) prior to hearing that person's story. It erases faces, and very effectively so. A particular accent, a style of dress, a person's skin colour or religious affiliations become an obscuring veil. That one characteristic becomes the only element of a story that is heard, however fictitious or misconstrued, any glimmer of another being comprehensively dismissed. Yet prejudice is not just about an Other whom we do not like; it is about their entire tribe. In dismissing a person's tribe, or what we assume to be their tribe, we are judging wholesale all who (we assume) share their depraved morality.

Because faces are erased, truth isn't what informs. Throughout history, and no doubt before it, defensive-aggressive tribes have accused each other of despicable and - to them - wholly immoral crimes: behaviour that would never be tolerated within 'our own tribe'. The enemy is always the kind of scum who boil babies. *Ergo*, because they are clearly so far beyond the bounds of 'our own righteous moral community', they can justifiably be de-humanized and treated as *objects*.

Honourable meeting, a *me and you* meeting, doesn't require us to like people. As human beings, we don't always agree. Indeed, as a philosophy deeply rooted in the peoples of Britain and northern Europe, Paganism isn't necessarily a call for peace, and meeting *face to face* can provoke confrontation. However, meeting with honour, our stories are told with responsibility, acknowledging the loyalties that will tug and bias understanding. When the stories told are well heard, we listen with respect given wakefully, generously, acknowledging the Other as a subject in his own right. We show our own face, revealing who we are, with the courage of our honesty.

Being with Children

One of the most detrimental places where we fail in terms of *me and you* relationships, particularly considering the shifting sands of human thinking, is with our children.

The ethical or moral validity of choosing to have children I shall discuss in the following chapter; here I am more interested in our relationship with them. That interest is heightened by the fact that I live in Britain, a country which is repeatedly criticized for its attitude towards children. As a nation, we are said to be the least child-friendly in Europe, and probably within the wealthy Western world. Indeed, the United Nations heavily criticized the British government in 2002 for its low level of care and support for children.

As someone who tends to avoid the company of children, I find the subject intriguing. To me, there is little more irritating than a badly behaved child. To have a quiet afternoon shredded by the screams of neighbourhood children is enough to provoke a psychotic rage. When the calm focus of a cinema or restaurant is disrupted by children's high-pitched and unpredictable chaos, I am among the first to complain and leave. Yet, now and then, I come across a most delightful child, one that confirms my suspicion that it is our society at fault. I don't dislike young human beings, I dislike the monsters we create by the way that we treat them.

Some Pagans hold to the belief that, as discarnate souls, we choose our parents. In its favour, the idea solicits a profound responsibility for how we have created our life and its resources. Most have no such conviction, perceiving the idea as another poetic thread within the tales of our lives: we neither choose nor are chosen to be with particular parents, instead simply emerging, through internal and external landscapes, our being utterly integral to its context, integrated, moment to moment, crafted by breath and blood, rain and mud. This emergence through initial connectedness generates a feeling of 'sameness', encouraging the bond needed to ensure the infant is accepted. With the new child's energy and consciousness interwoven with the stories of his parents, the parental response is to nurture and protect. If we are lucky, those connections provide a sense of ease and belonging that lasts.

It isn't long, though, before parent or child starts to perceive the other as Other. If the parent feels it first, without adequate consciousness to compensate with wakeful caring, the child will often carry the effects throughout his life: an undertow of a conviction about having been abandoned for no reason.

More usually and easily, it is the child who changes. Discovering quickly how laughter, movement and tears provoke different responses, a baby learns how to satisfy his cravings for food and attention, but as a toddler he begins to realize that the source of that satisfaction is a number of separate beings, each with their own currents of identity and purpose. Over the next few years, exploring the gap created by that separation, investigating the edges, the child begins to forge his own identity. Viscerally experiencing the efficacy of his actions, this growing individual develops a picture of his own worth, learning how to adjust in order to conform to the moral constructs, expectations and acceptability of the tribe.

In this first period of life, with growth fundamentally oriented around the desire for attentive caring, recognition and love, so much can go horribly wrong. If there is a lack of certainty about that love, the child's development into a balanced adult is compromised. It doesn't have to manifest as an all-out sociopathic disorder. If nature had allowed that, the human race would have faced its evolutionary dead-end in the very first centuries after hunter-gatherers began to settle. What is created is an ordinary human adult of our culture, prone to depression, with low self-esteem, carefully crafting a persona he thinks may not be rejected. Without honesty of self-expression, there is no hope of relationships based upon honour, let alone a connection where the love he so craves can be found.

Such a person is *ordinary* because the lack is normal in our culture. It is created by every parent who is too busy, too often absent, physically or emotionally. Not only is such parental behaviour socially and morally acceptable within our Western society, but the results - the depression and dishonesty - are equally common: normal.

Of course, when individuals whose belief in love was compromised at that early age themselves become parents, the chances are that they will play out their experience upon their children: it is, after all, all they were taught. So do the patterns repeat across generations. For some, however, the instinct is to compensate for their own need by smothering the child with a possessive and fearful enfolding. To the child, this need-based attention is no more nourishing than the rejection of being abandoned to a busy crèche or emotionally ignored. The child is no longer a person: he becomes an object, from which love is demanded.

Many traditions talk about this crucial period spanning the first seven years; that's how long it takes for every cell in our bodies to have been replaced naturally. As a *Pagan, I tend not to expect the world to be that precise, and perceive this first era to last until the first key milk teeth have fallen. The second stage is the journey from dependence to the foggy transitions of puberty. During this period, notions of difference and Other are becoming clearer and, while the first basis of decision-making (loving care and attention) may not have been sufficiently conscious to be termed as ethics, now the child is openly playing with ideas of acceptability. He judges himself against others, pushing to find the edges of the tribe's moral code. Beginning to formulate consequences and making his choices according to what makes sense, the child's ethics are constructed upon his desire for understanding. He is searching for the reins of his own life, needing to understand and be understood. Needless to say, if his life began without a surety of love, that desire for control is going to be all the greater. Indeed, here is where the effects of being treated as a concept and not an individual become alarmingly obvious.

To a child, feeling understood is not about intellectual concordance. It is far simpler: a child feels understood when, truly met (just *me and you*), he is listened to. A child's stories may be trivial in an adult's world, yet each experience nonetheless saturates his reality. In our culture, though, where children are set aside to be dealt with by under-resourced and all too busy playgroups and schools, seldom experiencing a wakeful and fully present encounter with parents, teachers or other carers (other than at times of trauma), the child who is truly heard is uncommon. In children's literature, from *The Famous Five* to *Harry Potter*, the heroes again and again are those youngsters whom the adults brutally dismiss ... and who, despite not being heard, gloriously succeed. Perhaps because the effects of not being listened to as a child reach into every part of an adult's life, these stories continue touch us. We get used to our truth being ignored, our creativity dismissed. Our ability to express ourselves honourably is compromised in line with a lack of fundamental courage, honesty and trust. Evading responsibility, not believing that credit or culpability is ever accurately assigned, our willingness to respect anyone or anything simply disappears.

Because the effects remain, it is brutally hard to watch another go through it. Having experienced insufficient loving care or attention, a child stomps into adolescence, thoroughly misunderstood, rejecting his parental tribe, hiding his face in disgust and shame. With determination, he establishes himself as a stranger in the house. Claiming independence, however illusory that may be, he perfects the art of mismeeting with every adult he encounters, evading responsibility, unwilling to be part of a tribe that neither truly knows nor respects him. With sadness and bewilderment, many anguished parents can identify the point, somewhere in the haze of puberty, when their child became a gormless and ill-mannered monster. But to many children, there was no moment of change: they were always treated as objects, and one day they got sick of it and walked away.

Our culture must stop treating children as objects - as a means to satisfy the craving to reproduce, as the achievement of a social expectation, as a public display of parental creativity, as an evasion of personal creativity, as a way to be loved and needed, and when any of those fail, as something to be blamed. We must acknowledge our children as people in their own right.

Yet why is our culture so loathed to listen to its children? From the very beginning, our children demand of us undiluted honour, not least honesty, responsibility and generosity. It can be terrifying. To ensure the security of not having to face ourselves, we legitimize the distance by proclaiming our adult authority.

As parents, most cultures endorse the mask of the role to the extent that children are required to call us by the role: *mother, mama, mum, father, papa, dad*. The child who uses his parents' names is considered precocious, as if the child were taking an unwarranted liberty in claiming an equality of individuality and importance. Consequently, a child can scorn a parent by refusing to acknowledge any value in their role, and use the first name instead. Of course, because using the role-names is traditional, many defend it, justifying that within the words there is often a well of genuine pride and affection. Yet I question it: as a habit, not thought through, it supports the *I-it* relationship. It allows the parent to wear the mask, hiding their face, declaring themselves the authority.

In the early 1960s, in his book *Centuries of Childhood*, Philippe Ariès reminded our culture that *childhood* is not only a human creation but a very recent one; throughout the long journey of humanity, children have entered the adult world just as soon as they were no longer dependent on their mothers. During the Renaissance, as products of the sin of sexual union, boys of the wealthier classes were set aside to be disciplined and trained, but the extension of childhood beyond the age of six or seven for every member of society didn't emerge as a cultural construct until the late nineteenth century.

As a construct, childhood protects the young. In mid nineteenth century Britain, industrialization still spreading like a plague, legislation began to creep in to deal with the appalling conditions in factories, mines and mills. The first to be given any defence against the dangers were the youngest in society, the number of hours they could work being cut, then the very youngest being denied the right to work at all. With the untended children of those working twelve hour days fending for themselves, it is easy to imagine the ensuing problems and the inevitable social uproar. We might assume that provision of schooling came from a caring and enlightened ruling class, but such legislation is more often reactive. In Britain, the Education Act of 1880 made schooling free and compulsory for all children between the ages of five and ten. Having been removed from adult society, they were then removed from the streets.

Obviously, provision for workers' safety and wellbeing was needed. Education clearly benefits any culture or tribe that has broken down into a state of poverty and disorder. Yet, that these two led so comprehensively to the creation of a separated world called *childhood* reflects how easily we de-face people. Children in the classroom, particularly the unruly who can't agree the purpose of the exercise, quickly become strangers, objects in line.

Some trace the construct back to Aristotle who saw children as immature human beings who, given sufficient time and an appropriate environment, would mature into complete and fully grown adults. It's a rationalist's binary declaration; in practice, it is an attitude that clearly rips into the social fabric a line of division. A child may not be as strong or experienced as an older person, but brought up well he is no more a fool than the average adult, no less insightful, creative or caring: no less valuable a member of society. Furthermore, his value is based not upon what he might develop into, but what he is *here and now*.

However, too many of our tribes' children are more problematic than valuable. In the early twenty first century, in what the rabbi and political thinker Julia Neuberger calls the 'risk-averse culture', protected from the possibility of any real experience, children are given lives of leisure, yet not the freedom to explore. Taught to distrust every stranger, they stay indoors in the relative safety of adventures played out in computer games and television shows. Neither given responsibility, nor learning what to do with it, the result is a tribe of incompetent, disrespectful and irresponsible pariahs, as young as seven years old.

Informed by nature, *Pagan ethics does not accept the construct of childhood. A child will not thrive if treated as anything other than a whole human being. From the point at which he begins to recognize the Other, every healthy human soul is capable of experiencing and learning respect, responsibility and honesty. Every child can and must learn how to interact with the courage, generosity and loyalty needed for a healthy human society, but he can only truly do so in an integrated world. Separating children from adults breeds endemic inhibition: children need to play but adults are supposed to be sensible. An identifying quality of many *Pagan communities is the evidence of adults who have refused to dry out, all grown up, but continue to dance and play, flexible and open enough to learn, knowing that we must always keep growing. Our playfulness and exploration allow us continually to make positive relationships that are respectful, however old we are - not only with our immediate family, but with the wider tribe of the neighbourhood, the environment and so on.

The anarchy of *Paganism is reflected in this lack of hierarchies of age and assumed authorities; learning the necessary responsibility and respect fundamental to self-governance within a tribe creates children who are co-operative and self-sufficient. This does not mean letting children run amuck, for discipline is needed in learning how to be free without imposing oneself on others: careening through places of quiet, yelling, thoughtless and inconsiderate, is not anarchic, nor acceptable just because the perpetrator is young. It is dishonourable action of a badly behaved child, an action reflected if amplified in the dishonourable behaviour of a damaged adult, grabbing resources (attention, security, control) through greed, competition, imperialism and war.

In many Pagan traditions, the discipline is manifest as the spiritual practice of the sacred circle. In *Paganism, the temple is not a permanent structure with rows laid out before an altar and priest, enclosed by a roof, walls and stone floor; often as simple and momentary as a circle delineated by the power of (shared) intention, sometimes walked, blessed by sound and the spirits of that place, its value is the moment set aside from the rush of life in which we remember the sanctity of nature.

That sacred circle of ritual, however, seeps into everyday living. Its boundary is a tool that we can share with others, allowing for safe space in which to explore, finding trust and connection. Indeed, just as the circle of the tribe protects its community, the circle created by a mother protects her child. The boundaries are always clear consistent in honesty and only flexible to allow for growth. When a child is brought up with clear boundaries, asserting authority over him is seldom demanded or required. As reason grows, with experience and the ability to conceive consequences, a child learns to judge his own balance between freedom and security.

In *Paganism, that discipline is an integral part of any relationship, and consequently central to spiritual practice. It comes as an awareness of boundaries, the edges of identity. From that animist *Pagan perspective, these may be the edges of another human being, but equally may be the tribal boundary of a family, religious or neighbourhood community, workplace or interest group, each with its own identity, ethics or morality, or indeed of any part of the nonhuman natural world. In discovering and honestly expressing our own edges, and acknowledging the Other's, we learn how to recognize and accept the difference. Feeling the edges, subject to subject, *me and you*, we find true empathy and connection.

Love, Trust and Freedom

The last kind of relationship to discuss here is the intimate adult bond. This is the relationship that most fully requires that we reveal who we are, and truthfully so. While the child is naturally open to his parents, only learning to protect himself as he discovers he is a separate being, as adults there are times when we choose to be open to another, to be everything but the stranger. We long to *know* someone and be *known*. We long to love and be loved.

For a few it is easy. A great many, however, wholly craving the closeness, fail to cross the distance, locked in the prison of separation, unable to grasp sufficient trust - as if not knowing quite which muscles to relax. Love: what a tangled and revered notion. For the human soul, it is both natural and hugely problematic. Like star dust, it is everywhere but so hard to find. As a force of nature, it so easily and commonly provokes the raw extremes of suffering and happiness.

Definitions are as broad. The Old English root is *lufu*, which has intimations of affection rather than passion. Going back further, the Indo-European base is *leubh*, meaning to like or desire, and this is how our culture most often uses the word: I'd love an ice cream, I loved that movie, I'd love to but can't. I am always intrigued by the Spanish way of expressing love: *te quiero*, which translates as I *want* you.

Discussing ideas with a colleague, he reminded me of a more *Pagan definition I have used: love is inspiration. When our soul is touched by another's presence, and our response is naturally to open to perceive and receive and give more, we feel love. Of course, I was not only referring to human love or love shared by human beings, but also the experience of being open with wonder, with appreciation, for a landscape, the ocean, the dance of a thousand butterflies, the golden sun sinking into an autumn horizon. The more we allow ourselves to be inspired, the more creative energy is evoked, the reverence and acceptance generating within us that exquisite mixture of fizzing excitement, confidence and calm.

Between human beings, that receptivity is often not so easy, and because it feels like such a high wave, the word itself shimmers with potency: it doesn't just (threaten to) flood through us, but may well have the power to carry us away. At the beginning of a relationship we tiptoe around it, anxious not to overstep some mark, sensing the word loaded with obligations. Some avoid it altogether, others using it for just that reason. Yet, sometimes it is the only word in our common language that comes close to the emotional torrent of joy evoked by being in another's company.

The rather archaic word *lief* (beloved) has the same etymological root, as does its derivative, belief, which literally means something that is held dear. The loss of this older sense of belief is to be mourned, for though the word retains an implication of what is precious, it has come to imply a certainty determined where there is no proof of fact. Because *Paganism does not require us to revere gods or spirits that we have no personal experience of, many in the tradition tend to perceive belief as illusory, as a notion that is clung to. When illusions and superstitions are pushed aside, after all, there is no need for 'belief'. Yet, *Pagan religious practice is based upon active and honourable relationship: in other words, connections that we nurture with those to whom we open our soul, those we hold dear.

However, the notion of clinging to a belief speaks of the problems that many experience with love. Indeed, having listed affection and desire, many dictionaries define love as an 'intense emotional attachment'. Love is often evoked within us when we find someone or something that will satisfy a need, yet behind that love (or need) is the insecurity of losing that resource.

Using the word wholly positively, the British psychologist John Bowlby crafted his ideas into what is called Attachment Theory. Further developed by a number of his students, this confirms the necessity of the healthy parent-child connection, exploring the inherent need within the infant human (or indeed primate) to be close to another person, and not just to satisfy the basic drives such as hunger. It is the security that we gain from that person's presence through the early years that allows us the confidence to grow into socially competent adult beings.

However, as outlined earlier in terms of loving care and attention, when that early childhood security is not adequately gained, the craving remains, extending into adult life. Attachment very often becomes no less than a crippling pathology. The insecure individual clings to anything that doesn't run away, and the more they hold on, the more rigid and fearful they become of what is the inevitable loss.

To the *Pagan, that we have chained ourselves is an act of dishonour, both to the gods (nature) and the ancestors: having been given the gift of life, to limit its value by being too afraid to live it fully is as irresponsible as it is disrespectful. Worse still, perhaps, is that our lack of courage leads us to dishonour the Other, the one with whom we are craving a closeness. Not only do we fail to give the best of ourselves, but we are liable to attempt to cast them into chains as well. For when we become attached, that person we cling to becomes an object, a *means to an end*, even if that end is entirely the alleviation of our fear of loss, rejection and isolation. Though we may call it love, such a relationship is wholly unethical.

We might wish it to be otherwise, at times even trying hard to convince ourselves, but love is a wild force, a *Pagan deity that calls out like the attracting power of a great magnet, flooding us with its single-minded aching for connection. Honour is not an inherent part of love. If we are not able to ride that force, finding the exhilaration of face-to-face connection and celebrate its expression responsibly, respectfully, honestly, it will easily reel us off our feet, provoking us in blind desperation to cling.

The sticky, heavy chains of attachment can be found regardless of what has inspired that love, and there are many different sources, forms and currents of love. The ancient Greeks identified four, and the abiding relevance of their distinctions over two millennia later reveals how little humanity changes. *Eros* is sexual love, a visceral desire that aches to sink into the experience of the other's physicality. *Agapao* is the word for love most used in the Christian New Testament, in older versions sometimes translated as charity: it is a pure love, wholly felt but in some way untouchable. It is the love we feel for a deity, a hero, a love filled with respect and open giving. *Phileo* is a love that inspires the heart, a deep affection that provokes loyalty; *philadelphia* is an important aspect of that, meaning brotherly love. *Stergo* is particularly used within families, the natural love felt by a parent for his child, a chief for his tribe; it is a love that inspires responsibility. In each case, there is the acute risk of holding on too tightly. An overt or previously hidden need that is being exquisitely fulfilled provokes a biting fear of loss. And when the soul is completely filled with the experience of another, the prospect of losing that Other is no less than annihilation.

It is this fear that provokes the notion of possession within relationship, and the *I-it* nature of attachment *allows* us to make that claim. When our own needs have overridden our ability to perceive the Other as an independent subject, the illusion that we can own another person slips in. Further, we justify the emotional flood by indignantly rationalizing our right to do so, listing obligations due to us, expectations, of what is apparently owed, considering what we have given ourselves - as if our own surrender into love (or need) morally necessitated its recip-rocation. So focused on our own needs and desires, dangerously failing to see the other's individuality, a catalogue of assumptions slip in to our understanding of the nature of the relationship: with this *I-it* mirror, we assume that the Other wants what we want, needs what we need. So often we are profoundly and seriously wrong.

Jealousy is one of the most destructive emotional tides of the human soul. It rises with the fear that someone else will take possession of that Other, themselves reaping the pleasures and denying us the possibility of sating our own needs. It is most prevalent where a relationship's founda-tions are constructed of assumptions. Anxiously urging us to remove the Other's individuality and freedom even further, negating their very personhood in favour of our own need, its current is one that carries us away from the equality of *me and you*. It is a raging storm of dishonour.

Once again we find those powerful words: courage, generosity and loyalty. In love, the first is often the hardest. It can take tremendous courage to let down our guards and allow ourselves to feel deeply, partic-ularly when we have been hurt before. Acknowledging the Other as a separate and different being, it takes courage to love, knowing that we don't and may never fully understand them. It takes courage not to slip into anxiety, suspecting or assuming the worst of our fears to be true, and instead to be honest, both to ourselves and the Other, expressing what we are feeling and communicating truthfully, and trusting that we will be heard openly. It takes courage to love without demanding what we might measure to be an equality of reciprocation. Indeed, without sufficient courage, though we may reach for intimacy, still self-defending we are likely to fail.

Good relationship also requires us to be wholly generous, never slipping from the soul to soul, *me and you* connection, acknowledging the Other's ongoing story, always awake to their needs - and the fact that their resulting priorities may well be different from our own. In listening with honour, we learn to hear and *accept* who the Other is: our *Pagan ethics don't provide the right to (try to) change that person, nor to expect them to change, even if we perceive that change to be healing. To love a person for who they could be is to dishonour who they are now: such love is for a concept not a person. Allowing the Other to walk their own road, we take responsibility for walking our own. If there is healing or change to be done, our focus must be upon ourselves.

Love requires the generosity of compromise. Without necessarily going to the extent of Lèvinas' *après vous* philosophy, if an intimate relationship is to work we must be willing to adjust our priorities, making choices that support the relationship rather than just ourselves. Very often we need to give something up that previously felt important, affirming that the relationship takes precedence. Yet, riding an undercurrent of doubt, any glimmer of reluctance negates the honour of that compromise, as do any assumptions that the other person will compromise equally. Generosity is crucial and invalidated by judgement and resentment.

If there is no loyalty to the relationship, there is no hope for it, and it is in the task of setting jealousy aside, accepting the Other's individuality, that we express our loyalty through respect. However, not only do we need to think about it, to consider its validity, but we need to *experience* it, to perceive and fully feel why the Other deserves respect. Nor can our decision be based upon judgement (deciding some element of their character is worthy); with wonder we open our soul to the Other's presence. Once again, to the *Pagan, nature's intricate patterns evoke appreciation and awe.

The nurturing of relationship is then very much based upon the way in which we honour the Other as a separate person. Open to who he is, I perceive the edges of his energy, the shape of his consciousness and identity. Where before, with the jealousy of insecurity, I may have felt those edges to be statements of separation and reacted badly, now those edges are a source of delight. For here is the realm of sensuality. Feeling the flickering touch of the Other's proximity, finding a heightened awareness of our own edges, thoughts move against thoughts, emotions touching emotions, energy stimulating energy, skin on skin.

Without consent, edges will always touch with friction, making us flinch and recoil. To insist on such a touch is as abusive and unethical as any declaration of *I-it* ownership. Indeed, to be threatened with another's intention to touch when we have no such desire can be utterly terrifying.

With consent, conscious proximity and the touch of edges is flirtation, the foreplay of deeper intimacy. Indeed, the *Pagan focus on profound relationships within nature brings this to the very heart of love: sometimes the open soul's receptivity becomes a desire to touch, to experience the edges ... then to dissolve into the loved one, to dissolve the Other into oneself, to merge, becoming one, momentarily losing the separation that is the natural gap between two people. Energy combines like fire and two souls, two cohesions of consciousness, lose their edges completely.

When it is all that we are craving, this merging in love can be powerfully exquisite. The liberation from the bounds of identity, of separation and self is an extraordinary experience of spiritual release.

As human beings, for the first months of our life held within the intimate embrace of our mother, there are no hard edges, and somewhere in the human soul is a longing to find someone with whom we can again dissolve the boundaries that separate. Just as is the case in a truly sound parent-child bond, when we merge in this way as adults, opening ourselves utterly to another, if there is to be a loving connection of equality and recognition, there must be trust that the encounter is truly *me and you*. For when the relationship is utilitarian, one party the object of another's need or desire, stranger meeting stranger, there is complete annihilation.

Sometimes our need for release encourages us towards that annihilation through submission. In fully consensual sadomasochistic relationships, where the trust is integral, the foundation forged of honour, the motivation is often the profound experience of being brutally stripped of the masks and scaffolding that allow us to pretend. Utterly naked in our honesty, drenched in the vulnerability of our humanity, the faux-identity destroyed, wide awake we can experience the cool flooding sensation of truth.

However, that need for release can also draw us into self-negating situations, where there is no ecstatic merging but the slow wearing down of boundaries, of edges and identity. A woman becomes the role she is given, a useful and acquiescent mother and wife; a man loses touch with his creativity, trudging through uninspired days of toil. Not only do we lose ourselves, but the loss becomes a habit, and one so common it is socially acceptable. The Danish nineteenth century thinker Søren Kierkegaard put it poignantly: 'The greatest danger, that of losing one's own self, may pass off quietly as if it were nothing; every other loss, that of an arm, a leg, five dollars, a wife, etc, is sure to be noticed'.

In part, this is an extension of what Hegel was exploring: self-consciousness needs another to recognize its existence, yet 'pursues the death of the other', longing to alleviate the alienation of separation, albeit knowing that to destroy the other would be to destroy oneself (or the mirror needed to experience one's own existence). What results is the perpetual tussle for dominance, however subtly played out, of who is reflecting whom, of which self shines most brightly through the encounter. All too often we find ourselves complicit in these games of insecurity, manipulation, guise and loss.

An ethics of honour requires us to take responsibility for our own actions: love may not be integral to honour, but freedom is. Crucial to our understanding, and integral to the web of our heritage, the Old English verb *freogan* means to set free, but also to love, probably referring to the freedom felt within one's own tribe, our family being wholly beloved and protected. *Freod* is friend and *friga* love; indeed, the Old Norse goddess Frigg, wife of Odin, is one of the most powerful deities of love in northern Europe.

Although the word is not found in modern English, the current beneath the Welsh word for love, *serch*, is another important part of British heritage. Often used for a forceful love, a passionate and erotic love, its roots touch the Greek *stergo*, reminding us of how key the family and tribe were to our ancestors, as they are in modern *Paganism. As with *freogan*, the freedom of protection and belonging provided by the tribe is paramount. Good relationship has, as its foundation, an acknowledgement of the Other as a free and independent individual.

However, accepting the need for freedom in any relationship, and especially an intimate relationship, is not easy. Where there is freedom but insufficient trust, the tiniest spark of insecurity can breathe into a blaze. And clearly, though an intimate relationship without trust can be rich with love and caring, it is far more likely to be based upon attachment and need; without a surety of reliability, there will always be a reluctance to invest, leaving it superficial. On the other hand, a love where there is trust is one that not only can afford integral freedom, but nurtures the freedom of both individuals as a valuable resource of growth, joy and learning.

But just what are we trusting? We cannot trust the future. The *Pagan reverence for nature's perpetual change encourages us to accept that all relationships contain the inevitability of their ending. At some point, the currents of life will draw us apart. As Heidegger spoke of the value of *being-towards-death*, so is the same true here: remaining awake to the transience of two human lives coming together - whether that transience is a half hour of wild sex or sixty years of loving marriage - can increase our awareness and appreciation of each moment. We no longer hurl down demands of the future, needing an assurance of permanence in order to cope with depths felt now. Nor do we surrender into the flood with reckless abandon, or refuse to do so because of the inevitability of an ending. Instead, remaining conscious of how precious the *here and now* is inspires us to express openly our thanks for all that is shared, never taking the relationship or the other person's presence for granted. We navigate our course, alert to the forces of nature, accepting the winds of change will always affect the journey and wherever it is that we are heading.

In *Paganism, what we trust is intention. With honour, we cannot demand that trust be reciprocated in every relationship; however, where we are investing energy and purpose in an intimate human connection, through *me and you* communication, without judgement or expectation, it is important to explore who we are and the threads of intention. Thus, I cannot *trust* that the man I love will be alive tomorrow, nor that he won't come across someone else with whom he longs to spend time; but I know that he knows me well enough to know what will hurt me, and I trust that his intention is not to do so. With honour, what more can I ask? Of course, relationships can falter if there is a lack of trust in terms of commitment, yet even here what more can we trust than the *intention* to remain committed? Anything more is idealistic. My point is not to dismiss the value of commitment, but to augment the importance of intention. For this is where the problems lie, in the dishonesty and hypocrisy of the unspoken undercurrents, where assumptions lurk, multiplying like a virus.

Even in a philosophy of anarchy it is important to recognize the value of committed intention: it is a beautiful gift to receive, a potent offering to give. Indeed, because anarchy relies on honour and not rules, it openly accepts the human craving for security, our ability to conceptualize generating ideas of both delightful and dreadful futures. Aiming to maximize the creativity of reason and emotion well balanced, anxiety is alleviated when we feel able to rely on the Other in terms of their presence and ongoing input, particularly where we are both investing in some form of shared creativity, such as children, a business, a home: a project that is more than momentary. So do we state our intention, crafting a road that clearly leads into the future. That many find it hard to vocalize or feel secure with words spoken privately only goes to reveal just how hard it can be; the institution of marriage, originally established to secure the protection of property and lineage in patrilineal cultures, has persisted to deal with this fear of change and betrayal.

In many forms of British Paganism, marriage is called handfasting, and despite our Western culture's statistics of divorce, it is hugely popular. Primarily the rite is witnessed by the gods, the ancestors, the land, and, perhaps most importantly in terms of human frailty, the couple's tribe or community. Though some Pagan traditions require a few vows that must be agreed, those passed through ancestral teachings or which secure loyalty to the tribe, the central vows are those the couple make to each other and these they write themselves, forcing them to think carefully about what they are doing. The rite does not bind a couple together 'until death do us part'; there is no sense that it is a bond made for life. Indeed some weddings only draw a couple together for a weekend, or a year and a day, at the end of which the two can decide whether to commit once more. A good many Pagans renew their handfasting vows, updating the basis of their marriage, actively and openly acknowledging the changes they have been through both as individuals and together; the practice keeps the bond poignantly relevant, vibrant and awake to itself.

Indeed, having had their vows witnessed in a sacred manner, and with the opportunity to renew their vows as often as they might wish, many Pagan couples consider themselves fully wed without seeing any reason for the legal glue - nor the wider tribe's morality that tends to come with it. In *Paganism, there is no sense of a norm in terms of a handfasted relationship. While the Church, and others keen to hold to a *status quo,* have been fearing for the future of marriage and the family with gay weddings and extended legal rights for couples cohabiting, the *Pagan perspective is quite different. Tribe and family are of paramount importance, yet far more worrying than the increase in 'different' household arrangements is the ongoing decline in people's ability to craft intimate relationships at all. Increasingly, adults in their thirties and forties are alone, wholly failing to build secure and healthy, viable relationships, unable either to trust or to compromise, at sea in a culture where there are so many choices and so many expectations of perfection and satisfaction. When a couple marry, there is too often a hypocrisy of family gloss, beneath which is empty depression, dishonesty and the clutter of broken vows.

After more than twenty years in mine, and having been the priest at the rites of countless others, I am a great *believer* in marriage. Yet the aspect I most value in *Pagan marriage is that each and every bond of commitment is entirely personal, and often quite deliciously so. The wedding vows carefully reflect the needs and idiosyncrasies of the individuals involved, and the way in which they are hoping to live their lives - and those vows are realistic: to swear to love each other forever is ludicrous, setting us up for failure. Having made those vows, when life is hard, we can return to them, remembering what we promised, what we *believed,* that witnessed statement of intention encouraging a couple to make an effort, to reconsider and re-craft the necessary compromises to engage with honour.

Marriage can and does work; and furthermore, where there is honour, a relationship based upon true intimacy and honesty, on generosity and responsibility, on mutual respect and loyalty, inspires the courage needed to deepen and broaden that connection. Indeed, regardless of the glue of convention or social rules, a human relationship can get better and better.

As if to emphasize that, I shall address one last issue here: the love affair. In terms of human relationship, in many ways it weaves together so many threads of *Pagan ethics that I shall use it as a means of summation.

Our Western culture may have a legal morality of monogamy, but underneath its ideals there is a clear tribal acceptance of the illicit love affair, expressed almost with a shrug of resigned inevitability. The paradox is tangled. Does a committed relationship have to be monogamous? Considering human history, the answer is clearly no. There are no laws against polygamy in the Christian Bible or Jewish Talmud. Indeed, where polygamy is legal, such as in parts of Africa, Church leaders emphasise that attitudes about monogamy are cultural and not religious.

Of course, taking more than one partner into a committed relationship doesn't guarantee there will be honesty, but neither does monogamy. The currents of life are neither predictable nor easy to ride, which is why *Pagan ethics, based upon honour, do not require monogamy. As long as we are able to communicate and engage with each other with honesty, maintaining our responsibilities and always increasing our respect for others, how many concurrent intimate relationships we have is entirely our own decision. Whether they are same gender, hetero- or non-sexual, co-habiting or at a distance, handfasted, married or fleeting, is entirely our own business.

Many polygamous cultures limit the number of wives to those that can be cared for equally. So in *Paganism, that soul to soul honour is essential: each person involved in an intimate bond is a subject in their own right, each relationship based upon *me and you* values. If at any time one of the individuals shifts from that place of equality in terms of value and respect, there is no possibility of honour. The moral code is simple: if you can't do it, don't do it.

And it isn't easy. I have known so many relationships crash and burn on the dishonesty of adultery, as have we all. Although I've witnessed many play with the possibilities of polyamory, *Pagan couples coping with the entrance of a significant Other into their lives, if there is wakeful honour where it doesn't work each relationship has nevertheless greatly benefitted from the journey of exploration, the honesty evoked and clarity shared. Where they do work, the freedom is glorious to observe.

Believing in freedom, recognizing that social rules are created upon a shared morality, but that too often that morality is founded upon fear, we can push the boundaries of 'normal' society. Within the clear parameters of honour, we can do as we wish. Crafting each step with honesty of intention, and with respect for life as it is experienced in the poignancy of *now*, it is possible to explore the wilder pathways of freedom - ethically.

CHAPTER SEVEN

THE VALUE OF HUMAN LIFE

Three ways to ensure a good life :
accept that you will die,
be always ready to die,
celebrate equally the living and dying.

Having established a set of parameters within which we can make ethical decisions about our human relationships, in this chapter I will extend that, picking up this globe of the human world, turning it over once again, this time to explore the issues of life and death. What is the *Pagan view in the debate about actions such as suicide, euthanasia, *in vitro* fertility treatment and abortion?

Inevitably, some *Pagan attitudes in this area tend towards the anarchic, and ideas around how we perceive the nature of death need to be discussed. However, the fundamental question is not about what happens when we die, but how, why and when do we value human life. In *Pagan terms, what is the point of being alive?

Meaning and Not Knowing

Questions about the meaning of life have always thrilled me. In my mid to late teens, stoned witless in the dark before dawn on some high-rise roof in a big city across the world, watching the moonlight and neon lights, deliriously alone, I'd pose the core question as if to the wind or the restless dead. For hours I would meander through landscapes of answers, not so much seeking certainty as washed through with the implications of every possible idea.

Cleaning up, crawling into my twenties, starting to learn about sanctity and honour, my need to find meaning was no less urgent. I'd seen too much violence at close hand, too much hunger and despair, and with the problems in my own body I had too much experience of pain to accept that the density and complexity of nature, and the slog of day to day living, could be entirely meaningless. My contemporaries, with a snide laugh, would shrug, "yeah, but what's the point?" The attitude to their own existence was played out in the complete disregard they showed for others' lives. As I stumbled onto the path of the seeker, it was meaning I was looking for, and consciously so. There *had* to be a course laid out, for without it humanity was surely doomed to flounder in the barbarism of not caring. Through those reckless years of my early twenties, blessed with the arrogance of youth, I was determined to find it.

Meaning: it's natural to suspect there is one. In one way or another the marketing campaign of every revealed and constructed religion has been based upon the claim that 'we have the answer! We know the truth! We can reveal the meaning!' Some believers smile as they inform me that such a niggling inner suspicion is merely the first step on the road to sweet realization, that there is indeed a fundamental meaning - one crafted by God. For those who can hold this conviction, life is given all the desired and necessary meaning simply through faith in God as the designer and creator of *everything*. Furthermore, by following God's laws, the solution is extended into every step along the road: every action, well guided, is saturated with that divine intent.

Yet, for those unable to transpose the mythology into reality, this teleological argument is clearly no more than the craving for certainty, laced through with ribbons of hope and carefully posing as logic. In a culture of ruling gods and superheroes, it creates the intuition that life is significant. If we know what the meaning is, after all, our lives are given purpose and thus more value than our crass living could ever provide. All we need do is simply walk the path described by that divine intention, experiencing its story. With a greater clarity about where we put our feet, and what the next part of the story will be, life is safer. We know how the song continues, so we can sing along.

While many *Pagans are polytheists, acknowledging countless deities - powers of nature - there is no belief in a supernatural deity, and therefore no one God the Creator whose intention floods all existence. There is no all powerful being who, disturbed by self-awareness, designed and manifested life for the purpose of self-exploration or self-glorification. With no notion of meaning being given from this external source, there is no sense of life itself being a divine gift, nor of any path or ethical code that gift might direct us to follow: there is no God the Judge, no divine morality. If we are seeking help with the question through the *Pagan perspective, then, the notion of deity provides no easy answer.

Religions based upon belief and authority are not the only players in this game of truth and certainty. Since the Renaissance began shifting the sands of human understanding, many have transferred their allegiance away from God towards science and the magic of technology. Increasingly buying into this 'more rational' advertising, conventional (non-heretical) society takes on board scientific perceptions as if they were fundamental and unalterable truths. Material life, having emerged through a series of coincidental and random happenings, has now neither meaning nor value given by some creator. All that remains in terms of purpose is the raw drive to reproduce, to maximise, to use up. In terms of scientific meaning, the only measure is life reproducing itself.

However, these are equally constructed answers, based upon the scientific rationalist and materialist view of life. They reflect the human psychological need for reification - making ideas, interpretations and observations more real than they are, as if they were timeless fact. Its core aim too often being to tame the natural world for human use, this *I-it* attitude is a very long way from the reverential and respectful position of the modern *Pagan. While *Paganism is inquisitive about nature, encouraging its adherents to question and learn, measurable scientific 'facts' are nothing to do with life's meaning, nor its purpose or value.

Of course, on the street, in the pub, unthinking society will shrug, not quite vocalizing the teenager's "whatever ... " but expressing the same thing. As the theatre director Richard Eyre says in his preface to an edition of Sartre's *Being and Nothingness*, the world Sartre describes is 'a familiar one to any contemporary reader in the West: a meaningless, godless and de-personalised world in which the words *ennui*, *angst* and *alienation* are much more current than *hope* and *compassion*'. To secular modern society, that life is meaningless is self-evident. Though deeper instincts may seep through when we hit a wall of trauma, inspiring us to cry out to some primitive sense of god, in the luxury of Western ease most realize that the ball is in their own court, even if only to grab mindlessly what they think society and the world 'owes' them. Given the resources available to us, life is as worthwhile or worthless as we craft it to be.

So ... we are each responsible for what we make of life. But in terms of ethics, this attitude is unhelpful. We are not, after all, simply looking at the mess we make of our own lives. If we are to develop criteria with which to value human life, we need to be drawing parameters that will be relevant when we are making decisions about other humans' lives. On what basis, for example, can we decide to create or take away life?

This first part of the chapter, then, seeks an adequate definition in terms of a *Pagan understanding of life's meaning, examining how we ascribe meaning to life, and in what ways that meaning provides a notion of life's value. Once criteria are found, we can look at the ways in which we express that value practically in terms of human life, how that value changes with differing circumstances, and whose judgment is valid when it comes to valuing a particular life.

Immediately, however, we face the problem of language, for in the above sentences there is still the vague implication that I am aiming to find some foundational truth about 'meaning'. I am not. The British thinker AJ Ayer, writing in the 1930s in the reckless arrogance of his own twenties, determined that truths could be divided into two: those supported by the meaning of the words used ('true by definition', such as mathematics), and those based upon the experience of the senses ('in principle verifiable', such as science). Able to judge any proposition as true or false by that premise, anything that couldn't be thus categorized he declared essentially meaningless. Consequently, there being no facility to judge a moral point as true or false, all morality must, Ayer decided, be acknowledged as based upon emotion, upon desires and attitudes; as such, it cannot be verified and is therefore meaningless. Any attempt to express value in terms of language is thus equally futile.

In his *Tractatus Logico-Philosophicus*, written fifteen years before Ayer, Wittgenstein explored the limitations of language in a way that appeared to imply the same thing: because language fails us, we cannot and therefore should not bother to explore the aesthetic, religious or moral, but instead focus on realms where fact can be explained. 'Whereof one cannot speak,' he said, 'thereof one must remain silent.' However, as one who read Wittgenstein as a teenager, perceiving in his words depths of genius and mystery, my perception of his thinking is still of the broader, less analytical camp: his statement wasn't a command but an observation. If we accept the exploration of philosophy to be not a search for facts, we can acknowledge every thinker's vision as if each had merely painted upon a canvas their interpretation of the same landscape - the world through human eyes.

Indeed, Wittgenstein never meant to dismiss the importance of the issues. Eight years later, in 1929, he clarified the necessity of attempting to communicate the inexpressible. 'My whole tendency and I believe the tendency of all men who ever tried to write or talk Ethics or Religion was to run against the boundaries of language. This running against the walls of our cage is perfectly, absolutely hopeless. Ethics so far as it springs from the desire to say something about the ultimate meaning of life, the absolute good, the absolutely valuable, can be no science. What it says does not add to our knowledge in any sense. But it is a document of a tendency in the human mind which I personally cannot help respecting deeply and I would not for my life ridicule it.'

I still read his words as I did at the age of nineteen, as a beautifully realistic attitude towards knowledge, and one that is wholly *Pagan: the quest for proven knowledge can distract. Accepting that we are always at risk of apparently invalidating an ethical argument or value judgment with subjectivity and emotion, yet knowing that in this arena we are not dealing with facts, I too emphasize the necessity of exploring life's meaning, in order to establish parameters within this area of ethics.

In her discussion of Sartre, British thinker Mary Warnock defined the key problem to avoid with the wonderful phrase, the 'spirit of seriousness'. Our task is to ensure we don't 'pretend that values are absolute, given somehow independently of any human subjective judgment. This spirit makes us pretend that the quality of being desirable or undesirable is somehow a quality of the things themselves, like redness or roundness'. It is not.

Over and above the 'spirit of seriousness', I am aware too that I risk constructing here just another framework of value, albeit based on a *Pagan worldview. In an attempt to avoid doing so, I shall look first at how a few key thinkers have deconstructed meaning, and hope that a glimmer of the *Pagan perspective will be revealed in the rubble.

Meaninglessness and Becoming

The place to start is Schopenhauer, perhaps simply because he makes such a thoroughly comprehensive job of it.

Misogynistic and invariably depressive, Schopenhauer described life as determined by the relentless and primordial drive he defined as self-preservation: the *will to live*. The development of human consciousness and reason is a part of this impulse, manifesting the idea of reality that is our tangible world. Yet this Will has no other purpose. Blind and irrational, beyond its own drive it is completely senseless. Insatiable, it permeates everything, creating futile lives, fraught with conflict and suffering. As human beings, nothing guides us but this Will of existence, indifferent and yet tortuously powerful. As he strove to find peace through what he perceived as this storm of volition made worse by human self-awareness, he wrote, 'Everywhere in the world is desire, because all

- everywhere - is will'.

If life is crafted of meaninglessness, its very fabric utter futility, there is absolutely no purpose to life; our task is simply to find a way of living without too horribly suffering its useless torrent. Not until Book IV of *The World as Will and Representation*, written with his darkly poetic eloquence, does he lay out his ideas of how it may be possible to achieve release from this storm, and here he describes three media for peace: aesthetics, ethics and ascetics. The first, he felt, was most powerfully found in music, for drenched in music the Will's drive is no longer all-powerful. Music, he said, expressed the Will disconnected from its harrowing manifestation as life. Wholly noumenal, 'when music suitable to any scene, action, event or environment is played, it seems to disclose to us its most secret meaning'.

It is within this noumenal realm that we find empathy, and thus our source of ethics. For beneath the projected world he perceived that we are all connected. When we do not allow the Will to overwhelm us, we are able to feel compassion for fellow travellers struggling through the storm. Further, how we disconnect from the power of the Will is through the discipline of asceticism. By stepping out of the contained and defensive notion of self, denying self-interest, we find stillness. The *will-to-live* ceases. Yet there is still no meaning.

From a polytheistic *Pagan perspective, his view appears similar to that of the revealed religions: one brutal, judgmental force saturates all existence with its single intention, denying life on earth any intrinsic value. However, there was no greater realm of heaven and hell for Schopenhauer to anticipate. Taking these ideas into his own thinking, Nietzsche embedded them into his criticism of Christianity, which he perceived to have successfully obliterated the value of life through its devoted focus on an externally given meaning and an afterlife. However, unlike Schopenhauer, Nietzsche fought the weight of nihilism: 'What does not kill me, makes me stronger'. He saw the human task as being to return meaning to life. Crucially, though, this is not about discovering any natural or inherent meaning, for he was sure there was none: instead each individual is given the task of creating their own. Meaning is forged through the state of *becoming*, a state he called the 'will to power'.

Sometimes attributed with being the first existentialist, the French thinker Blaise Pascal, writing in the late seventeenth century, questioned the value of life without the divine benefaction of meaning. Three centuries later, as the first philosopher to accept the label of existentialist, Sartre wrote, 'There is not human nature, because there is no God to have a conception of it': human life is devoid of any meaning or value until we ourselves begin to fill it. This is not just about what we do, but about crafting our very humanness, our identity, defining ourselves and our life's journey. 'Man,' he said, 'with no support and no aid, is condemned every moment to invent man.'

At the heart of *Being and Nothingness* is Sartre's wry look at just how we do create ourselves, for within this essentially meaningless world, as human beings we have complete free will. If we acknowledge his experience of Nazi-occupied France, his words are further emphasized: however little we have, however dire life is, there is nobody to blame but ourselves if life is or seems worthless. If we haven't the strength to make choices, we will perpetually fail, lacking the necessary commitment to create anything of value. The absurdity of existence will confront us, challenging us to wake from the irresponsibility of our evasive stupor, to grasp all that is needed in order to craft our essence into meaning.

Here is where *Paganism and existentialism find a weave. Exploring the significance of the individual as a free subject, both rational and irrational, passionate and thinking, existentialists have challenged notions of meaning, purpose and value within a world that they perceive to be clearly indifferent. Although some Pagans do reach to mythic gods who they believe care, the *Pagan will readily acknowledge the merciless indifference of nature towards humanity. With no god-given reason to live, no opportunity to defer to an omnipotent deity, responsibility lies solely with the individual and their willingness to choose. The autonomy of freedom leaves us awake, seeking truth within and around us.

Dismissing conditioning, social pressure, economics and genetics as excuses for 'bad faith', and declaring the compulsion to establish these as causal to be a 'futile passion', Sartre's emphasis was on our ability to *imagine* our potential and walk towards it. Here Sartre speaks of the search for authenticity and freedom. When we identify with the moment and its limitations, when we believe we are something, we become trapped by our self-awareness and, unable to express our authentic self, instead play at being that self, languishing in 'bad faith'. Regardless of our circumstance, he claimed, we can always envision and transcend the facts of the moment, for we must always be choosing, creating, *becoming*.

The assembled reality of our lives Sartre calls our 'facticity', and although getting stuck in this mire is so badly compromising of our freedom, awareness of it is essential. In *Paganism, this is what makes up the stories of an individual or tribe, its accumulation of being, the time-broad consciousness that goes to create our identity and edges. These stories continue to manifest the immediate world and the resources at hand. Yet, in keeping with Sartre's thinking, the tribal, genetic or personal stories within a *Pagan soul do not diminish the need to question, to be wakeful and heretical, and to find one's own path. The search for truth is fundamental, and as we walk the journey, we continue to create those stories as wellsprings of and for our future creativity.

Heidegger, from whom Sartre derived the notion of authenticity, also expresses this very *Pagan perspective: being authentic, wakefully true to self, requires us to live our own lives, not to get lost in expectations, fears and conventions, in the guises of acceptability and social coping mechanisms. Authenticity is about *becoming* one's true potential. Many readers of what can seem densely complicated thinking note that Heidegger didn't imagine authenticity could ever be a perpetual state of being, instead remaining a goal reached at exquisite moments of presence. When we lose ourselves, what Heidegger called 'fallenness', there is no hope of living honourably.

John Stuart Mill termed it beautifully in his classic work, *On Liberty*: 'because the tyranny of opinion is such as to make eccentricity a reproach, it is desirable, in order to break through that tyranny, that people should be eccentric. Eccentricity has always abounded when and where strength of character has abounded; and the amount of eccentricity in a society has generally been proportional to the amount of genius, mental vigour, and moral courage it contained'.

Presence and Consciousness

Within the rubble of meaninglessness, then, we find the first and perhaps most crucial *Pagan notion of value in terms of human life: authenticity. To the modern *Pagan, the validity of this perspective is not simply that it makes sense within his own soul, his own generation, but that it sits solidly within the flow of his blood, his ancestry and the long stretch of his heritage: it is fundamental to his humanity. Authenticity, as described by both Heidegger and Sartre, expresses a foundational concept of *Pagan spirituality, in that it is about being fully awake and present, and thus capable of responding to the Other - human or non-human - with immediate relevance and reverence. It is humankind in sustainable relationship with his environment.

To analytical philosophers, and others demanding verifiable facts, language provides no way of establishing certainty in terms of meaning, and thus does not allow us to explore an ethics based on value. Authenticity, to the *Pagan, is more than sufficient, for it is an expression of self-perception of the experience of truth, of becoming (being in the current of life's changing) in the *here and now*. It is not easy to achieve, but it is a standard by which the *Pagan's path is directed.

With this first treasure in hand, as a foundational understanding, more can be recovered from the rubble, not least the necessity of personal responsibility and choice - which to the *Pagan is integral to honour. For here we find it laid out with authenticity, not as a tool of analytical thinking, of pondering and deciding, but as an experience of presence.

Only within that presence can truly honourable relationship be crafted: wholly where our feet are, breathing in the air about us, aware of all who stand with us, listening to their tales, and responding through the truth that is the easy flow of life changing. Here is integrity sufficient to offer moments of surety within that experience of immediacy and honesty. Allowing ourselves to ride the current, allowing the Other to do the same, now do we have a chance of grasping the notion of value.

Moving through the rubble, I return to Sartre, for his ideas draw me on to the next key *Pagan treasure: consciousness. Sartre's freedom, formed of Cartesian dualism, was based upon the understanding that the spirit could not be bound by the world - except when an individual chose to act in 'bad faith', relating too closely to the dense material world. As a dualist, Sartre considered consciousness to be 'nothing', a gap at the centre, moving upon the tides of intention, ever pulled between past and future. It could only validly be defined in relation to something else. Indeed, because of our perpetual state of evolving, becoming, changing and choosing, consciousness 'always is what it is not, and is not what it is'.

From a *Pagan perspective, in that he focuses on the currency of inter-action his view holds some water, but it is also limited by being thoroughly disconnected through the dualistic binary division. Consciousness, he said, was 'a wind blowing from nowhere towards the world', which recalls for me the raging Will defined by Schopenhauer, whose dark nihilism describes so much of the devastation of a world without meaning. For Schopenhauer, consciousness was the appearance of the Will through the self-awareness of the intellect: the medium through which the Will creates the idea of the world in which we exist. Because the Will, however, is such a powerful and primitive force, there is no easy positivity within it. Irrational, its freedom is terrifying, which was one of the most shocking aspects of his thinking; if consciousness were crafted of reason, life would be safer.

In the Grail stories, amongst the key myths of our British heritage, the search for that sacred and mysterious cup is for many construed as a search for the meaning of life. At one of the many climactic points, the young knight Parsifal - stumbling through the reckless arrogance of youthful immortality and confusion - at last asks the wounded Fisher King the question he is bound to ask, "Whom does the grail serve?" The first time I heard the tale, the answer given was the shockingly simple "Itself". Having wandered, barren and despairing, for so long, when the King remembers and speaks this magical response he finds himself healing, once again finding his potency in a land that is equally starting to regenerate. The storyteller, a wild feminist bard, left me with such a clear flood of understanding: the grail was the womb, the cup of life, the wild goddess of regeneration, life giving birth to life. While this Pagan goddess is an ageless flow of intention and purpose, a force of nature sustaining herself through reproduction, the story reminds me of Schopenhauer's blind, irrational and self-driven Will.

To the *Pagan and animist, both mythic goddess and philosopher's Will are forces of nature, and both seething and evident within human nature. Indeed, as many monotheists envision their God as a father and judge, or brother of love, here too are elements of human nature. Each force has its own intention, woven with energy, and as such each are expressions of consciousness. The way in which this adds to the *Pagan notion of the value of human life is definitively *Pagan. For here we return to the view of consciousness being inherent within all nature.

Defining consciousness simply as inbuilt intention, natural purpose, fuelled by the energy of life, does not of course equate to meaning. However, laying the understanding once again upon the foundational experience of authentic being, walked through the honour of generosity and respect, from that extraordinary courage of total self-honesty, respon-sibly, the meaning shines gloriously. This is not a meaning inherent in every being that is sublimated to a greater cause. What the *Pagan perceives is purpose within every aspect of nature, crafted of its own meaning and aching to play that out. The American philosopher Martha

Nussbaum refers to this as valuing any being - human or nonhuman - as the individual it is in itself, and allowing it to flourish in its own way.

Each human being holds within it the purpose of each cell, each muscle and limb, of his own human and individual journey, and those of the tribes of his blood and choosing. That this purpose not only drenches but crafts a life into being provides it with value; to the *Pagan, this value does not need affirmation through reflection, but because nothing is isolated, each being in perpetual relationship with some other aspect of nature, the reflection that measures value is ever present.

When later I read and heard the Grail myths relayed by others, and heard the Fisher King's answer to the young seeker as the more commonly told, "the grail serves those who serve", it took a while for me to understand. The intention was here not the inner drive of innate purpose, easily comprehended by the *Pagan animist (we must be what we are, and revere the current by being fully so), but the call for ethical action. Here the Fisher King's wound is healed not by the celebration of self, be that individual or tribe, but by the creativity of honourable relationship.

No life is isolated. Heidegger, among others, felt Nietzsche's emphasis on personal success to be far too individualistic, not sufficiently allowing for the necessity of relationship. In *Pagan terms, as the Grail myths tell, the beauty of perfect autonomy, of natural anarchy, is only honourable and thus sustainable if it is lived through an acute consciousness of the ecology of the web. Further, this awareness of our interaction shows us just how well we are doing. So is each life that we encounter of exquisite value, for it reveals our place in the web.

What then is the value of human life in *Pagan terms?

Accepting the difficulties of subjectivity and judgment based upon emotions, and the resulting limitations of our language, we still have no hope of discovering a premise of value if all we do is think about it, analyse, deconstruct and measure idea against idea. Instead, in order to find value, we must experience it for ourselves. As the extraordinary thinker and mythologian Joseph Campbell said so beautifully, 'People say what we're all seeking is a meaning for life. I don't think that's what we're really seeking. I think what we're seeking is an experience of being alive so that our life experiences on the purely physical plane will have resonances within our innermost being and reality, so that we actually feel the rapture of being alive'.

Utterly insignificant in the big picture of existence, each human life is potentially vast. We can each be *übermensch* in Nietzsche's terms, grasping and expressing the fullness of our true potential. Through presence, self-reflection, reaching to communicate authenticity, the integrity of truth, living with honour, awake to the web, instead of constructing some notion of worth, we can discover the exquisite value of life.

However, on that basis, we cannot judge the value of another's life. Other than by observing how that individual experiences their own living and expresses that outwardly, we can have no idea. To judge is to project our own needs upon another soul.

As a statement of ethics, let us see how that plays into the practicalities of human living. When does such an attitude become problematic?

Suicide and Being Dead

Suicide is an issue that articulately expresses many of these *Pagan perspectives.

If we acknowledge an individual as having responsibility for what he makes of his own life, we must also allow him responsibility for how he might end it. In *Paganism, there is no God, nor any other body wielding authority, whose judgment on such a decision has any validity. Indeed, the very idea that someone would prevent another from ending their life would be an act of force that negated the individual's freedom, implying that their life was in fact not their own. Yet in a culture that does not accept slavery, who might justifiably claim ownership of (authority over) another's life is an incomprehensible question. With its emphasis on the importance of self-governance, such an idea is entirely counter to *Pagan thinking.

This extends to the objection made by those libertarians who perceive suicide to be an act of self-sabotage against personal freedom, erasing the option of further decisions; the choice is still ours to make, even when it apparently ends our freedom to choose. In this ethical arena then, and perhaps more than any other, autonomy is fundamental.

What does compromise our human freedom are the flooding tides of desolation and depression, now at epidemic levels in Western society. Unable to function or think clearly, an individual may stumble into fantasies of suicide, particularly if legal or illegal drugs are further complicating the chemical mix, paralysing parts of the brain. These urges can be temporary, provoked by loss or trauma, and to make critical decisions when emotionally flooded is always dangerous. Blinkered by the experience of suffering, seeing only pain ahead, we risk behaving with clumsy dishonour, lacking courage, dismissing our responsibilities, forgetting loyalties. Yet, even dishonourably done, through the selfish fog of despair, the decision to end the suffering by taking our own life is still ours to make.

Schopenhauer, a man who had journeyed extensively through the dark valleys of despair, supported the right to commit suicide: 'it is quite obvious that there is nothing in the world to which every man has a more unassailable title than to his own life and person'. However, he also spoke of the risk of being overwhelmed by suffering, acknowledging the difference between submitting to the dreadful torrent, letting despair overcome reason and killing oneself through an act of destruction, or stepping aside from the force of Will and choosing to end the nightmare by taking one's own life, fully awake to the nature of existence. With a clear head, mindful of the threads of connection and relationship, fully present in our authenticity, we can commit suicide with honour.

With each sunset, each autumnal release, death is witnessed within *Paganism. The festival of Samhain each year brings an ease and familiarity about the subject, even to those who are untrained in the mysteries of the tradition. The stories and songs of the dead are retold, the dying that winter brings is welcomed, the lessons brought by the cold and dark overtly acknowledged, encouraging what Heidegger termed 'being-toward-death'. Indeed, the medical term *apoptosis*, which describes the natural process of cells dying without damaging neighbouring cells, is poetically derived from the Greek meaning falling leaves. Without this dying, there would be no regeneration. Within our bodies, this happens on a cellular level (ten billion cells each day), yet to the animist it is evident everywhere: individuals letting go, consciousness dissipating, allowing renewal within the tribe, within the whole ecosystem. Spiders, clouds, stars die in the same way.

From a *Pagan perspective, this death is not an ending. Death doesn't bring the complete annihilation of consciousness. In thoughts, memories and stories, in the consciousness within each cell of our decaying physicality, in the waters of our body that drain into the oceans, in each relationship that was influenced by our living and dying, in everything with which we have shared energy and intention, our existence continues. It may remain in the recognisable cohesion of our identity, or dissipate into the broader tides of emergence and release, but it is not gone.

Death is not binary, not a black or white process. Even modern science admits the lines are blurred. Consciousness is an unsolved mystery. As a result, the scientific definition of death varies: in the USA, a person is dead when the whole brain has ceased to function, while in Britain it is only the brain stem which must have failed. It takes complex technology to ascertain either, the necessity being that in most cultures a person's moral status changes completely at that point of death: they can no longer suffer or die, nor value their own life. Whether the spirit has flown or disappeared, the dualist perceives the body as no more than waste. Moral obligations are transferred to any kin and their immediate sensitivities.

In the natural philosophy of *Paganism, without need for proven and delineated categories, there is less uncertainty, more acceptance. The focus on *becoming*, pivotal in existentialism and *Pagan understanding, does not lose validity when we are speaking of death. At the most essential level we are consciousness, still moving within nature. Death does not remove us. Because we continue as a member of the tribe, albeit now as ancestor, our moral status continues.

Through my own experience with people who dance the precarious edge of suicide, Pagan and non-Pagan, and having meandered within that place myself, I perceive a very clear distinction: between those who do not want to live and those who want to die. The former are crying out for help, desperately needing to re-establish the functionality of their *life*. Without that help, finding themselves unable to make the suffering disappear, they want to disappear from the suffering, and death appears to offer that option. At the crucial moment, however, the soul clings to life. Overwhelmed by fear, such people wish that they could let go, but they have not yet crossed the river.

The latter have. Whether requesting help or acceptance from others, or just to be left in peace to walk their chosen road, their situation is totally different from the person who does not want to live, and needs to be acknowledged as such. Here we find authenticity, and so the possibility of honour. When we let go of life, choosing to do so and gently turning our face away, an extraordinary peace fills us. However old we may be, whatever our situation, we find ourselves present, awake to the flow of time with all its stories. Indeed, the most gracious act is to die with that sense of peace, of conclusion and resolution.

Euthanasia and the Tribe

Yet having turned away, then to be kept alive with medical technology, the peace becomes a wasteland, a grey emptiness, the lack of dignity provoking shame, rage and isolation. So is the debate on euthanasia equally bewildering to the *Pagan. Why anybody would want to keep an individual alive, in crippling pain or dreadful disability, when that person is requesting the release of death, is utterly baffling. Ensuring another's painful and undignified death against their will is historically what human beings have done with those outside their moral community, those beyond the pale of their tribe, the enemy, the vanquished and the outcast. Our society now insists we do this with those we love.

Euthanasia is simply the act of bringing a life to its end before it would naturally do so. The word comes from the Greek, simply meaning a good death, and what greater gift can we give our loved ones than a good death? With acceptance, with song, with listening and care, as they walk the path that we can only glimpse from afar, it is honourable to help in any way that we can. For what is a more disgraceful - graceless - way to behave than to draw out the suffering? When a person has lost the ability to be courageous through the storms of pain, they also lose the most positive sense of pride, of belonging and identity; to be complicit in that loss is profound cruelty. To die with honour is as important to us today as it was for our ancestors millennia ago.

Lives are not owned, but they are shared. Each one of us is a part of the identity of the tribe of each community and environment that accepts and supports us. So is our dying also shared. When someone dies, a part of the tribe dies, released into the realms of story and song. When someone chooses to die, or requests help with their release, the task left to those who live on is to let them go with honour: with generosity, loyalty and courage. Using the emotional lever of fear or grief to hold someone alive can never be justifiable.

To be so completely accepting of suicide, and the assisted suicide of euthanasia, may to some seem dangerous. Surely people will die who should not have to, who could be saved! Yet to the *Pagan, this argument is nonsensical and invasive. When we die, we have not lost anything. We are simply moving, changing, shifting like the wind. Our life expectancy in a Western society may be four score years and more, but there is no need for us to live those years out or be judged for not wanting to. Our task is to live with honour, whether for ten years or ninety. Our desire is to die with honour, to be *free* to die with honour.

Euthanasia comes in different forms. The voluntary euthanasia spoken of above is essentially assisted suicide. The individual gives full consent, for their wish is to die. That our Western society, and currently British law, maintains that this is unacceptable is, to the *Pagan among many others, completely and shockingly immoral.

In the arena of medical ethics, it is non-voluntary euthanasia that is more seriously debated: this is where, for some reason (such as coma or infancy), the person isn't able to communicate their wishes as to whether they would prefer to die, nor how much they value the life that they have. In his book, *The Value of Life*, British philosopher John Harris states that non-voluntary euthanasia is widely implemented in our British medical system, and as obviously as voluntary euthanasia should be permitted, this non-consensual practice 'should be outlawed or in its relatively few benign forms more closely regulated and supervised'.

The practice of selective treatment is one form, where decisions as to how to treat a person in terrible pain are languaged in terms of what is actively given and what is not. The problem here is that our society evades the key issue. We shoot horses, but instead of mercifully lifting a severely and terminally disabled child out of his suffering by releasing him from life, we withdraw that which will enable him to continue to live. Hiding in the legally acceptable intangibles of 'negative responsibility' is clearly not honourable. The point is whether he suffers, and though the result is the same, selective non-treatment is a longer and often more painful way to die.

The same is true of resuscitation decisions: priorities are made as to who receives the trauma care and who does not. The medical profession once again evades the issue. As Harris says, 'what is disturbing is that it is not acknowledged to exist, and the decisions are seldom scrutinised'. The practice of using the 'double effect' of pain treatment is equally prevalent, where a patient is not made aware that an increased dose of analgesic morphine will foreshorten his life. This too is non-voluntary euthanasia, and without facing the issue directly, there is no clarity, no transparency: no honour.

For John Harris, by far the most serious form is lack of government spending, and the way in which the National Health Service budget is used. With the technology to save lives but not the money to fund its use, professionals throughout the system are daily prioritizing who lives and who dies. As one of the most respected voices currently writing about medical ethics, his words are forceful. Once again he refers to the way the framework of our society, here through government and NHS management decisions, allows and supports a culture of evasion: 'a traditional but inexcusable myopia as to negative responsibility has allowed this area of euthanasia to flourish while the government and other agencies continue to show moral disapproval for the only morally acceptable form of euthanasia', assisted suicide.

Here, the *Pagan stance that requires us fully to hear how another values his own life, instead of imposing our own judgment, becomes problematic. The question remains: given limited resources, how do we prioritize between one life and another? Already stated is the irrelevance of age, for the *Pagan attitude is not that long life is allotted as a natural right, but that a valuable life is created day by day, living wakefully and honourably. A child is not saved before an old man because of his youth and innocence, or because he deserves a chance to live.

It is tempting to measure a person's worth upon the moral quality of their life - do we spend limited resources on a heavy drinker with liver disease, an obese overeating diabetic, a smoker with lung cancer, unwilling to change their lifestyle and with no apparent ability to bear responsibilities? As Harris says, effectively this would be a sentence of capital punishment for what the tribe (currently) declares to be immoral behaviour.

However, in *Paganism no individual is perceived as isolated; each person's identity is interwoven with that of their tribe and their landscape. Just as when someone dies, a part of that tribe also changes its conscious form, so when someone is given the precious energy of resources - the time, attention and money that provide healing, medicine, education and care - so are we nurturing that element within the tribe. As a result, how we engage with the tribe that supports us is of critical importance. Where a person is not giving what they can to the tribe, the tribe naturally has less to give in return. Needless to say, in *Pagan terms, we are not only members of human tribes, but also of those of the environment. How responsible we are within an ecosystem in itself reflects just how much will be proffered in exchange.

This is harsh. Yet Nietzsche's sense of each individual reaching to achieve their potential, pouring that creative energy into the culture as a whole, is fully *Pagan: it reflects nature. The weak struggle. However, human nature is equally nature, and the force of human empathy is as strong as its reason, provoking the need to support those incapable of positively contributing. Nietzsche has been interpreted as dismissing this need as socially destructive, perpetuating apathetic and uninspired culture, and perhaps in the throes of his not infrequent frustration that is what he meant. The *Pagan attitude is less dismissive. There is a place for empathy and care, but not without limit.

Moral debate, whether philosophical or political, often speaks of the mentally disabled, the severely physically disabled and the sick, the very young and the very old, as those who are not able fully to contribute to society. Here is surely where our empathy needs to kick in. However, such questions outline the need to define more carefully the notion of contribution. Inevitably, the *Pagan does not base true value upon the vulgar measures of capitalist culture. The competition that fuels economic growth and progress is founded not only on natural human curiosity and creativity, but on forces of insecurity that skew our ability to interact honourably.

From a *Pagan perspective, the value an individual brings to their tribe is derived from how fully they are living with authenticity and honour. This means striving always to interact through honourable relationship. For what we give to those we are in immediate relationship with, we give to the tribe: our partners, our children and parents, our work colleagues and those we talk with when we shop, pay bills, arrange events, seek guidance, as well as the landscape of our natural environment. If we give resentfully, minimally, if we can't be bothered to make an effort, we receive little in return. If on the other hand, wholly present and responsible for our giving, we give openly, with generosity, courage and respect, doing our utmost for the sake of the tribe, even when there is not much to give, what we receive in return is abundance. Naturally, consciously, we act in a way that evokes reciprocity.

It may be said that such a system could not work on a national level, such as through government health services, but I disagree. *Pagan ethics begin with the individual and the way in which they interact, person to person, the way they craft each of their relationships. As we extend from small tribe to larger organizations, there is no point at which that premise need stop. Where it does, the honour is lost, for the interaction becomes person to abstract, with all the related *I-it* disfunction. In a culture of sincere relationship, even the hardest decisions can be made with honour.

The Cost of Life

While *Pagans revere the gods of nature, including those whose currents provide us with the basics of life - birth, breath, hunger and so on - we do not *worship* life in the way that many in Western culture appear to do. Medical practice, with its modern technology, too often now works to create and sustain life regardless of its quality or value. For a doctor sworn to save lives, a patient who dies is a demonstration of his failure. It is an attitude aggressively supported by the enormously profitable pharmaceutical industry, providing drugs to extend lives at vast costs - albeit only where there is money to pay. In the US, particularly, health insurance companies add to the mix, taking vast sums that leave people expecting miraculous care in return. Death is (in comparison) wholly unprofitable and unacceptable. Life, even on forty two tablets a day, dazed and adrift, wired up to an assortment of tubes, drips, pipes and pumps, has to be worth it.

Yet the very notion of life at all costs is antipathetic to *Pagan sensibilities and ethics. When it comes to walking the road, experiencing each step, life is just not worth some costs - to the individual, their tribe or their environment. In *Pagan terms, the work of a doctor, a healer or carer is measured by the quality of peace, not in days of breathing.

This worship of life no doubt develops from the animal instinct to survive, augmented by our human self-awareness, weighed down by our fear of the future and the horror of death. As a force within human nature, some may assume this survival drive is important in *Paganism: life is surely sacred. Yet this is to misunderstand the philosophy, mistaking reverence for submission. Lust is a force of nature, to some *Pagans revered as an extraordinarily powerful deity. It seethes through me with its urgency, hunger and desire, but I don't respond to its every craving. Instead, crafting a relationship with it, coming to understand its drive (its energy and consciousness) within my own soul, I can play and explore its current, wakefully, honourably, instead of submitting to the flow when the results would otherwise provoke hurt or chaos. Human nature, with its reason and self-reflection, offers the ability to consider and choose which tides and floods to ride. The craving to stay alive is (usually) even more powerful than lust, but equally a force of nature that we must learn to ride, for in doing so we also learn when to let go, slipping off the current. Life is indeed sacred, but without the pathological attachment generated by fear of dying, we don't have to submit to a desperate need to survive.

The desire to reproduce is yet another tide. Like lust, for some it is an easy current to ride, one that can be readily managed (a person freely deciding when to have a child) by working consciously with the desire and its inner energies. However, like lust or indeed anger or love, when its expression is blocked that force can become enormously debilitating. Immersed in its worship of life, the medical industry once again takes advantage, stepping in with some elusive miracle cure, like IVF.

In vitro fertilisation is an articulate manifestation of human curiosity and creativity, one that has developed out of that collective survival instinct which ensures any such ideas are socially acceptable. In *Paganism, however, it doesn't sit so comfortably.

Undergoing *in vitro* fertilisation, a woman takes a range of fertility drugs that provoke her to produce up to two dozen eggs; these are removed and fertilized with her partner's sperm in a warm petri dish in a lab. Between one and four of those are then implanted in her womb, depending on her age and the clinic's practice, in the hope that she will accept one and successfully hold the pregnancy to term.

In this hugely competitive and lucrative industry, success rates are manipulated by clinics, drugs companies and researchers. According to NHS statistics, currently in Britain treatment that results in pregnancy is at a rate of around twenty seven per cent in women under thirty five years old. The figure drops to ten per cent within five years, and crawls to negligible over forty five. The statistics of women taking home a healthy full term baby lie at around ten percent. Government figures for the financial year ending March 2004 put the number of women who had IVF treatment at nearly thirty thousand. Pregnancy by normal means has a two thirds success rate.

The key ethical issue from a *Pagan perspective is about the unnecessary use of resources. If we acknowledge human autonomy, accepting that people should be able to do what they wish (and can) as long as they don't harm others in the process, then the ethical dilemma is how much suffering is caused by precious resources going into fertility treatment instead of elsewhere. This is not solely about government funding IVF with tax-payers money; more holistically, resources consumed are curiosity and wit, care and time - as well as money - that could be used to relieve suffering in more ethical and tenable ways. Further, there can be no excuse of ignorance about the population issue: this can't be dismissed when considering whether to bring another child onto a planet already massive overpopulated by humankind, with its untenable consumption of the global environment. The unnecessary use of drugs is another issue that must be acknowledged here, knowing each drug's brutal history of long-term testing on nonhuman animals in captivity in pharmaceutical laboratories.

After all, nobody has an inherent right to create a child. The UN Declaration of Human Rights (article 16) states that every person has 'the right to marry and found a family', yet this is based upon ensuring these options are not limited by race, religion or nationality. To declare the bearing of children to be a right is wholly to conflate desire with necessity. As the Mary Warnock says in her book *Making Babies*, 'if we allow wanting and needing to slide into each other, with the consequence that there may seem to exist a right to whatever is deeply wanted, then the dangers of the rhetoric of rights, the borrowed authority, escalate'.

The claim to a *right* is, as I described in Part One of this book, a call to belong to a particular moral community, a tribe that will support those needs we feel most pressing. For a person to declare they have a right to bear children is to demand membership of that tribe which so clearly worships life, a tribe that will support an emotional desperation to fulfil a primitive craving to reproduce, without asking too many questions about justification.

Of course, the *Pagan wouldn't call for legislation on this from a ruling authority: that would be counter to its foundation of natural anarchy and autonomy. It is, however, crucial for each individual to make their decision fully awake to their own motivations, authentic in their honesty, and responsible for the effects of their action throughout nature's web.

In some religious traditions, IVF is deemed immoral for entirely different reasons: the Catholic Church have problems with its dependence on the sin of male masturbation to make available the sperm. However for many, regardless of faith, the most complex problem is that of the redundant embryos - and there are usually more than a dozen from each treatment. It is this issue that provokes the most instinctive discomfort.

A couple may be given options as to what is done with these unwanted embryos. They can donate them to another couple in what is called 'embryo adoption', but this is infrequent for a number of emotional reasons. They can instead have them frozen in liquid nitrogen, preserved for later potential use though the efficacy of thawed embryos drops significantly (current estimates state that there are over half a million frozen embryos in the US). The third option is usually that taken: to allow them to be discarded with other human tissue waste. They are thrown away.

Experimenting on Life

The alternative is the subject of fervent current contention: embryos can be donated to laboratories for stem cell research. Most scientists in the field claim that the best source for this cutting edge experimentation is the embryos that are a waste product of IVF treatment.

Three days after fertilization, an embryo is a tiny bundle of four to ten cells, smaller than a pin prick, each with a nucleus containing the necessary DNA. This is allowed to grow into what is called a blastocyte of fifty to three hundred cells, taking from four to seven days, at which point the embryo is then dismantled: the stem cells are removed, killing the embryo. Undifferentiated primitive cells, these precious stem cells have the ability to become any of the two hundred and twenty types of cells that make up the human body.

In 1990, the Human Fertilisation and Embryology Act made it illegal in Britain to carry out research without being registered to do so, or to keep embryos for more than fourteen days. In 1995, under Clinton's presidency, the United States made it illegal to use federal money for stem cell research that killed the embryo, and in 2006 Bush vetoed any change in that law, against the advice and wishes of most of the American government. Adult stem cell research, particularly using umbilical tissue, is proving to have potential, but most declare it profoundly limited. American biochemist Paul Berg, testifying before a House of Representatives subcommittee, expressed the frustration of most in the field: 'surely, obtaining cells from legally obtained abortants or from early stage embryos that are destined to be discarded in the course of IVF procedures and making them available for potentially life-saving purposes would be viewed as ethically permissible if not a moral imperative'. Indeed, research shows possibilities of embryonic tissue being grown to make tailor-made cells for grafting into adults, addressing problems such as radiation and burns, anemia, Parkinson's disease and immune deficiency disorders.

If spare embryos are going to be discarded (killed) anyway, why not use them to help other lives? Although still most often expressing the values of a culture that worships life, easing suffering from disease would seem a more valuable use of precious resources than creating more children for an already overpopulated world. To object on the point of disposal is either ignorant or disingenuous: contraceptive pills and devices (such as the IUD) that disallow fertilized eggs to take root effectively kill embryos. Berg mentioned aborted material: government statistics for 2005 put the number of abortions at 186,400 in England and Wales, 84% funded by the government. Only one per cent of these were deemed necessary because of the risk that the child would be born handicapped. If a culture allows abortion and contraception, where potential human beings are daily killed in numbers, it is surely simply a lack of understanding and familiarity with stem cell research that makes it feel unacceptable.

Of course, those whose religious beliefs attribute a sacred soul-form to the body from the moment of conception, thereby making the cell bundle a 'person', will be horrified at any process that actively or obliquely kills it, rightly calling it murder within the framework of their definition. Indeed, even those without such religious convictions argue as to just when an embryo does indeed become a human 'person'.

Science tells us that the embryo must develop into a foetus eighteen weeks old before it might have the necessary physical infrastructure to feel pain (89% of British abortions were performed at less than thirteen weeks in 2005); thus, if we take this on board, there can be no pain, suffering or indeed self-awareness felt by the tiny growing form, these often being the simplest definitions of what constitutes a person. I shall be delving into the debate as to what makes a 'person' in the next chapter, but the reason I have omitted to do so here is to restate an important *Pagan perspective.

Honouring the Stories

To the animist, consciousness is everywhere. As a bundle of cells develops with its own coherence, its consciousness emerges, at first openly sharing its sense of being with its immediate and surrounding environment. Slowly it forms its own identity, its edges, finding self-awareness: in a human child this last stage begins well after birth. It is a long way from that point at eighteen weeks of gestation, let alone four days from conception. The cells that make up its growing form, nonetheless, are alive with consciousness.

Research has recently led some scientists to consider what has been fundamental to animist and *Pagan understanding in this respect. American neuroscientist, Candace Pert has been exploring what she calls the 'biochemicals of emotion': neuropeptides (amino acids) and receptors, thought to have been present only in the brain, are now being found all around the body, transmitting information, providing what is referred to as cellular memory: glimpses of consciousness in flesh, blood and bone. Following organ donation - from a simple blood transfusion to more complex transplants - recipients feel changes in their identity. Many may put it down to the gift of a renewed life, but to some memories come of experiences they haven't lived, memories held within the organ that they've received. To the *Pagan, this is not an ethereal soul implausibly attached, but deep in the subatomic matter, consciousness as stories, awake and vital in the patterns of energy, dancing in response to patterns around. As a result, many *Pagans will not take part in the technology, even though it may save countless lives.

Another key argument widely used against stem cell research, and abortion, is that the killing of an embryo or foetus is the destruction of its potential. This too holds no water in *Pagan philosophy. Though it is important to prepare for the future, to be honourable in our actions bearing in mind the road ahead, a *Pagan does not live for the future, nor dependent upon it. To do so would be to live without authenticity, not adequately present and therefore unable to make fully honourable relationships.

The value of a life is its value *now*. The relationships we make are relationships with what exists *now*. Though an embryo does not have sufficient self-awareness to value its own life, the parent who wants it born shares its intention. Indeed, when that growing bundle of cells is within the mother, soul to soul, she shares energy and consciousness with that being within her womb. Even if the embryo is not inside, those cells still share with its parents, its genetic tribe, the stories of that blood line. Thus, though we cannot own another individual or soul, there is a duty of care within a tribe for its own stories, its own people. Those who hold that obligation act honourably only when they accept their responsibility, whether for an unborn child or the remains of someone who has died.

From the *Pagan standpoint, establishing that honourable interaction with and with regard to those who hold the stories of the tribe, whether alive or dead, must be based upon *consent*. It's a word easily written, but not easily enacted. What is consent? The *Pagan doesn't imagine it as simple. In practice the wellspring of care and responsibility is wholly dependent on just how much understanding there is of the intricacies of each thread of relationship, each twist of the story that colours and directs the course of individual intention. Yet when there is sufficient awareness, and we are able to feel the currents and ride them together, consent is naturally expressed. Decisions emerge.

Seeking to know himself, striving to forge wakeful honourable relationships, the *Pagan works to improve his ability to interact with authenticity, present in the flow of *here and now*, fully responsible for his actions. Acknowledging consciousness as intrinsic within all nature, his perception is underlaid by an acceptance of natural connectedness, which in itself evokes his experience of the web, the rich ecology that is the environment of each decision to be made.

Human life has inherent value. Yet that value is worthless unless life is wakefully grasped, explored and celebrated, in the myriad relationships that make up nature. And that value is diminished if it is clung to; for human life must be allowed naturally to emerge and recede, moving upon the rivers and tides of human consciousness: our stories.

CHAPTER EIGHT

THE VALUE OF NONHUMAN ANIMALS

Three ways to belong to a tribe :
sharing fear, sharing guilt,
sharing joy.

In his book, *Minds and Bodies*, the uncompromising British philosopher Colin McGinn addresses the ethics of how our human society treats the rest of the animal kingdom, the nonhuman animals. 'Do not expect,' he says, 'to find me in any way *balanced* on the question: this is not really an issue on which there are two sides.' Written in his wry but direct and thoroughly perspicuous style, his words give me courage where otherwise I might have taken more cautious steps, treading through the minefield of this particular moral issue, for I too can find no justifiable moral standpoint that supports the current state of abuse. McGinn calls it 'humanity's worst moral failing'. I agree.

In keeping the topic to one chapter, there are many points I will not adequately cover here. My aim, however, is to ensure that *Pagan philosophy is expounded while addressing the key issue: the *use* of nonhuman animals for food and clothing, as resources for scientific experimentation, for the excitement of hunting and sport, and, held in captivity, for company and entertainment. It is hard to imagine any reader not fully aware of the current situation, but I will craft an overview, if only to establish the evident problems. Briefly then I will look at the history of human attitudes, before looking at the arguments now used to support the continuing abuse, philosophical and more mundane, together with how each holds no water for a *Pagan today.

The Species Barrier

It always intrigues me how most British (myself included) don't instinctively consider themselves to be European, despite the fact that the islands are indisputably a part of that continent; indeed, most of Europe perceives the British as an idiosyncratic, slightly wild if innovative culture on the edge of their world. There is a glimmer of defensiveness on both sides, tribal boundaries made clear with every little dissimilarity in culture and morality.

As humanity we play a similar hand, yet in a far more damaging way: we determine ourselves distinctly and morally removed from every other kind of animal. The perspective is embedded in our language. The word *animal* is most commonly used as if denying that we too are members of that kingdom. Patrolling the boundaries, we protect our position, clarifying moral status as we claim superiority, demarcating our species territory as if it were blatantly obvious.

To counter this ingrained bias, I use the term 'nonhuman animal' here whenever I want to distinguish from human beings, keeping to 'animal' when my point includes our own species; I am aware of the term's clumsiness yet choose not to avoid it, to ensure a continued wakefulness to the prejudice. Prejudice, after all, can be hard to perceive. Like a river current we can ride it unaware of its force until something stirs the water, lifting us on its waves, rocking the complacency of our journey and provoking us to see clearly the situation we are in.

In our twenty first century Western culture, it is widely accepted as *fact* that the colour of our skin is no measure of our humanness or humanity. Yet less than a century ago, hundreds of millions of darker skinned human individuals were considered unequivocally less human and globally conferred a lower moral status. Upon their backs the world's developed nations accrued (and continue to accrue) their wealth, free to exploit those not part of their white moral community.

Today, the way humanity treats nonhuman animals, with even more brutal disregard, is no less shameful and problematic a situation. Making a comparison with the horrors born of racism and sexism, Mary Midgley wrote, 'The dialectical road-block so far thrown up at the species-barrier is not less crude than these were, but far more so, because it has received even less attention'. In the late eighteenth century, Jeremy Bentham called it an 'insuperable line', one we hold on to with determination, between those we are willing to have suffer and those whom we can't bear to see in pain.

To the *Pagan, it is hard to grasp how anyone can maintain belief in these distinctions, especially considering the impact such beliefs have. In this era, we have not the excuse of ignorance Bentham could have held to: we know we are primates. Literacy and information technology leave few corners of our culture untouched by news of human violence, selfishness and brutality: the notion of human superiority has nowhere to fit within the thinking soul's patterns of logic. Committing to his religious journey, the *Pagan learns how to deepen his relationships, exploring the connectedness of consciousness within the web of nature; the option to be complicit in the abuse of nonhuman animals simply disappears.

In wider Paganism, however, including both the priesthood and non-trained community, various surveys place the percentage of vegetarians and vegans at a little over half: given the average in Western society the number is significant, but many find the figure dismally low for a religion ostensibly based upon the currents and songs of nature. How we treat nonhuman animals is a highly emotive topic. Within Paganism, as outside it, debates explode into storms of emotional shrapnel. The clothes we wear, our hobbies, the sports we follow, the pets we keep, the medicines we take, all contribute to the way each small tribe crafts its identity, delineating a moral community, declaring who is in and who is not.

It is the food we eat, however, that provides the most overt and defining statement of our ethics. Declining an invitation to the greyhound track or a quiet day angling on the river, not wearing leather shoes or taking *Night Nurse* to fight a cold, is far more easily ignored than being unable to eat the food served at a gathering because it is soaked in animal juices. Food is, after all, at the core of any culture. The food we eat describes our lifestyle. It is the first bond between parent and child. Declaring one's diet different from that of the surrounding community is a poignant proclamation of ethics, of both belonging and rejection.

We begin then by looking at the current situation with regard to the use of nonhuman animals as a food source; for this unnecessary killing for food, whatever level of sentience the creature possesses, is the most basic and widespread expression of human relationship with other animals on the planet. Moment by moment, it perpetuates the human attitude towards nonhuman animals as entirely beyond the pale of our moral community.

Using Animals as Food

Meat is defined in the Oxford English Dictionary as 'food; nourishment for people or animals; solid food' - as opposed to drink. Only the fourth entry refers to meat as being food in the form of animal flesh.

As a concentrated source of protein, in days when calories and nutrition were hard to come by, to the omnivorous human another animal's flesh would have been a treasured food. Evolutionarily, through the stories of our ancestors that hum in our blood, we are built to crave such foods, as we are those rich in sugar and fat, in order to ensure we make the most of them when we can get them. That the word *meat* now (when spoken without a source noun, such as *nut*) refers solely to animal-flesh-as-food is indicative of this natural craving. The word, with its history, is still saturated with that natural prejudice: the implication that animal flesh not only equates to but completes our understanding of what solid food is, or at best should be, obliterates any sense that the animal whose flesh is eaten has any moral status whatsoever. We need solid food; we need meat; full stop. Except that we don't.

If the raising pens and slaughter houses were visible within our society, the world would be a different place. Many vegans believe that were the average person to witness the reality of the animal industry, they too would become vegan. A good number would, but many just for a while. I am not so optimistic about humanity or our ability to perceive what we see. I wonder if, instead, the violence of the raising pens and slaughter houses would simply drench society more fully, habituating a more extreme violence within our species. We would be just a little less 'civilized'. For already, from an animistic understanding, those who consume the flesh and milk of nonhuman animals are ingesting the toxicity of a long heritage of suffering, stories passed through blood and genes, generation upon generation, of traumatic loss, persistent abuse, desperate boredom and fear. These stories don't just disappear. Just as so much ancestral consciousness seeps into the mud through the natural cycle of burial and decay, so does the consciousness of what we eat move through our body, affecting who we are, providing the fuel for who we can be.

That this suffering exists cannot be denied. Peter Singer, in his classic text *Animal Liberation*, makes his point succinctly by solely quoting from trade journals where the facts are stated in order to advertise the industry. In the 1997 edition, he refers to a 1987 journal boasting that 5.3 (American) billion chickens are killed annually for eating in the United States. That is 14.6 million every day. Artificially fattened in tiny wire cages, these birds are killed at seven weeks old, the last few weeks being in the dark to dampen aggression. Deranged by the extreme stress of their conditions, birds' beaks are cut, without anaesthetic, to stop them pecking each other to death. In the egg production industry, five genetically altered, drug enhanced and debeaked hens fill a twelve by twenty inch cage, expected to lay up to three hundred eggs in a year. Calcium deficient, most struggle with the trauma of broken bones. Slaughtered when productivity dips at around eighteen months, their bruised and battered bodies disappear into processed foods.

Cattle and pigs experience equally horrific abuse. Developments in hormones mean that the average cow yield twice as much milk now as she did forty years ago, and thus spends her three to four year life suffering the excruciating pain of deficiency and stress diseases such as ketosis, laminitis, mastitis and milk fever. Impregnated every year in order to continue lactating, her calf is usually removed within twenty four hours, the males slaughtered for food. Castrated without anaesthetic, branded, kept in unnatural, cramped, overcrowded or isolated conditions, transported long distances without water, cattle retain the stress of their experience in their bodies, just as humans do. Pigs are kept in similar conditions. With more innate intelligence than most dogs, the majority are pathologically bored; their tails are cut off (without anaesthetic) to minimise the damage of their inevitable aggression. Sows, kept in crates that don't allow them to turn around, are expected to litter twice a year, and slaughtered when they can't.

Sheep have the natural advantage of being usually either healthy or dead: because a sheep simply won't survive such treatment, they are more likely to lead lives that faintly resemble the children's storybook picture of a farm. However, the abuse of tail-docking, drug use, parent-baby separation, the diseases of overpopulation, the trauma of transportation, markets and slaughter are no different for these creatures. Neither mulesing (cutting off folds of skin under the tail, without anaesthetic) nor grinding adult ewes' teeth to the gums is permitted in Britain, but such practices are common for the sheep raised elsewhere whose products (body parts) end up in British households and kitchens.

Though increasing number of consumers believe meat labelled free-range is an ethical alternative, standards are still very low. The majority endure the fear and confusion of markets, heading to the same brutal slaughter houses. Though considered unnecessary for birds, mammals are supposed to be stunned unconscious before being strung upside down, and shunted along a production line to have their throats cut. Nowadays, electric currents are used to stun; any human who has been electrocuted will happily describe the excruciating pain of such an experience; furthermore, although a shock may paralyze, it may not erase awareness. An animal needs very little sentience at all to be conscious of the stench of death and terror, particularly amongst those of its own species: many killed in this way have a good deal more than a basic awareness. The blood and muscles, every organ of the body, are flooded with the chemicals of fear.

Religious strictures of Islam and Orthodox Judaism require that animals to be eaten are slaughtered while conscious. What rage and terror must be provoked in an animal that, fattened beyond its natural size, is yanked up and held upside down by a leg that breaks or dislocates from the weight of its own body, slowly shifting along the line waiting for its throat to be cut that it may bleed to death. For those who don't eat *halal* or *kosher* flesh, it should be remembered that only a small part of these nonhuman animals' bodies goes to the religious market, the rest being sold into general trade.

Not many human beings would choose to work in such an environment. Across the world, the industry employs the least advantaged of society, working for minimum wages and below, in conditions where accidents are rife: little care is shown for any life.

American philosopher David deGrazia describes the industry in the simple phrase: 'massive unnecessary harm'. All three words are crucial, but the second is the one that needs the most emphasis. As Singer says, 'those who, by their purchases, require animals to be killed do not deserve to be shielded from this or any other aspect of the production of the meat they buy'.

Over and above the absolute dishonour paid to the animals involved, at a time when we face urgent environmental issues, and starvation in many areas of the majority world, the current use of nonhuman animals for food makes even less sense. Figures given in Keith Akers' *The Vegetarian Sourcebook*, quoted by Singer and others, state that an acre of oats produces six times more calories than if that grain were used to feed pigs slaughtered for pork, and twenty five times more than if it were used to produce beef.

Western culture's message about protein needs is tantamount to propaganda for the animal industry. According to the American Institute of Medicine's Food and Nutrition Board figures, daily we need around 0.8 grams of protein per kilo of body weight; taking into consideration the digestion of whole plant food (as opposed to processed vegetable foods such as tofu) compared with non-fibrous animal flesh, the figure has been raised for vegans to one gram per kilo, a requirement easily fulfilled by a simple vegan diet. Pregnant or lactating women and athletes may need a little more (1.1 - 2 grams). The WHO put the figure at 0.75 grams. However, over consumption of protein in the US is between fifty and a hundred per cent, causing kidney disease, obesity and calcium-deficiency among other problems. Returning to Akers' figures: where an acre of land can produce between 300 - 500 pounds of vegetable protein in the form of beans or peas, if that crop were fed to livestock, it would yield 40 - 55 pounds of protein in the form of animal flesh, or 75 - 175 pounds in the form of nonhuman mammal milk. Not only do we need less protein than most Western diets provide, but our production of it is inefficient.

For those who still buy into the lush advertising about nutrition expounded by the industry, Akers states that an acre of broccoli produces twenty four times the iron than that acre used for beef, and five times more calcium than milk. An acre of oats produces sixteen times the iron of beef. This inefficiency is criminally unintelligent in a world where millions are dying of hunger and malnutrition.

An increasingly precious commodity, half of all water consumption in the United States is used for animal rearing. One pound of beef has required fifty times more water as that pound in wheat. According to professor of ecology David Pimentel, production of animal protein takes eight times more energy as plant protein, the vast majority of which is still provided by fossil fuels.

If we add the destruction of habitat and top soil, the pollution from manure and urine, from a massively unnatural population of these food-source nonhuman animals, the damage to the environment is clear. Indeed, looking at global warming, twenty six per cent of Britain's methane comes from livestock animals, where 800 million are slaughtered each year for the food business. According to vegan writer Joanne Stepaniak, that figure is the United States is nine billion (American).

Those numbers don't include the billions of fish or crustracea that are suffocated, boiled alive, or die from decompression, dragged up from their deep sea world. The situation is equally clear, or even more obviously untenable. The destruction of water environments - rivers, mangroves, seas, reefs and oceans - is globally well documented, yet still ignored. The battles over fishing rights and quotas are a noisily political and undeniable statement on how effectively humanity is devastating ecosystems with its *I-it* attitude of arrogance. The artificial farming of water creatures is rife with disease, stress and overcrowding. Though fish and reptiles have nervous systems in many ways unlike mammals', they have similar nerve pathways and display many recognizable pain responses; fish emit a sound vibration, albeit inaudible to human ears. Indeed, according to an independent enquiry set up by the RSPCA, the evidence that fish feel pain is no less than for other vertebrates. For someone to deny that these animals suffer distress is a blatant expression of determined human ignorance.

Leather, suede, fur and other hides are not by-products, but an essential part of the animal industry's financial base. Pulled wool adds to the value of slaughtered lambs, whose flesh price is even lower than cattle, thus supporting an industry that takes any extras it can glean. Cattle skin provides a similar boost: between five and ten per cent of the end value. Aborted calves make the softest suede. Gelatine, made from the collagen of the connective tissues in cattle's bones, knuckles, lips and so on, is used not only in foods but hair and nail products, pharmaceutical and nutritional supplement capsules, photographic film, among other things. Indeed, that animal products are used in so many parts of our lives, including the production of rubber and steel (animal fats), refined sugar (charcoal bone filters), beer (fish bladders), prescription drugs, perfume, tennis rackets and woodshine, makes them hard to avoid.

Using Animals as Company and Entertainment

Of course, some animals are acknowledged to have faces. Indeed, many people treat a few chosen nonhuman creatures with more care and consideration than they do other human beings. Some of these relationships are a pure delight, with mutual respect underpinning an authenticity of care. This is often most exquisitely seen with companion dogs trained to help humans who are disabled, blind or deaf, where the necessity of good connection requires the nurturing of an honourable relationship. Yet, for the vast majority, the incredible hypocrisy of choosing to care deeply for a dog, while eating bacon without a moment's consideration for the pig (a generally more intelligent creature who has suffered a life of traumatic abuse), is not only rampant in our society but perceived to be rational and acceptable.

A pet's purpose (like a racehorse or greyhound) is often solely the pleasure of its 'owner'. Many are used and abused through breeding fashions, tail docking, isolation, lack of exercise or poor relationship. Hundreds of thousands of pets are put down each year, abandoned, crippled by genetic weaknesses and ailing from poor diet.

Domestic cats, bred delinquent and dependent, are hugely destructive of indigenous wildlife. According to the Mammal Society, there were an estimated nine million domestic or feral cats in Britain in 1997, killing over two hundred million small native animals, including mammals, birds, reptiles and amphibians. Neither native nor (if they were) in anywhere close to naturally occurring or naturally tenable numbers, they have a considerable negative impact on local ecosystems. Dogs may cause fewer immediate environmental problems, but, like cats, just keeping these pets fed supports many of the worst practices of the animal industry.

We don't need to seek out the worst practices of badger baiting or bullfighting. Zoos and aquaria often now claim to be conservation based, but few keep endangered animals, have any kind of successful breeding programmes or release animals into their native environment. The idea that animals are kept safe from the dangers of the wild is yet another expression of human fear of death: life at all costs. Captivity can provoke psychological trauma, desolating boredom and pathologies from lack of stimulus. Although protection from natural predation can mean some lives are extended, the trauma of being caged can not only severely compromise the quality but also shorten lives.

Using Animals for Science

It is hard to recount the facts amongst those who don't want to know, who don't want to change their lifestyle, and harder still to discuss without feeling currents of emotion. Singer was heavily criticized for pointing out the commonalities between the holocaust and the current abuse of nonhuman animals. Nazi doctors were given free reign to experiment on those they determined beyond their moral community - Jewish, Russian, Polish and disabled human beings - in just the same way that governments permit experimentation on nonhuman animals today. Yet it is a valid comparison, one that wakes society, for every individual who buys from a company that experiments on animals is complicit in this ongoing torture.

According to the BBC, in 2005 eighty five percent of experimental procedures used rodents, eight per cent used fish, four per cent used birds, the total number being close to three million animals in Britain alone. Nearly five thousand nonhuman primates were used, a figure that is rising (up eleven per cent from the previous year). Yet, despite administering phenomenal suffering, the vast majority of testing on animals is both trivial and futile, results often having no possible correlation with human responses, psychological or physiological.

Quoted in Singer's *Animal Liberation*, the British government declared that, from examining drugs marketed between 1971 and 1981, new drugs have 'largely been introduced into therapeutic areas already heavily oversubscribed ... for conditions which are common, largely chronic and occur principally in the affluent Western Society. Innovation is therefore largely directed towards commercial returns rather than therapeutic need'. Indeed, in 2004 the Home Office admitted that no comprehensive research had been carried out to check the value of animal testing for human medicine.

Tens of thousands of animals, famously beagles, have been forced to inhale tobacco smoke, yet the connection between smoking and lung cancer came from clinical observation of human beings, not from the animal laboratories. It was human clinical investigation that isolated the AIDS virus and defined its course, with human cell and tissue cultures initiating and processing the development of medicines now used. Despite decades of funding animal testing for cancer research and heart disease, nothing of any value has emerged. Where significant reductions have been made in ill health, the causes are almost always simply improved diet, environment and general welfare.

Although in Britain nonhuman animals can no longer be used for cosmetics testing, there is no such prohibition in the United States. Elsewhere legislation can be even slacker. Chemicals and products - for pharmaceutical, military, industrial, agricultural, beauty, personal care and household uses - are unnecessarily tested on hundreds of millions of nonhuman animals. These procedures include what is known as the LD50, where sixty to a hundred individuals are continuously subjected to injection, inhalation, ingestion or other exposure to a product until half of the group die, providing the often meaningless statistic of what is a lethal dose for fifty per cent of a particular nonhuman species.

Abusive experimentation also looks at psychological models, using pain stimuli to study behavioural responses, addictions and trauma. Yet the human context and its needs are usually so different that such tests are worthless. Where they are not, the research is idiotic. That infant monkeys deprived of comfort, reared in total isolation, develop physical weaknesses and psychopathic disorders is something any mother could confirm, simply by watching monkeys in their natural habitat: It is common sense. That researchers can claim millions of dollars to abuse monkeys in order to 'prove' it, expresses no more than a profound sickness within the scientific community.

Historic Attitudes

Why do we treat nonhuman animals in this way?

Aristotle was unambiguous in his assertion that humans were animals. Through his studies of nature, he made it clear that we should never feel disdain for another creature, 'for in everything in nature there is something wonder-inspiring'. Having witnessed and felt that wonder, it is hard to abuse or kill the individual, or even to compromise its dignity or ability to live its life in its own way. However, acknowledging human reason as a quality that grants superiority, he clearly placed human beings at the top of the *scala naturae*. This declaration was influential in a human world that was shedding its fear of (and reverence for) nature, and initiated a firm tradition of anthropocentricity. It is a stance that also justified his support of slavery. Believing his view in tune with nature's purposefulness, he stated that those without reason were the 'property' of those with.

Through the millennium of its development, Christianity adopted and advanced this apparently phylogenetic hierarchy with human beings as the God-blessed holders of the crown. After all, in the Bible (Genesis 1:26) God commands Adam and Eve to 'have dominion over ... every living thing that moveth over the earth'. The term is unambiguous: the Hebrew *radah* means to subjugate. The mythic couple were to 'be fruitful and multiply and fill the earth and subdue it' (Genesis 1:28); again the Hebrew is clear, *kabash* being to conquer completely. In Genesis 9, God gives Noah the whole of nature, but not as modern Christians like to think, not to care for as stewards or guardians. The words are: 'The fear of you and the dread of you shall be upon every beast of the earth, and upon every bird of the air, upon everything that creeps on the ground and all the fish of the sea'. It is a religious root-myth that gives eternal souls - or inherent value - solely to human beings.

In the thirteenth century, Thomas Aquinas affirmed that other animals were inferior. Plants, he said, are for animal use and animals for human use and that perfect order must be maintained. Anything else is unholy. Despite mystics and thinkers such as his contemporary Francis of Assisi and the Jewish Maimonides, both of whom wrote at length on the need for care and respect, recognizing that all beings existed for their own sakes and not simply humanity's, nonhuman animals remained objects to be used. When Descartes declared that animals were mere machines, their cries being not pain or sentience but instinctive response, he was reaffirming an attitude society wanted to hold to. Though divine reason is evident in God's creation of the nonhuman world, reason was given only to humans to use. Man, he said, was not an animal at all, but a 'thinking being'.

This attitude allowed as daily practice what within modern culture would be deemed unspeakably cruel. Dissection of living creatures (before anaesthetics) was a central part of the developing science; indeed, the word *vivisection* literally means cutting up the living. Dogs, bears, cockerels and other creatures set to fight to the death were considered entertainment. Yet this cruelty was simply indifference. Upon the dunes of human understanding at that time, animals were beasts, existing beyond the field of reference that was comprehended morality.

The eighteenth century saw the beginnings of change, with an increasingly educated and growing middle class. Kant, riding the winds of change albeit cautiously, acknowledged nonhuman animals' sentience and capacity for pain, yet dismissed their moral status on the grounds of their lacking reason. Human benefit superseded any and all consideration they may require. We must, he wrote in 1780, acknowledge another human's freedom, and limit our own accordingly, treating each individual as 'an end not a means'; nonhuman animals are, however, means to ends, and 'that end is man'.

Within that decade, Jeremy Bentham was challenging the attitudes that were so much the framework of his era. His words are sadly still radical for some today: 'The day may come when the rest of the animal creation may acquire those rights which only human tyranny has withheld from them'. Indeed, his words reflected Leonardo da Vinci's, three centuries earlier: 'The time will come when men such as I will look upon the murder of animals as they now look on the murder of men'. In Britain, change came more quickly than in Catholic southern Europe; where society was losing its reliance on the Church and its theology, benevolence became a fashionable idea, with charity, care and concern finding ground within Christian understanding. A creature's *suffering* needed to be considered.

In 1792, in outraged response to Mary Wollstonecraft's *Vindication of the Rights of Women*, the academic Thomas Taylor anonymously wrote the satirical *Vindication of the Rights of Brutes*. Horrified by the claim that women - wholly irrational and naturally lesser creatures - could be equal to men, he postulated that if her ideas were valid, they could be extended to provide rights for 'beasts' as well - dogs, cats and horses - a notion he saw as both ludicrous and dangerous. By his argument, he declared, her ideas were clearly absurd.

Despite such ingrained bigotry, throughout the nineteenth century the undercurrent of change continued. The first bill to protect animals was passed in Britain in 1822. Named after the MP Richard Martin, its focus was specifically livestock; in order to get it through the parliamentary process and into law, the bill was worded to protect a person's animals as property, not the animals themselves. The Society for the Prevention of Cruelty to Animals was established in 1824 by Martin with a group of reformers, achieving its Royal prefix from Queen Victoria in 1840. The Vegetarian Society emerged a few years later, in 1847. Although Darwin's presentation of evolution was attacked as a sinful and soulless vulgarity, the first protests against scientific research on unanaesthetized animals were starting at around the same time.

It may sound as if a new thinking had been set in motion. Yet, a century and half later, that I have to write this chapter at all is an expression of how little headway has in fact been made. I could potter through the little steps of change in attitude and legislation, but those steps don't get far. It may no longer be acceptable to beat a horse to death in a London street, but horses are brutally tortured in the quiet of laboratories day after day, and it is easy enough to eat one if it has been killed by a slaughterman in the privacy of his bloody abattoir.

Persons or Things

In the same way that the wealth of any political empire is founded upon the blood and suffering of other humans, so is our Western society sustained by the suffering of nonhuman animals. I have no doubt that the opulent and prosperous imperialists of Britain's colonial trading companies feared an apocalyptic (and global) descent into poverty should slavery or exploitation be disallowed. It may feel as hard to imagine a world without the human use and abuse of nonhuman animals. The arguments are certainly as vociferous.

The English thinker John Gray said, 'the chief difference between humans and other animals is simply that humans have acquired enormous power'. When my stomach churns, my body responding to the smell of decaying or cooking flesh, and I wonder why it is taking so long for humanity to stop the abuse, Gray's words answer my bewilderment. As McGinn says, 'the more powerful will always tend to oppress the less powerful, if they can get away with it'.

Indeed, in a crowd of unthinking people, if I question why we still use animals as we do, the answer is more often than not as McGinn says: 'we do it because we can and we like it'. The industries that base their wealth on the resource of nonhuman animals may depend on the wallets of an unthinking population, but more important are the justifications for the abuse raised by those who benefit from it, whether industrialists, politicians, scientists or simply consumers, arguments put forward by those who *do* think.

The key issue is essentially whether or not a creature has inherent value. As such, the foundation of the debate is at the heart of human morality.

That human beings are, as Simon Blackburn termed, 'ethical animals', ever judging, comparing, evaluating what is worthy of their time, energy and resources, is here particularly poignant. For if something - be it an individual or tribe, human or nonhuman - is afforded inherent value, a decision has been made to continue that process of evaluation and consideration, in order to maintain an appropriate ongoing ethical relationship. We care. Where it is decided there is no inherent value, however, the very need to think slips away: the judging has been done.

For many centuries, the decision was made for us by the tribal 'educating' authority of the Church, preaching with a surety that only humans had souls. In the materialist world of modern Western society, corporate power with its advertising sidekick perpetuates a secular version of the same stance. Implying that any necessary moral considerations have been carefully dealt with by those in control, with fallacious images they reassure us that we don't have to think. Happy cartoon cows offer us their milk with a smile; cheeky turkeys eagerly wait to be sliced up and packaged. We don't have to care.

But the debate is now rising into popular consciousness. Given our genetic similarity with primates, given the obvious barbarity and injustice of humankind (now that the majority world's corruption and terror is spilling onto Western streets), given the decreasing belief in fairy tale theologies (in Europe, if less elsewhere), the general public are asking questions. Do nonhuman animals have inherent value? In other words, do we (should we) *care* about an animal's desire to live its own life, without human intervention? Is each individual animal's life, human *and* nonhuman, valuable in itself, regardless of any usefulness we perceive it may have to us?

Care: it's a powerful little word and I use it here consciously. Its etymology speaks of an intensity of response, the Old English from which it is derived, *cearu*, meaning anxiety, concern or grief. In everyday language, it is an often used word, especially with its suffixes - careful, careless or carefree. Indeed, it is because it is an apparently mundane and common word that I use it, for the question is one that is thoroughly integral to how we live, day to day, meal to meal, choice to choice. Do we *care*?

For many, the argument comes down to the notion of personhood.

In this respect, the Oxford English Dictionary lags behind current philosophy, for their definition of a *person* is 'a human being regarded as an individual'. Although for many millennia, by no means *all* human beings were considered persons, that *only* human beings could be persons is a limitation that continues to be overtly expounded by many monotheistic faiths. Crucial to the debate, it is an attitude that seethes as an undercurrent beneath much thinking elsewhere.

Defining the word is not a trivial task. Lifting it from assumption into clarity is important, not least because the word, as used in everyday language, implies two things that together lay out the *all* humans/*only* humans problem. Firstly, a *person* can (and therefore ought to) take responsibility for their own actions; capable of ethical awareness, this allows a person membership of the tribe's moral community. Secondly, a *person* is someone we care about.

In philosophical circles the definition is debated with subtler edges. In the seventeenth century, Locke described a person as 'a thinking, intelligent being, that has reason and reflection, and can consider itself as itself, the same thinking thing, in different times and different places'. In this century, John Harris simplified it to 'any being capable of valuing its own existence', meaning someone who has a desire (or unwillingness) to experience the future. Like Singer, he makes it clear that a person need not be human at all: the notion is 'species-neutral'.

The word is derived from the Latin *persona*, meaning a dramatic or theatrical mask, yet if a person is seen to be someone who takes an active and autonomously reasoned role in life it must be conceded that there are many human beings who are *not* persons. Clearly, the very young and those whose faculties are compromised by illness, disability or age, do not qualify. Because there are humans incapable of responsibility, not all humans are persons.

Answering the question as to whether it would be acceptable to let thousands of humans die if they could be saved by experimentation on nonhuman animals, Singer challenges those supporting experimentation, asking whether they would be prepared to perform their experiments on orphaned human infants - in other words, on an individual of their own species who is not a person. I hear it as a valid challenge, for the vast majority of laboratory animals are as or more alert and aware of their surroundings and what is happening, and equally able to suffer, as an infant human. We could equally suggest severely mentally disabled humans. Without that willingness, where the scientist feels morally justified in continuing to use nonhumans, his attitude is revealed as unambiguously species-prejudiced: an assertion that only humans can be persons.

Referring to an American court case of 1977 debating experimentation on bottle nosed dolphins, Mary Midgley quotes the judge who stated that nonhuman animals were simply 'not under the penal code'. Before the law, he declared dolphins to be property, not persons at all. Persons, it was clear, were human beings.

Society is reluctant to deny an innocent human being (of our own tribe) the status of person, for those without this protection are effectively cast beyond the pale. In order to embrace the individuals incapable of reason or responsibility, the defining boundaries are blurred. We speak of a youngster growing up and becoming a 'person in his own right', implying that before this time his status has been kept for him by parents or others of the tribe. We behave similarly with nonhumans we have taken as pets, conferring them with honorary personhood in order to establish their right to be cared for. In this, then, it is not that all humans are given the status of persons, but all members of our tribe. Those who are not must take their chances: we protect our own.

Clearly then, although in much Western philosophy the lack of ability to reason has equated to a lack of personhood or inherent value, in practice it clearly does not necessarily lead to ejection from a tribe's moral care. This is not analytical laziness but instinctive human response. There is, after all, scant evidence to show that an individual's reason will ensure his actions are broadly morally acceptable: as Hume said, we utilize our reason simply to justify our emotional drives, and the more intelligent or capable of reason a person is, the more cunning their ability to achieve this.

Humankind's capacity for cruelty is, within nature, literally extraordinary: we describe someone who behaves with violent disregard as a 'beast' or an 'animal', but very few nonhuman animals would or could act with such knowing brutality. That human beings are believed the only species with reason and self-awareness sufficient to judge their own actions by a standard of morality makes their lack of consideration yet more abhorrent. Though some humans behave violently when flooded with emotion, cruelty is clearly not a symptom of lack of reason in the majority who know full well the consequences of their actions. Glancing through the media at global politics of war, genocide, rapacious greed and suppression, each situation is but an office, playground or family dispute writ large. Reason does not equate to morality. What humanity lacks is, all too often, simply the willingness to care.

It is easier to take the capacity for responsibility as a measure of morality, but there is here no valid corollary with inherent value. Because nonhuman animals are generally believed incapable of taking responsibility for their actions or making ethical decisions, they are classed as nonpersons, beyond necessary care. For many, it is as simple as that. As the laws of the street tend to be based upon simple reciprocity, usually through unspoken contracts of expected behaviour, when someone fails to act according to a shared morality that individual is not given the benefit of a moral response: he forgoes his moral rights. Because a fox kills hens conveniently trapped in a wire enclosure, unaware that this is unacceptable within a human tribe's morality, it is acceptable acceptable for that human tribe to chase to exhaustion one of its fox tribe and tear it apart with dogs. The fox is, after all, beyond the bounds of human morality.

Thus, although thinkers may articulate rationally constructed definitions of personhood, the simplicity of the Oxford English Dictionary's words is closer to the real use of our language. For most human beings, the need for reason or responsibility is wholly flexible. A person is someone we care about, someone we are willing to take into our tribe.

Kant summed up the attitude concisely. He declared there to be *persons* and *things*. Setting aside his philosophical definition of *person* (rational and moral), there is no need to debate the meaning of *things*. A person is not replaceable, not because of their specific and unique qualities, for no daisy or butterfly has an exact copy, but because the very notion of personhood provides that individual with inherent value. Wrong done to one cannot be erased by good done to another of the same species. A *thing*, however, can be used, abused, thrown away, and replaced.

Such an attitude is incompatible with *Paganism. By limiting relationship to the human *I*-subject and the nonhuman *it*-object, the premise provides the necessary convenience of being morally free to use another being for one's own benefit. That this *I-it* interaction is blatantly dishonourable within human relationships may be more widely accepted (if not adequately practised). The *Pagan extends this understanding further, and without dilution, to his relationship with nonhuman animals.

For by removing the human delusion of anthropocentricity, it is self-evident that all animals have inherent value. From a nondualist perspective that value is not determined by whether or not a creature has a soul, a 'ghost in the machine'. Each individual hums with nature's consciousness, forging its own intent from resources and influences, finding its own identity. Beetle, buzzard, rabbit, human, spider, bat or manta ray - each one is the centre of his own world, his existence from emergence to decay unquestionably significant within his own native environment, within the patterns of that ecosystem's consciousness, the natural web of life. As American philosopher, Tom Regan explains so vigorously, 'We are each of us the experiencing subject of a life, a conscious creature having an individual welfare that has importance to us whatever our usefulness to others'.

This is not an idealized view, based on sentimentality (an emotion that has no aim to provoke change); *Pagans tend to be far from sentimental. Their profound reverence for nature, inspired by exploration, experience and understanding, equally accepts the merciless as the beautiful. Nor is this the overemotional mush of the animal-lover. It is a rationally balanced attitude that perpetually informs of the absolute necessity of tenable relationship, individual to individual, awake to the simplicity and complexity of each ecosystem, each environment, from initial encounter to symbiosis.

To imagine it impossible to craft a relationship of sufficient mutual understanding with a nonhuman animal is merely a declaration to reject any intention to do so. As a society, we are already in relationship with other animals (all animals): one all too often drenched in brutal dishonour. It doesn't take much wit to increase receptivity to listen, that we might have a hope of interacting without abuse or exploitation. Of course, in doing so we risk sacrificing our ignorance and having to change our way of life. Yet for the *Pagan this is essential, for all suffering feeds into the songs of life: the shared environment of this planet, its food, breath and water.

To the *Pagan then, the whole notion of who is - and who is not - a *person* is simply and comprehensively irrelevant. The very term is a means by which human wit uses apparent reason to justify selfish action, obscuring the prejudicial attitudes and assumptions that lie beneath. The challenge is to be wakeful to how the word is used, if humanity is to change its current acceptance of this 'massive unnecessary harm'.

It is not simply in response, but as a natural development of *Pagan language, that to the animist every creature is acknowledged a person, for every individual (human and nonhuman) is as deserving of consideration and appropriate care. Every animal has inherent value. So do *Pagans refer to all animals, not as persons, but in the colloquial: as *people*, individuals of the tribe.

Thinking and Awareness

The problem of inherent value shifts a little if we adjust its centre from personhood to the notion of sentience. Here the crux of the argument doesn't appear to depend upon the humanity of the individual or our affection for him that allows us to acknowledge him as a person; instead, it is about how much that individual is really aware of his world. Sentience, from the Latin *sentire* meaning to think, is not about self-consciousness, but the ability to feel and experience through any rudimentary consciousness. Bentham's words, written just over two hundred years ago, are still pertinent and often quoted: 'The question is not, Can they *reason*? nor Can they *talk*? but, Can they *suffer*?' So does Singer's emphasis kick to the point still not adequately addressed in our society: where our actions cause a being to suffer, 'there can be no moral justification for refusing to take that suffering into consideration'.

Though Singer has been a truly heroic voice in the fight against animal abuse, in this area of his argument his words can *permit* it. For, in a situation where all things are fully considered, if one individual's suffering, however extreme, may alleviate the suffering of many others, then it can be justified. To Richard Ryder, Singer's utilitarian scales of suffering and consideration are not an adequate base for ethics; worse, our culture weights the scales with greed, power and apathy, cleverly dressed with reason, further shaming itself by how lightly it weighs nonhumans. So can the extreme suffering of billions of nonhuman animals be considered justified to balance the appetite of a fraction of human beings.

Utilitarianism can be a powerful tool of egalitarianism. However, it is not based upon inherent worth, not on the individuals themselves. Instead, it measures the aggregate level of happiness or least suffering generated in all those involved or affected by an action; in other words, if a good crowd of people are happy, a small group can acceptably be left to suffer (unprotected by the tribe's morality) in order for that happiness to continue. To Ryder, the point is not complicated: to knowingly cause pain can never be ethical. If we are willing to accept some degree of suffering in others, then our judgement will ever be skewed.

Further, just how much a creature suffers can never be fully understood. Upon the slow current of progress gained over the past century, few now doubt that nonhuman animals can feel pain. As animals, we all react to painful stimuli and move to avoid it: nociceptors pick up potentially damaging sensations and respond as a basic defensive mechanism, revealing that pain behaviour evolved before the conscious experience of pain. For many philosophers, however, what is important is how much sentience is required to allow not just the ability physically to react to pain, but the neurological capacity to remember it and the language to express it. Flinching from discomfort doesn't prove a creature is feeling pain (as a human might understand it); here is a tighter definition of suffering. Yet if an animal's sentience is judged by brain size or complexity of nervous system, we are using the limited ideas of a healthy mature human to comprehend another creature's experience of existence - which is absurd.

Within human beings, there is a capacity for suffering which, like a jar, some fill with trivial discomfort augmented into catastrophic crisis, while others deal with terrific levels of physical and psychological trauma while still functioning capably: intelligence is not an accurate or consistent measure of whether an individual will respond one way or another. Indeed, limited awareness or understanding of a situation, the inability to anticipate or predict what will happen next, can either provide an ignorance that lowers the suffering, or provoke confusion and panic as the whole system is flooded with immediate sensations.

Within Locke's definition of person, and integral to the idea of suffering, is this issue of whether a creature suffers more if they can perceive the future or recall the past; it is used most assertively when considering whether killing someone is morally worse if - removing the problem of suffering by ensuring a painless death - that individual has a sense of a life to be lived.

Setting aside the fact that the animal industry does *not* kill painlessly, the issue is whether or not a being believed incapable of conceptual thought has any significant interest in remaining alive. If not, and flesh food were produced from animals who had lived comfortable lives and were killed without trauma, could it be ethical? If an individual has no dreams and hopes of achievement, then death doesn't deny him these (and thus, the argument states, the suffering is reduced). In *Pagan terms, this is yet another overanalyzed and unnecessary philosophical tangle, and a profound misunderstanding of consciousness.

In a soul where ideas can be laid out chronologically, it can be hard to remain in the here and now, instead slinking back with nostalgia or resentment, or slipping on into fantasies about what is to come. In *Pagan thinking, such linearity is not altogether an advantage. Authenticity, as described in the previous chapter, is very much about being able to be where our feet are - aware of the horizons of time that create our inner landscape, yet not losing our immediacy or presence. Furthermore, capacity for conceptual thinking is not a binary black or white, a *can* or *can't*, but a spread of evolution and variance.

Being unable to deconstruct awareness into yesterdays and tomorrows doesn't necessarily leave us stranded in some gap without context. Working with nonhuman animals, with very young human children, with drugs that knock out areas of the brain and those affected by disorders like autism, it is easy to see that without chronology experience of the present is more naturally saturated with both past and future: memories, journeys, relationships, are more accessibly present as patterns of consciousness. Time is very much an environment, one that can be explored. A nonperson may not have a clearly conceived future, formulated with language into separate ideas, but killing that individual still erases the experience of being that stretches in all directions, within the broad landscape of time and space.

Such a perspective is not scientific; it is a wholly valid worldview based upon human experience of losing capacity to perceive time and as such held firmly as fundamental with animistic and *Pagan understanding. Its value here is not as a statement of fact projected upon nonhuman animals, but as an idea raised, expressing acceptance that we do not know how other animals perceive the world. Because it may be close to this, our chances of honourable relationship are increased if we take this into consideration.

In many ways, this has been the attitude of The Great Ape Project. Instigated by Singer with Italian philosopher Paola Cavalieri (and others) in 1993, the GAP has been working towards a United Nations declaration of rights for great apes, including the right to life, liberty and freedom from torture. Any caveats to these rights are no different from those applicable to human beings; in other words, the GAP calls for the great apes to be welcomed into the wider human moral community. Singer denies that there can be any 'sound moral reason why possession of basic rights should be limited to members of a particular species'. The *Pagan would agree, for he continues, 'At a minimum, we should recognise basic rights in all beings who show intelligence and awareness (including some level of self-awareness) and who have emotional and social needs'. While not dismissing such a need in other nonhuman animals, the GAP 'merely asserts that the case for such rights is strongest in respect to great apes'. In its 1999 Animal Welfare Act, New Zealand granted special rights to apes as 'non-human hominids', assuring them protection from being used in research, testing, or teaching 'unless such use is in the best interests of the non-human hominid itself or its species'. In mid 2006, the Spanish parliament asked its government to approve the GAP's declaration (a decision was postponed). Needless to say, arguments similar to those of Thomas Taylor have erupted.

Not only do nonhuman animals have inherent value, but as conscious creatures (a part of the ongoing creativity of nature, fully integrated within its web of being) they have an entirely valid interest in avoiding suffering and staying alive. None of us avoid pain and death for very long, for those are necessary elements of nature too, yet as human and nonhuman animals our intention to avoid them is crucially natural. Upon the lines of philosophical logic, that interest confers rights. *Rights*: it is a word I have barely used in this chapter, and consciously so, for I have dealt with many of the arguments without feeling the need to raise the term as a flag.

That not all humans speak English has been an excuse for many within our heritage (and current society) to deny equality of rights to those whose world is languaged differently from our own. The same is true of nonhumans. Rights are expressed declarations that claim a place within a moral community, to share a tribe's understanding of acceptable behaviour and protection against those who don't. Using the term *person*, claiming a level of sentience, we extend our community of care as and when we wish. Just as we speak out for the young and disabled, those unable to speak for themselves, so must we speak out to make the claim for belonging for those who do not speak our English - or our human - language, as the GAP is doing.

To justify the current abuse on the basis that nonhuman animals have no rights is to determine that species-biased belief as a fact. It is not a rationally balanced conclusion. Such a determination is either knowingly fallacious or based upon obstinate prejudice. My chapter here then does not fight for the rights of nonhuman animals, because I see no value in the debate. To object in the style of Thomas Taylor, as many do, is simply absurd. Animal rights don't provide an orang-utan with the right to vote in the Scottish parliament: they are relevant and appropriate considerations, based upon the life that the individual should be able to lead. As McGinn says, 'One can only satisfy one's desires if one is alive and free to act in appropriate ways.'

Nature and Necessity

Where arguments are not based around the issues of inherent value, they tend to lose philosophical rigour. A few are, nonetheless, worth exploring here. The first is one often used by Pagans or those attempting to use Pagan thinking to denounce the *Pagan standpoint. It calls upon nature itself.

As humans, we like to think of ourselves as predators. Soft skinned and clawless, we hold extraordinary weaponry crafted by our adaptability and cunning. Though we are still prey to the elements, the rest of the animal kingdom is now our prey. It's a claim that makes a man feel tall.

However, in reality, there are very few natural human predators. As a species, now more than ever, we are scavengers, willing to eat the meat of dead animals, already a little sweet with decay, that we find in our local butcher shops and supermarkets. Our natural skill, to *find* food, is indeed far more important a factor in our heritage than our ability to kill. The ability to think, to adapt, inspired by ideas and opportunities, exploring our creativity, is what has brought humanity this far, and will take us on from here.

In *Pagan Dawn*, the Wiccan John MacIntyre states that a vegetarian or vegan ethics is out of step with Paganism. He goes on to explain how nature functions, the predator being as dependent on his prey as the prey is to the predator, the cycle of death feeding life maintaining the necessary balance of populations. 'This is', he writes, 'natural and good because most living things depend on it. It cannot reasonably be considered either harmful or exploitative.' His argument is one used by many who still use nonhuman animal products within Paganism, most of whom, like MacIntyre himself, are strong proponents of free-range and organic production. That many don't hold to the standards when it comes to buying meat, milk or shoes - for reasons of economy, time or apathy - and thus fully support the harmful and exploitative factory farming industry with the votes of cash, is a sad reflection of the community. The hierarchy of strength is paramount here, though, the more powerful humans finding a moral justification for oppression of the less powerful. MacIntyre: 'As natural omnivorous creatures, it can no more be wrong for us to kill other animals for food than it can be wrong for other predators to do so.'

Although many within the Pagan tradition perceive human society to have lost touch with the cycles of nature, MacIntyre states that it is because human beings have meandered too far from accepting themselves as a part of nature that they are now able to believe they can and should live without eating animals. If we were still needing to catch, skin and bone a rabbit or pigeon for the pot each evening, or herding our own sheep and slaughtering in the backyard, we would indeed be very much more in touch with the blood, suffering and injustice that are the balances of nature than many are now in our gentle culture. It is an interesting and useful point, for complacency and ignorance is a terrible defence. However, the element missed here is the faculty of human understanding, and reason.

Certainly, we are omnivorous: it is natural for human beings to sate their hunger by eating animal flesh - or indeed anything edible at hand. However, it is also natural for us to sate our craving for sexual inter-course; yet where such an action causes suffering, it is not acceptable. With my own entirely natural human sexual appetite, I could seduce a man with feminine guile and enchantment, drawing on his libido until his reason was submerged by animal desire: that would be entirely natural. If he were married, however, and in a monogamous bond, my behaviour would be transparently unethical; a few hours or days of pleasure, sating desire, could cause profound suffering for everyone involved. Equally, it would be entirely natural for a man to take a woman, raping her by force: the natural predator and prey instinct often reaches for justification with the rational defence that the woman won't feel any long term ill-effects. As human animals the list continues: it is natural physically to attack someone who provokes a rush of irritation or anger, to have as many children as the female body will bear, to dance, drunk and free, all through the night to the pounding of drums in a suburban street.

Yet our human nature is not just the ability to satisfy desire, whether through force, or wit and cunning. Nature has provided us with the ability to consider the consequences of our actions. We must think as broadly as our intelligence allows. If we are to interact with honour, ethically with validity, our behaviour must not be based upon what we *can* do, but what our reason guides us to do, directing the fuel of our emotional and instinctual drives. Conscious of the web of an environment's relationships, human and non-human, we adjust.

So does another Pagan priest write, again in *Pagan Dawn*, 'It would be a more positive fulfilment of the Pagan Federation's first two principles if people's responsibilities went beyond their personal tastes, and protected creatures with no choice or voice'. Those principles, set out in Chapter One, describe a respectful and responsible relationship with and reverence for nature, through its gifts and cycles of life and death.

In other words, although it is natural for humans to eat animal flesh, if we are to act with ethical validity, we must not fail to take into account the broader picture. Killing a nonhuman animal in order to eat is, in our current Western culture, entirely *unnecessary*. That simple fact wholly negates any ethical justification for doing so. It is killing (or being complicit in killing) for pleasure.

This principle of necessity is crucial. In *Paganism, there is no law against killing. If a *Pagan finds himself in a situation where he feels he needs to kill in order to survive, if he is able to perceive well, that moment will provide the information he needs to craft his decision. The same is true for illness: unnecessarily using drugs tested on animals to get over a bout of flu or a period of pain is plainly incompatible with *Pagan ethics. If we face the edge of endurance, then we need to think more carefully about what is or is not necessary: what or who is more important. Sometimes, even at such times of crisis, the ethical choice is not to support the drug companies and legislation that perpetuate the abuse of others.

Using Reason to back Desire

An equally weak argument posed states that hundreds of millions of animal industry creatures would not be alive at all if it weren't for the trade in flesh-meat, mammal milk, hide, furs and so on. Human beings have given them the sweet gift of life, albeit a life of slavery, torture and premature death. Is such a life better than not living at all? The question is farcical from the *Pagan perspective. Firstly, as I have explored in the previous chapter, life at all costs is an irrational and selfish declaration. As individual identity emerges, cohering out of the consciousness of nature, if that experience of being is little more than suffering, life may not be worth living. Furthermore, to imagine otherwise is dependent upon the worldview that each individual is an entirely separate entity, yet that is incomprehensible from a *Pagan perspective. Every individual's suffering seeps into the wind and water, the blood and mud of the land and the community, wholly integrated with the ecosystem that is the web of nature. It is not only by ingesting the fear-drenched flesh and blood of an abused animal that we are affected by that suffering; we share the same world and its resources. We cannot help but be affected: irritated, depressed, confused, exhausted. As a species, it is self-sabotage to cause such suffering. It is madness to create life for that purpose.

Another blinkered argument states that humanity cannot afford not to raise animals for food, considering the world's bulging population and how much of our planet's land is insufficiently fertile or unsuitable for growing crops - land that can, however, maintain a population of grazing herbivores. The *Pagan answer is simple, for this is not about how a scant living can be made on 'marginal land': over a third of all grain produced worldwide is fed to animals, incurring a significant loss in protein, calories and nutrition in the conversion to flesh or dairy products. The issue is thus about distribution of wealth, an issue I shall look at in a later chapter.

The argument posed in support of the current state that most bewilders me is perhaps this: if an animist believes there to be consciousness in all 'things', then surely we are as unjustified killing carrots as we are killing cows. How we care for the environment, together with plant-consciousness, is a subject for the following chapter, but while we are addressing the value on nonhuman animal life, I shall answer the question knowing it will be developed later.

Firstly, *Pagan ethics are not blinkered by a consideration solely for animal rights; they are based upon least unnecessary harm. No plant feels pain like an animal does: it would be wholly disadvantageous for a creature to have evolved the capacity for suffering without achieving the ability to move away from the cause of it. A carefully sourced vegan diet, as a result, will inevitably generate less suffering than one based on animals.

However, what we are seeking is not a balance that fundamentally requires Singer's utilitarian scales of consideration; the principle is once again one of necessity. The unnecessary *use* of plants, trees, land and water is equally unethical as the unnecessary *use* of animals, human and nonhuman.

The 'screaming carrot' is an argument seldom taken seriously. It is posed by those for whom the use of nonhuman animals is central to their lifestyle, in order to provoke the vegan into an irrational corner, and it is clumsily done. As McGinn says, 'it is bad enough to mistreat animals for blatantly selfish reasons, but to defend this mistreatment by means of transparently shoddy arguments is almost as objectionable'.

*Paganism, like nature, teaches that relationship is all. If or when necessity arises, the choices we make must be those that allow for ethically (or indeed morally) viable relationship. Where we fail, someone suffers, sometimes to the point of extinction.

The Animist's View

The premise of necessity and the subsequent need to prioritise returns us to a more thoughtful level of argument. Worrying about carrots is futile, but where is the cut-off point in terms of how we place our priorities? If

*Pagans value nonhuman animals' lives, does that include insects, and are we talking bees or fruit flies? Do we include water creatures? According to marine ecologist, Jacques-Yves Cousteau, the average octopus is considerably more intelligent than a dog. But if we measure value on intelligence we stumble again into speciesism: it is not acceptable within modern society to *use* a human of lower intelligence for our own benefit, thus to avoid the prejudice it cannot be ethical to behave in that way with another species.

Singer has been clear about the premise, saying that 'the only legitimate boundary to our concern for the interests of other beings is the point at which it is no longer accurate to say that the other being has interests', which he defines as the ability to experience pleasure or to suffer. These he measures through the creature's pain responses and the similarity of their nervous system to our own. Acknowledging how hard it is to understand the data, he is considerably less sure about where the line needs might be drawn. In the first edition of *Animal Liberation* (1975) he placed it 'somewhere between a shrimp and an oyster', but interestingly has since questioned whether even these basic molluscs should also have the benefit of the doubt.

To the *Pagan, the notion that there could be such a specific cut-off point in terms of a creature's inherent value is hard to comprehend. Here we move towards the crucial tenets that underlie the *Pagan standpoint. As individual animals emerge from the consciousness of nature, rich as it is with memory and potential, each one forms, growing, becoming, according to its source consciousness and its environment, finding its own innate purpose, its place in the world, its natural intention. This is its soul-song.

Each animal, human and nonhuman, is crafted by the deep need to play out that song. In other words, to determine that beneath a certain level of phylogenetic complexity a creature has no interests (and, as a *thing*, can therefore be used) is ethically unsound. That is simply moving the goal posts of species prejudice. Interests are more than the utilitarian's pleasure or pain; they must be acknowledged as an animal's inherent need to express its unique being.

American philosopher, Martha Nussbaum comes close to this perspective with what she terms her 'capabilities approach'. Individuals, she said, must have the freedom to flourish in their own way. Primarily writing about human justice, she recalls Aristotle's encouragement of the study of nature, for 'there is something wonderful and wonder-inspiring in all the complex forms of life in nature'; so does she reach to extend her ideas across the species barrier, acknowledging our shared animality. In fact, 'that the human maker of principles is imagined as a needy, often dependent animal being prepares the way for that extension'.

It is with that wonder that Nussbaum advocates the necessity to allow all creatures the opportunity to *flourish* - and for each to do so 'as the sort of thing it is'. Because each species has different needs, it is necessary to keep in focus that 'each life has multiple and heterogeneous ends'. Her words appear fully in tune with the *Pagan understanding of the inherent value and individual intention or purpose of each individual animal. For when we are receptive to the wonder, it is extremely difficult (and instinctively unethical) to deprive that being of any aspect that allows it to continue and thrive in its own existence. Nussbaum: 'With due respect for a world that contains many forms of life, we attend with ethical concern to each characteristic type of flourishing, and strive that it not be cut off or fruitless'.

It is always hard when considering nonhuman animals to ensure that we are not making up an anthropomorphized list of needs, desires and problems, slipping into projection and sentimentality. Yet, such problems are often as evident within our own species: all too often we disastrously fail to comprehend our parents or children, let alone our immigrant neighbours. Indeed, Nussbaum is more confident, encouraging 'sympathetic imagining', ever bearing in mind that we can get it wrong. The necessity of listening, so important a part of *Paganism, is indisputable: in the poetry of *Pagan language, we remember that each creature has a story they tell with each action and reaction, a story (or expression of consciousness) that not only becomes evident if we are willing to perceive, but which equally outlines what that individual needs in order to continue to live and tell that story in the most wonder-full way.

Relationship is all.

Honourable Interaction

So do we return to the premise of honour.

For the *Pagan attitude towards all animals must be one of generosity, loyalty and courage. We may utilize ascetic discipline in order to rein in our natural selfishness, or take on another's limiting rules so as not thoughtlessly to go chasing the raw cravings of our animal soul, seeking satisfaction with no consideration for others. However, it is generosity that most effectively and healthily guides our behaviour in this regard, allowing us to take responsibility for what we give and what we take.

In our loyalty, we do not look simply to the small tribes of our families and common-interest communities. *Pagan loyalty extends, through subject-to-subject interactions, inspiring ongoing respect, out to broader tribal boundaries. So does the *Pagan learn how to speak for those who cannot stake their own claims for consideration, embracing nonhuman animals into his own community of care.

Of course, choices always need to be made, and priorities rated. Within this broader moral community, human needs do not automatically take precedence. That can take tremendous courage, and where it doesn't we must question whether we have evaded the true situation and chosen the easy road of self-preservation over honour. It takes courage to let fall the veils of ignorance, to know exactly what the costs are of our actions, to stand in our honesty, present in our authenticity, and decide just what is necessary, and what is not.

A world without the abuse would be significantly different. For some it is so hard to imagine that the first steps towards it seem futile. Yet each small step adds to the winds of change that will shift the sand dunes of human understanding and potential. We must each begin by addressing our own lives, and every way in which we perpetuate through complicity the ongoing abuse, checking at each step the sticky and insidious under-currents of species-based prejudice and hypocrisy.

As Singer put so articulately, writing in the mid 1970s: 'To protest about bullfighting in Spain, the eating of dogs in South Korea, or the slaughter of baby seals in Canada while continuing to eat eggs from hens who have spent their lives crammed into cages ... is like denouncing apartheid in South Africa while asking your neighbors not to sell their houses to blacks'. In Tom Regan's campaign for the abolition of all nonhuman animal use, he questions the ethical validity of ending factory farming while still rearing animals for human benefit: 'You don't change unjust institutions by tidying them up'.

Money is a powerful resource. Those who profit from exploiting animals lose their profit if we stop buying their products. The wakeful *Pagan isn't just attentive about his diet, but actively and wakefully minimises support for all forms of animal abuse. Not buying or consuming animal produce for food is just one step; beyond that, there are the household products, cosmetics, toiletries, clothes and shoes, that contain or are crafted of animals. The *Pagan stops buying products that are grown with chemicals or that otherwise damage ecosystems which nonhumans depend upon, or thinks twice about the true need, seeking out the most wakeful and least abusive compromise. It is not an easy path that can be achieved without thinking. It takes research. We have to make an effort if we are to care.

The use of products, including drugs, that have been nonconsensually tested on animals needs careful consideration: who is more important? And if we remove the fear, the selfishness of tribal insularity, how can we respond with honour? Who is being given the chance to flourish and who is paying the cost, by being denied that opportunity themselves? Although there are many organizations that we can support, which positively seek out alternatives to nonhuman animal testing for medication, we are still facing a series of national laws requiring the continuance of the abuse. In many cases there appear to be no effective alternatives to necessary drugs. However, more often than not, the use of drugs is neither effective nor necessary: there are non-chemical ways of dealing with most trivial discomforts, and some not so trivial.

Furthermore, the fight against most Western diseases is only going to be won by a shift in lifestyle, diet and stress. Indeed, across the developing majority world, most deaths are caused by the same things that killed Europeans for generations: poor sanitation, nutrition and health care. The amount of money poured into animal testing could be used to address these basic problems. That would be an expression of authentic care.

Again, Colin McGinn sums it up in his usual uncompromising approach: 'Becoming a vegetarian is only the most minimal ethical response to the magnitude of the evil. What is needed is a complete revolution in the way we deal with other species'. As Regan says, the current situation 'that allows us to view animals as our *resources*, here for *us* - to be eaten, or surgically manipulated, or exploited for sport or money' is a 'fundamental wrong'.

If we are to honour the other members of this animal kingdom, we must acknowledge their subjective experience, each individual upon its journey through time. We must bear our own responsibility for how our actions affect and influence the Other of any species, and each tribe that rides upon its own intentions, honest in the expression of our own needs and desires.

Four and a half centuries have passed since the great Polish scientist Nicolaus Copernicus pushed our race to remember the fallacy of geocentricity. It is time to release fully the equally fallacious myth of anthropocentricity. Only then will we, as a culture, find the necessary momentum for the radical upheaval necessary to stop the abuse of nonhuman animals. No longer complicit or actively involved in such unnecessary violence, no longer ingesting or numb to the trauma of constant suffering, human society will have a chance for extraordinary change. McGinn again: 'The deepest form of exploitation and institutionalized death in human history will have been eradicated, making other forms of oppression psychologically harder to bring about'.

CHAPTER NINE

THE VALUE OF THE ENVIRONMENT

The three elements of home:
knowing the land,
being known by the land,
knowing our grandchildren's children will know home here as well.

As a child, I was fascinated by a paperweight that gathered dust on a window sill in my parents' house. Hemispherical, within its perspex dome was a tiny house in a forested valley upon which, if turned upside down, a magical snow would gently fall. An enclosed world, it was the silence that most intrigued me; I wondered what sounds might be heard within that little dome, the sound of that tiny snow storm, of the empty house.

I was not much older, perhaps six or seven, when first it was explained to me how our medieval ancestors had viewed the world, their cosmology describing a vast dome of sky, the stars, sun and moon circling the stillness of the earth. Gazing at the picture in the big book lying open before me, I felt again the intense silence of being outside the dome, and was struck by how dreadfully lonely God must feel. I recall the relief of remembering the image was not real, and running outside to sit in my tree-house alone, to gaze up at the skies, as if reaching my hands into the infinite space, knowing (determining) that there was no enclosing lid. Whoever the 'God' was they spoke of in Sunday school, I felt sure he was not on the outside looking in; he was right here, with the ants and the birds, and me, in the tree.

My story isn't sentimentality. That first experience of being conscious of a significant and limiting worldview was important. When considering the planet on which we live, and the ethics that determine how we interact with and within its nature, our attitude towards the world is clearly the foundational factor. This is even more crucial when thinking about *nature* than when addressing the more specific issue of (human and nonhuman) animals, for here we cannot juggle and trade ideas about sentience and rights, nor can we play with notions of contracts agreed. We need simply to acknowledge and admit what we perceive the earth to be.

Furthermore, reviewing the ideas and realizations that have crafted and adjusted the dunes of human understanding not only helps us to see why we might hold the attitudes we do; through an awareness of the roots that still in part nourish the present, we can better know ourselves and the beliefs that underlie our actions, which in turn allow us more effectively to adapt, taking the steps of any necessary change - and given the current state of our planet's environment, it is clear that we *all* need to be a part of that change. Yet, knowing the history also allows us to acknowledge the heritage of our people, which offers us the chance to comprehend the shared moralities and the heresies, both of which have brought us to the situation we are now facing.

I begin this chapter, then, by reviewing and discussing a few of those worldviews. It is not with an old Pagan understanding that I start, however; for to present such a profoundly *simple* perspective would be too easy for a reader to dismiss.

Nature as Creation
Let us imagine that dome.

In the medieval monotheisms (of Christianity, Judaism and Islam), God was believed not only to have created the world in six short days, but had done so with systematic grace: everything had its place, everything had its purpose. Carefully illustrated and disseminated by medieval theologians, upon the divinely inflexible hierarchy of this Great Chain of Being the cherubim held sway above the seraphim. Men, being taller and more prosperous, were better than women, and the darker the skin the further down was one's place. Among the 'beasts', the lion was above the dog, the frog was deemed lesser than the lizard, the ostrich more blessed than the duck. Lower still, the oak was acknowledged worthy of respect while the yew was the basest of trees, and beneath the plant kingdom, gold was a graceful rock while dirt was rock's imperfection. God was at the top, and at the very bottom was nothingness; human beings' existence was at that specific point exactly halfway between pure spirit and pure matter, for *uniquely* we were created of both.

Centred upon the geocentric cosmology explained by early astronomers such as the Roman Egyptian, Ptolemy, the Chain of Being did not exist within a hemispherical dome but a whole sphere, encircled by the stars, sun and moon, and enclosed within the limits of God's creation. In a world before widespread science could accurately predict or explain nature's moods, from wild storms to contagious diseases, such an ordered understanding of the world was readily accepted. It expressed a connectedness of all things, providing a satisfactory sense of integration, with the special nature of humankind carefully secure within the complete, divinely crafted system.

This integrated model of life is not entirely distant from the *Pagan's vision of nature's web of being. In tune with modern ecology, of course, in *Paganism there is no sense of one species or element being any more holy or intrinsically important than any other. However, while that foundational interconnectedness is nowadays not hard for most to comprehend, it was the importance of the hierarchies that persisted, and still does albeit with the subtlety of an underlying assumption. Such age-old certainties are hard to release. In the United States, in sharp contrast to the rest of the West, Young-Earth Creationists continue to hold to an idea crafted by Bishop Ussher, Primate of All Ireland in the early seventeenth century, whose calculations revealed that God's act of creation had been completed four thousand and four years before the birth of Christ, on Sunday 23 October. (YECs do admit that he may not have been *entirely* accurate, and accept the earth may be as old as ten thousand years.)

To a modern Pagan, such a conviction is as bewildering and fantastical as the hierarchical Great Chain of Being, or indeed any belief that the Bible might stand up as a scientifically or historically valid text. When words of myth are taken as fact, whether or not interpreted for one's own benefit, the Old Testament's commands that humanity must *conquer* nature, holding *dominion* over her, become an easy reason for bestowing upon the Abrahamic faiths full culpability for the current environmental crisis.

Creation stories that tell of a perfect world that was lost are another important influence, particularly where taken literally, as was for so long the Bible's account. Hurled from grace, denied access to ease and comfort, humanity is left to live in a world where it takes blood, sweat and tears to survive. Nature becomes the enemy, demanding hard toil through relentless struggle. Shaking possible sources from the myths, some thinkers have posed ideas that the story speaks of that enormous change, around ten millennia ago, when small bands of roaming hunter-gatherers began to settle, claiming land, domesticating herds, creating larger communities. After many hundreds of thousands of years of moving with nature, the impact of this comparatively recent change is often underestimated. The intense hardships of early agriculture, the need to work from dawn until dusk, would have been profound, as it continues to be for a great many human beings today. The notion of a divinely-blessed garden paradise would be, for anyone dependent upon the unpredictable injustice of nature, a glorious dream.

The Greek myth of the giant Prometheus who stole fire from the sun to give humankind warmth against the cold, an act that led to Pandora opening her jar and releasing strife and cruelty across the world, describes an earlier fundamental change to human life. And like the Hope that was left in the jar, like the process of turning to agriculture, this fire was a double-edged blade.

That nature is merciless has not just provoked Christian antipathy. As I outlined earlier in this book, Plato's distinction between the Forms and the increasingly tainted reproductions of their original perfection - matter

- provides a clear pre-Christian source within our Western philosophical heritage of contempt towards nature. Adapted and disseminated through early Christian writers such as Augustine, the effective dualism of Plato's vision was the strongest thread in European philosophy, together with the belief in that enclosed sphere of creation and its inherent hierarchy.

It was his student Aristotle who crafted the first construct of a *scala naturae*, a ladder of nature which is seen as the root of the Great Chain of Bring. Often arranging its order from no more than the appearance of a creature, he placed the reasoning intelligence of mankind in a privileged position. However, Aristotle's vision was quite different from Plato's: encouraging wonder at and study of nature, he dismissed the notion of a soul separate from the body, perceiving a far more fully integrated world. Disappearing for a millennium in the West, his writings continued to inspire eastern Mediterranean cultures, providing inspiration for the classical era of Islamic culture which, between the ninth and twelfth centuries, produced extraordinary literature, astronomy and scientific work.

Re-emerging in Europe in the twelfth and thirteenth centuries, mainly through Moorish Spain, when his ideas were translated from Arabic into Latin, their introduction was philosophically revolutionary for the West. For centuries, thinkers had been pondering no more than earlier Christian thinkers; Aristotle, however, posed a new way of perceiving creation. Indeed, in thirteenth century France, the Church tried to ban the teaching of his works in the new universities, a prohibition that was largely swept aside by the enthusiasm of their followers. A rapidly growing number of commentaries began to formulate a newly scientific way of thinking across Europe.

Christianity was widespread throughout Europe at this time, but among an illiterate population still hugely dependent on nature the old traditions persisted, old gods and heroes revered alongside the All-Father and saints of the Church. Amongst the educated, the natural philosophy and magical explorations of the alchemists were accepted. When

Shakespeare was writing in the late sixteenth century, his depiction of magic, spirits and the surreal were an accurate representation of contemporary attitudes. However, perspectives were beginning to change. *The Tempest* was first performed nearly seventy years after Copernicus posed his theory that the earth encircled the sun, an idea that lit the touchpaper igniting a scientific revolution lasting well into the eighteenth century.

One key figure at the start of that revolution was the extraordinary sixteenth century English scientist, William Gilbert, whose work significantly advanced the process that took Galileo to redescribe the skies. His seminal research was on magnetism and static electricity (it was he who gave us the term *electricity*), and his language is a beautiful expression of the old attitudes of his day; in *De Magnete* he spoke of magnetism as the soul of the earth, spinning on its axis. 'We deem,' he wrote, 'the whole world animate and all globes, all stars, and this glorious earth too, we hold to be from the beginning by their own destinate souls governed and from them also to have the impulse of self-preservation.' He declared the earth was far from 'brute and soulless', but an integral part of the 'fair order of the glorious universe'.

A rigorous thinker, basing his ideas on careful experimentation, he took pains to distinguish himself from natural magicians, avoiding reference to what he perceived as the occult forces of attraction and repulsion, spirits with autonomy and their own unseen agendas. Instead, he spoke of the 'orb of virtue' that surrounds a magnet, extending in all directions, drawing 'towards a common source, towards the mother where they were begotten, towards their origin, in which all these parts will be united and preserved and in which they all remain at rest, safe from every peril'. Yet like another genius of the era of changing attitudes, the German Johannes Kepler whom he inspired, his words were heard as superstitious reverence for a Pagan goddess, and thus dismissed.

Indeed, this attack on all that was believed to be superstition provided the quickening current of the new science with a powerful momentum - and gave another key figure the force of his colourful rhetoric. Francis

Bacon, seventeen years younger than Gilbert, would have been poignantly aware that in 1600, the year *De Magnete* was published, the Italian Giordano Bruno was burned at the stake by the Christian authorities in Rome for refusing to deny the validity of Copernican theories. Bacon, fully dedicated to his own social and political ambition, would not have risked such treatment. Instead, his work reads as a tirade against nature, the focused aim being to reverse the tragedy that evicted man from the Garden. God, he believed, was the perfection of reason that underpinned creation, and by scientific observation, experimentation and inductive reasoning, man would gain access to paradise once again, this time through domination over the natural world. Each scientist must strive to control 'Nature with all her children, to bind her to your service, to make her your slave'.

Nature, through its tides of birthing and nourishing, has inevitably been described as female, and this was what Bacon and his fellow revolutionaries wished to destroy. His aim was no less than the exorcism of the soul of nature, and thus its separation from any notion of the sacred. Like Shakespeare's Kate, written during Bacon's lifetime, nature was a wild, irrational and unpredictable creature that needed to be tamed: each scientist was to be a conquering Petruchio.

This is not a retrospective perspective, created by modern feminists. Bacon's attitude was typical amongst the thinkers of his time, declaiming the need to 'overcome' and 'subdue' her, to 'discover the secrets still locked in Nature's bosom', and thus to 'penetrate' her. It had been Eve, after all, in the mythology of his Christianity, who had caused the original Fall, corrupting Adam and provoking their eviction from paradise. Men, better blessed than women, provided with the power of reason, were the inventors; the scientists would be humanity's saviours, releasing mankind from its toil and misery. Reason, backed by God, would turn out the dirty goddess, and take nature for his own.

In the Islamic world, the task had been completed some centuries earlier. Islam had not felt threatened by the new science, as Christianity did later. Indeed, from the eighth century onwards the initial translating into Arabic of Greek, Latin, Sanskrit, Syriac and Pahlavi scholarship had been sponsored by the Abbasid caliphs at Baghdad. Perceiving the scientific theories and discoveries as a vibrant understanding within what was still a fluid and self-realizing religious culture, this acceptance was effective in sweeping aside the older animistic traditions that had honoured nature's inherent sanctity.

Born thirty two years later than Bacon, it was René Descartes who sealed that transmutation in the West. Establishing with his dualist perspective a vision of nature as a machine, he carefully reduced it to its soulless and inert component parts. Indeed, it was his uncompromising clarity that helped take down the Great Chain of Being. The pirate-adventurers funded by European royalty and nobility were finding their worldview bruised by the stature and dignity of black 'savages'; Descartes swept aside the problem by dismissing the ordered if complicated hierarchy of medieval thinking. His simpler worldview was of a God of perfect reason, and rational (white, male) mankind, both raised well above the dry mechanics of the rest of the world. Science, he determined, could and soon would provide knowledge sufficient that people would 'see nothing whose cause they cannot easily understand, nor anything that gives them any reason to marvel'.

God, as the source of all creativity, imagination and inspiration, expressed through rational purposefulness, was wholly distinct from dull matter which existed as a resource to manipulate and use. Clearly, any sense that nature was other than a divine repository for human benefit would limit progress. Although he died in 1650, it was in 1660 that the Royal Society was founded in London, and through that organization his ideas were so widely and comprehensively disseminated. From its inception, the Royal Society had the ear of the British monarch; it provided clarity as to what was acceptable, informing policy and politics. In *Science as Salvation*, Midgley sums up its aims: 'The campaign waged by members of the Royal Society, and by seventeenth century mechanists generally, was not, as their atheistical successors often suppose, a campaign against religion as such. It was primarily a campaign against the *wrong* religion - against what seemed like nature-worship, against a religion centering on the earth, and apparently acknowledging a mysterious pagan goddess rather than an intellectual god'. The Royal Society declared its objective to be the promotion of 'a truly masculine philosophy'.

Why this conflict began, and indeed why the mechanists won, shaping the dunes of human understanding, is a question increasingly considered. Midgley has stated that its success 'was not due - as we were brought up to believe - solely and directly to its scientific correctness'. While enormous progress was made, the accuracy and validity of the new science of mechanistic beliefs were not consistent. However, as the current surged, flooding through Europe, its momentum self-propelled it further, provoking extraordinary change. The industrial revolution inspired increasingly ingenious technologies, funding its imperialism of piracy, all of which required a moral freedom to exploit nature in its very form. Education, wealth, literacy and printing all expanded opportunities, including for women, some of whom were beginning to clamber out of their rank subservience. Furthermore, what must have felt like an eternal curse of extreme poverty, weighing down the populace, was by the eighteenth century beginning to lift. As the working classes scrambled from its slippery grip, there was little capacity to care about how this new glimmer of ease had been generated. Capitalism was emerging. What had been a long and unchallenged heritage of male domination was starting to look less secure: what was required was a response that, presented as an ancient sacred doctrine of male divine reason, would once again unquestionably establish society as a noble patriarchy. Reason became synonymous with virtue, with God.

Sacred or Secular, but Ever Changing

At this point we find the Romantic movement of the late eighteenth and nineteenth centuries, as I have described in an earlier chapter, revolting against the hyper-rationality of the Enlightenment and the rapacious destruction of the countryside and rural life, presenting again the importance of emotion, beauty, experience and intuition. William Wordsworth, noted as the first of the English Romantic poets, declared the effects of the industrial revolution 'an outrage to nature'. A counter-cultural rebellion of reverence emerged through the poetry of Coleridge, Tennyson, Byron, Keats, Shelley and Clare, in the art of Turner and Constable, and of course the genius of William Blake whose words, 'Nature is imagination itself', contradicted the new science so completely. Expressing his ideas as if in tangential scribbles around one of his classical engravings, in *Laocoön* he wrote, 'Art is the tree of life. Science is the tree of death'. Clearly one of the most important rebels to fight the worldview of mechanistic and inert nature, he described the new scientific perspective as 'Newton's sleep'.

Together with the American Transcendentalists such as William James, Ralph Waldo Emerson and Henry David Thoreau, whose writings were inspired by the earlier European Romantics, these individuals were often overtly pantheistic, polytheistic and even animistic in their worship of nature. Their input should not be underestimated. However, like many Pagans today, together with artists and poets, environmentalists and conservationists, midwives and carers, their work is like a broad and slow-moving river, carrying with it the soul of the people and their relationship with the land: love, grief, beauty, companionship, compassion and care, these are the poignant harmonies that suffuse their words.

Concurrent with Blake, the French naturalist Jean-Baptiste de Lamarck proposed the first ideas about evolution. Though ridiculed by his contemporaries, he was praised by the likes of Herbert Spencer and Charles Darwin, publishing fifty odd years later in the mid nineteenth century. Lamarck was certainly breaking new ground: the characteristics of nature were, he claimed, not fixed at all, but through an ongoing process of adaptation and development, species changed. Though he held to the notion of some universal *scala naturae*, he proposed that this ladder was ever-changing: at the time, the idea was so radical it was hard to comprehend.

Spencer, who coined the term 'survival of the fittest', further developed Lamarck's work. He believed aggression was integral to the naturally refining process of evolution, each part of nature adapting, managing its environment, failing or changing and thriving, from - as he said - 'gas to genius'. Darwin made the next move, stepping further from the conventional Christian anthropocentrism. Disagreeing with Spencer, whose approach was clearly saturated with the traditional attitudes towards the inferiority of nonhuman animals, Darwin declared that adaptation created not improvement but variation. Dominance and predation (or asserted superiority) was not the key. Nature's strength was in the peaceful coexistence of species, mutual interdependence, common bonds and symbioses, not aggressive competition. It was diversity that allowed for success. Although Darwin's name is better known on the streets of Western culture today, Spencer's worldview clearly tussles to retain its own dominance.

The nineteenth century saw a good number of theories and discoveries that, together with evolution, increasing drove a wedge between the Church and science, and by the end of the century a deep opposition had grown between scientific dependence upon (and celebration of) reason and religious faith. God - as a patriarchal source of objectivist reason - was being removed, as the goddess had been a few hundred years earlier. What was developing was a secular scientific materialism that had upon its altar nothing but reason.

Today, as Christianity continues its steady decline in much of the West (if not in the United States, at war with terror), scientific imperialism retains its power and momentum. With Bacon whispering in its current, it declares itself the world's saviour, through technology, medicine and even entertainment, extending the reach of reason beyond what is actually empirically verifiable. Matter (or nature), exorcised of its spiritual sanctity, is believed still to be empty, inert and soulless.

It has not been plain sailing for devotees of this paradigm. The mechanistic worldview has begun to crumble. Einstein's theory of relativity, laid out a little over a hundred years ago, together with the expanding reaches of quantum theory, has taken apart what were believed to be entirely stable components of Newtonian mechanics. Nature is beginning to be perceived, by cutting edge scientists at least, as a dynamic and perpetual flow of tides, currents and eddies, interconnected.

So does *Paganism once again rise, revealing the strength of that broad and ancient river, singing the songs of the current, not just through old heroes like Blake and WB Yeats, but scientists like James Lovelock and Fritjof Capra, even quantum physicists like Richard Feynman. The biochemist Rupert Sheldrake writes, 'As soon as we allow ourselves to think of the world as alive, we recognize that part of us knew this all along. It is like emerging from winter into a new spring'. Of course, these writers are not expressing a religious perspective, but their ideas whisper of nature's wonders and potential in ways that wholly reflect the *Pagan view. Albert Einstein didn't deny his religious perception: 'Try and penetrate with our limited means the secrets of nature and you will find that, behind all the discernible concatenations, there remains something subtle, intangible and inexplicable. Veneration for this force beyond anything that we can comprehend is my religion'.

Having been torn apart by the brutal alliance between materialism, patriarchal religion and rationalism, *Paganism has been cleansed of sticky superstition, leaving a religious worldview that retains its awe and reverence for nature, for its mystery and its revelations, its patterns of reason and its tides of emotion.

Environmental Crisis

As a *Pagan, I see that broad slow-moving river all around me, in a child's curiosity, in naturally inspired creativity, in music, in the berries of the hedgerow, in the white water of love and the surging flood of grief. Hundreds of millennia of human stories move through us, just as they have moved through our ancestors.

My words don't idealize the past. Unlike Spencer, I see not progress in evolution, but the cunning adaptations that allow for brief periods of success. Nor do I imagine our primitive ancestors were nature-loving: the effects of their consumption were simply limited by lower levels of population, the effects of their pollution and violence limited by their less damaging technology. Within every era, there have no doubt been individuals who have espoused the ideals that I lay down here as *Pagan ethics, attitudes based upon a dedicated and visceral love of the natural world, but they have not been the majority. Within that broad and most ancient river, human beings splash, fighting, drowning, declaiming and grasping, provoked by the greed, selfishness and delusions of base fears. As cultures change, the sands of our human understanding shifting, that essential blinkered ignorance and lack of care that allows for exploitation of others maintains its position as the executive perspective. It is no wonder we are in the state we are in now; it has been bad for a long time, but now that our toys are bigger, the mess we've created is critical.

Archaeology speaks of our atrocious record. As early as nine thousand years ago, the lush forests of the Middle East were razed for agriculture, whispering of Eden's destruction. By a thousand years later the effects of deforestation, soil erosion and coastal changes, with the disease and famine of pockets of overpopulation, were leading to the collapse of early civilizations. The rulers of Ur, around 2700 BCE, passed laws to protect the few remaining forests. Greek writers such as Hippocrates and Thucydides speak of the ecological crises of their time, in the fourth and fifth centuries BCE, Plato mourning 'the mere skeleton of the land' that remained.

When Descartes was writing, the pollution from coal and woodsmoke in the cities of Europe was unbearable. The diarist John Evelyn describes London as more like 'the suburbs of Hell than an assembly of rational creatures'. Efforts at regulating deforestation persistently failed with growing industrialization and the constant needs of shipbuilders, particularly navies. In 1690, Governor William Penn in his new American territories declared one acre of forest must be preserved for every five cleared.

By the time Spencer and Darwin were writing, the artist John Ruskin described every river as 'a common sewer, so that you cannot so much as baptize an English baby but with filth, unless you hold its face out in the rain, and even that falls dirty'.

Despite the words written in protest and despair, legislation, sanitation and advances in medicine, change was painfully slow and wholly focused upon human wellbeing. In 1935, Robert Sterling Yard described the creation of The Wilderness Society, in its magazine which he edited, as 'born of an emergency in conservation which admits of no delay. The craze is to build all the highways possible everywhere while billions may yet be borrowed from the unlucky future'. By the Second World War, the smog was still so bad in many industrial towns that lamps were needed through the day.

It was perhaps the effects of the hydrogen bomb that truly woke the world to the need for change. In 1962, Rachel Carson laid out the truth about pesticides in what is now seen as her most affecting book, *Silent Spring;* '[t]he *control of nature,*' she wrote, 'is a phrase conceived in arrogance, born of the Neanderthal age of biology and philosophy, when it was supposed that nature exists for the convenience of man.' The first oil spills in Britain and California in the late sixties, together with the first photographs of the earth from the space, all went to provoke the United Nations Conference on the Human Environment in 1972, following which came more legislation and the creation of government agencies. Through the 1980s, a dawning realization rose on the problems of the ozone layer, acid rain, toxic waste and climate change, yet still the situation is not fully addressed.

Fear is never a sustainable motivation for action, nor is it a healthy basis for creativity or relationship. To provoke our Western culture into responsible behaviour, to drag it from its fattened complacency and the greed rooted in its memories of millennia of poverty, seems a Herculean task. At times, the shock tactics used by Lovelock (as a scientist), Al Gore (as a politician) and David Attenborough (as a television presenter) appear to be the only way; but, after a moment's concern and maybe a chill of guilt, nothing changes.

Centuries have been passing of decreasing contact between the urban majority of our Western society and the damp green growth and wide skies of a world not fully controlled by mankind. Just as the daily slaughter of millions of animals and the ingestion of their fear leaves its mark on the mental and physical health of our population, so is this disconnection felt as an underlying loss and tension. Our tribes are incomplete without the company and guidance of the nonhuman elements of our landscape, and that absence provokes a deep grieving, an ache that is hard to pin down. So endemic is the feeling, it is presumed a normal part of humanity. Our culture compensates, encouraging the escapism of consumerism, drugs and stories (predominantly now gossip and television) to ease the pain, if temporarily. Indeed, societies are increasingly built upon these replacements for forest and meadow, for mud and rain. As the American thinker George Sessions points out, 'In technocratic-industrial societies there is overwhelming propaganda and advertising which encourages false needs and destructive desires designed to foster increased production and consumption of goods'. How quickly people have forgotten what has allowed human beings to thrive, joyful and alive, for hundreds of thousand of years.

According to the biologist and writer EO Wilson, in what he calls a 'biotic holocaust', more species are now becoming extinct (as a result of human activity) than at any time since the end of the age of the dinosaurs: one every twenty minutes. The Soil Association reports that an apple might be sprayed up to sixteen times with some thirty six different chemicals before it reaches our shopping basket, many of which cannot be washed off, leaving pesticides to be ingested by those who eat it.

World Heath Organization figures say twenty thousand human beings die each year from pesticide poisoning, with as much as a quarter of all pesticides being used on cotton: a further eight thousand chemicals are used in its processing to create fabric.

The details continue. Waste products from nuclear energy remain lethally toxic for a quarter of a million years. National Geographic reported that during the last two years alone, the Arctic Ocean has lost fourteen percent of what was permanent sea ice; how much this is caused by human pollution is debated, but most scientists agree we are at *least* a significant influence. The Kyoto Protocol requires its signatories to reduce greenhouse gas emissions to five per cent below 1990 levels; by 1999, the US were 11.7% above and rising. In Britain, carbon emissions from electricity generation (particularly coal-fired power stations) are still increasing. The British government says we need to reduce emissions by twenty per cent by 2010, sixty per cent by 2050; Greenpeace's executive director, Stephen Tindale, puts the necessary figure at ninety per cent if we act within the small window of opportunity currently open. Any delay would mean reduction will need to be even quicker.

Environmental awareness is topical, and increasing. My son's school texts speak of the issues while my own education in the 1970s didn't mention them at all. If one were to ask the average unthinking Joe Public if nature mattered, his answer would be an unequivocal yes. However, if he were to say why, every one of his reasons would be based upon human need: we must look after the natural world so that human beings can continue to thrive.

*Paganism as Dark Green

On paper, without the poetry of ritual, *Paganism can look like environmentalism, and some agnostics or atheists question the point of unnecessarily making a *religion* out of what appears to be a simple love of nature. The challenge is often based upon an assumption that all religions worship gods whose key priority is humanity, gods who perpetually watch and judge human rights and wrongs.

Remnants of old superstitions in popular culture dictate that if you do something wrong, you will somehow be punished. As Midgley writes, in a crisis the human tendency is not necessarily to think out rational causes, but to believe consequences 'flow directly from the moral obtuseness that goes with greed'. Human guilt and fear make us alert both to figures of authority and who might take the blame. So have many environmental protest groups and writers been criticised for creating a culture of fear, directly or indirectly stating that the earth, her self-regulating systems pushed off balance by human interference, is judging our species and condemning it to extinction. James Lovelock's Gaia theories have been interpreted in the same way: the tenable spectrum within which life is possible is alarmingly thin, and when necessary equilibria are lost (temperature, salinity and pH levels, gases in the atmosphere, volcanic and tectonic activity, and so on), we shall pay the price. Life on earth will disappear. That he uses the name of a goddess further provokes his objectors to assume he projects onto her human or (other) monotheistic qualities.

*Pagan gods may be merciless but they are not judgmental; they don't care about humanity. Rain is simply rain. As Darwin said, with each tiny adaptation, nature continues in all its diversity, and will continue with or without humanity, both providing for human life and continuing to challenge its tenability. Nietzsche expressed human insignificance within nature in a piece so rich with his inimitable wit it is worth quoting in its entirety: 'Once upon a time, in some out of the way corner of that universe which is dispersed into numberless twinkling solar systems, there was a star upon which clever beasts invented knowing. That was the most arrogant and mendacious minute of world history, but nevertheless, it was only a minute. After nature had drawn a few breaths, the star cooled and congealed, and the clever beasts had to die'. His concluding comments are scathing: 'One might invent such a fable, and yet he still would not have adequately illustrated how miserable, how shadowy and transient, how aimless and arbitrary the human intellect looks within nature. There were eternities during which it did not exist. And when it is all over with the human intellect, nothing will have happened'.

A master of cynicism, Nietzsche may go further than is necessary to express the point, but his extreme attitude is useful as a tool of emphasis. Understanding that human life is not special in any way, *Paganism is very much a *deep* rather than *shallow* ecology.

It was the Norwegian philosopher, Arne Naess, who coined the term 'deep ecology', making a distinction between management of the environment for sustainable human benefit, such as Al Gore's anthropocentric Christian position of human stewardship of nature, and a truly earth-centred perspective. As a utilitarian, Singer's view focuses on the importance of sentient beings, for 'if a being is not capable of suffering or of experiencing enjoyment or happiness, there is nothing to be taken account of'. Similarly Richard Ryder does not consider the environment deserving of direct consideration, for it does not feel pain; the value of ecosystems 'lies solely in the pain and pleasure that they give to painients'. Damage to the environment is 'bound to cause suffering to animals who inhabit these features' and should therefore be 'of concern to painients'.

Deep ecology, on the other hand, is not dependent on the needs of animals, human or otherwise. Like *Paganism, it is not about the environment, in the same way that veganism is not about abstaining from eating animal products. It is an attitude towards life, a complete worldview. Initially writing on the subject in the early 1970s, Naess called his ideas *ecosophy* (etymologically, the *wisdom* of the *household*), making it clear that he was speaking from a philosophical and not scientific standpoint, for he saw ecology as limited by its scientific methods. His aim was to refocus the way in which our society perceived nature by locating moral priorities within the natural as opposed to the human world.

Three terms continue to be crucial within deep ecology, all of which are central to *Paganism, the first being *inherent value*, which needs no further explanation. The second is *biocentric equality*, or the perspective that all within nature is of equal value. The last is *self-realization*, which Naess called the 'ecological self'; it describes the way in which we expand our sense of identity to allow for a connectedness with all of nature. He talked of this state being one of human psychological maturity.

Writing on environmental ethics, the American philosopher John Rodman garners similar themes. An effective environmental perspective, he suggests, needs to embrace 'a theory of value that recognizes intrinsic value in nature without engaging in mere extensionism; a metaphysics that takes account of the reality and importance of relationships and systems as well as individuals; and an ethics that includes such duties as noninterference principle, limited intervention to repair environmental damage in extreme circumstances, and a style of co-inhabitation that involves the knowledgeable, respectful, and restrained use of nature'.

Addressing environmental problems is not about limiting emissions of carbon and methane, recycling and planting trees. The attitudinal shift that deep ecologists seek to effect is from the self-assertion of the competing isolated individual to the acceptance of an integrated systemic world.

Naess' self-realization is to the *Pagan an instinct to extend what we consider to be our tribe - those with whom we share support and morality - to include the ecosystems of home. It is reflected in the ecologist Aldo Leopold's seminal work, *A Sand Country Almanac*. Writing in 1948, Leopold explained the basis of his 'land ethic' as one that 'simply enlarges the boundaries of the community to include the soils, waters, plants, and animals, or collectively: the land'. By shifting our vision, humanity can adjust its position from being the 'conqueror of the land-community to plain member and citizen of it'.

Of course, opening our tribe to others requires us to craft relationships with them, to learn how to co-operate and communicate, and indeed to share. If the environment is strong, beautiful, thriving and supportive of human life, such a task is not so challenging. But the earth as a whole is now unstable, and many ecosystems are losing their ability to sustain human life. As Midgley wrote: 'For three centuries we had been encouraged to consider the earth simply as an inert and bottomless larder stocked for our needs. To be forced to suspect now that it is instead a living system, a system on whose continued activity we are dependent, as system which is vulnerable and capable of failing, is extremely unnerving'. To welcome such a world into our tribe, and thus offer it the protection of our shared morality, requires courage.

The only way it can be done is by relinquishing the competitive and domineering *I-it* attitude towards nature. Acting honourably, with authenticity and presence, we begin to care about nature for nature's sake.

What is Nature?

Exploring more carefully *Pagan ethics in relation to our planetary home, finding a *Pagan perspective on nature's value and how we should therefore engage with it, it would be useful here to clarify just what is meant by the word *nature*. To recall the beginning of this chapter, in order to elucidate the *Pagan worldview we need to explore just *what* the *Pagan perceives the earth to be.

Through the centuries of the emerging new science, nature was all too often defined in terms of an opposition. With his customary lack of charm, Descartes wrote, 'by nature I do not mean some goddess or some sort of imaginary power. I employ this word to signify matter itself'. John Stuart Mill was more comprehensive, considering where the word lacks honesty, suggesting how often it expresses an evaluative judgement. Nature is understood to be either 'a collective name for everything which is' or 'a name for everything which is of itself, without voluntary human intervention'; it is, however, also used to describe 'what ought to be; or for the rule or standard of what ought to be.' Considering what is deemed *unnatural* does indeed reveal attitudes about nature, shedding light on often hidden layers of human prejudice and assumption. Further, that what is seen to be unnatural has changed and continues to change, differing so widely around the world, expresses the true extent of diversity amongst human cultures.

The word is derived from the Latin *natus*, meaning birth. The Greek for nature is *phusis*, its root *phu* also relating to birth. Yet to limit what is natural to the state in which something is born discounts growth and learning. A child's innocence is natural, but if the behaviour of an educated adult is not (being consciously honed or nurtured, not in itself nature), we discount too much. If it is natural, the term loses any meaningful limitation as we risk accepting any nurtured action: medicine, abortion and biotech slip in the door.

In common language, actions declared unnatural are those unacceptable, immoral, counter to social and/or state law; unnatural entities are usually *things*, objects that can be patented, owned, controlled, used, lacking any inherent value. As an example, in twenty first century Britain, reviewing the popular press, anal sex (regardless of gender) is just beginning to shift its status from unnatural to acceptable within a free society; biotechnology and its products have a long way to go. With no clear boundaries, subjective opinion (preferably shared by the tribe) is the customary guide to its definition.

As a complicated and complicating word, I put it to the groups I gathered to discuss Pagan ethics. The conclusion forged was simple.

Nature: that which has soul.

Within a *Pagan context, the phrase not only makes sense, but lacks unnecessary slack for ambiguity or judgement. However, in order to understand it beyond the *Pagan context and as a basis for how the *Pagan perceives and thus values the world, it needs elaboration. I shall do so obliquely by posing the core question: what is the *Pagan attitude towards nature?

Bearing in mind the dualism and materialism of the last four centuries, and that allegiance to both worldviews persists within Western society, there are two threads which express *Paganism here most poignantly:

sanctity and connection. I shall begin with sanctity.

Sanctity and Connection

The foundation of *Pagan religious practice is based upon the tenet that all nature is sacred. In animistic terms, this is derived from the understanding that all nature is inspirited: in other words, every creature (every part of nature's creativity) is made up of natural energy and the directed momentum that emerges through intention, or consciousness. Both this energy and the directing consciousness exist as the base building blocks of existence; where they cohere, sticky with intrinsic purpose, larger forms come into being, intentions developing. From quanta to molecules, elements to storms and butterflies, moons to galaxies, entities come into being, driven upon the currents of their own nature.

This fuelled consciousness, in *Paganism, is the soul of a being. So far in this book I have argued that human and nonhuman animals have such soul; now I extend that to include the rest of the environment: as a whole and as each of its component parts, nature has soul.

Martha Nussbaum wrote of each individual creature's right to flourish 'as the sort of thing it is'. Rodman writes of the moral obligation 'not to treat with disrespect or use as a mere means anything that has a *telos* or end of its own - anything that is autonomous in the basic sense of having a capacity for internal self-direction and self-regulation'. Kant, among others, gave this status solely to human beings; Rodman suggests it apply to 'all living natural entities and natural systems', for everything from wombats to rain forests have 'their own characteristic structures and potentialities to unfold'. In many ways we are reaching again to Aristotle's entelechy: nature's energy finding its purpose through each individual's telos rightly expressed.

William James acknowledged how little humanity in general is capable of perceiving the inherent value of nonhuman life. In the late nineteenth century, he wrote, 'Not a being of the countless throng is there whose continued life is not called for, and called for intensely, by the consciousness that animates the being's form. That *you* neither realize nor understand nor call for it, is an absolutely irrelevant circumstance. That you have a saturation-point of interest tells us nothing of the interests that absolutely are. The Universe, with every living entity which her resources create, creates at the same time a call for that entity, and an appetite for its continuance, - creates it, if nowhere else, at least within the heart of the entity itself'.

Telos, the word used by Aristotle, is close to the *Pagan soul: the story of a being's existence, of every note of its song, each twist of the weave of energy and consciousness, creates not only experience but refinement of intention. A soul's inner purpose, like its telos, is the summation of its being, its state of flourishing. So to the *Pagan, the soul provides all that is needed to back a claim for inherent value, for the soul contains that core intention to be, and to flourish as that being. Although humanity does not provide nature with its value, it is through acknowledging each soul's intention that nature is accorded the status of sanctity.

The second word adds to this comprehension: connection. For if energy and consciousness are the defining features of nature, there can be no *separation*. All of nature is interconnected. This is not simply at the level of symbiosis, the webs of interdependence and threads of relationship that exist within any ecosystem. At the microcosmic level, energy and consciousness are fundamental to every whisper of nature, every breath of life. Life is shared.

Like nature's energy, consciousness is not tightly bounded, not held within the singular boxes of separate entities. It exists within the fluidity of ever-changing experience. Through observation and reflection, inter-action and reflection, a creature's sense of being is perpetually shifting, tidally expanding then receding.

As a part of nature, the hawthorn is not just an individual tree, but an ecosystem in itself; further, it is a part of its particular genus, of all trees, of its environment; heading in the other direction, it is made up bark, leaves, cells, molecules, chemicals and so on. Every layer we can identify, and those in between, is made up of cohesive forms of being, fuelled and moving within their own purpose, their own telos. In the same way, I am not just Emma, but a part of my family, my bloodline, a number of communities, my nation, the environment of the valley in which I live, my gender, my species, mammals as a whole, the humming of life.

Each and every relationship of my living, as I breathe, move and eat, sharing creativity and space, depends upon how I identify myself at any given time, and on what level those relationships take place. Atoms move through cell walls, sound vibrations make the air dance, I murmur to my baby son who sucks upon my breast as has every mammalian infant for millions of years. Instinctively currents of compatible intention are found, pools of shared consciousness, in whatever way is most appropriate for that interaction. Every creature does the same - molecules of water within a torrential storm, rushing down a river or down an otter's gullet, atoms of calcium in an ancient clam shell or the rolling hills of chalk. Each of us, and each part of us, responds moment by moment to each threat and to each opportunity.

To the *Pagan, this sense of connection is crucial to living with honour. Arne Naess termed it *self-realization*, the way in which we learn what we truly are as human beings, as nature. If we are only able or willing to identify ourselves as separate, competing human egos, we will not find peace. Yet when the web is understood, the connection is a visceral experience, allowing a deeper level of rational comprehension and emotional empathy within and across apparent boundaries of identity and tribe, a real sense of heritage and the stories that are lived again and again. It is an experience that evokes courage, allowing for true generosity and loyalty. It breaks apart our jaded awareness, filling us with wonder and respect, provoking an unavoidable sense of responsibility for how we engage through that connectedness, and a hunger for true honesty, a truth through which each relationship hums with vitality and potential.

When the cynic ridicules the animist, declaring that the lake does not care if it is being polluted, he is missing the point, making the common and misguided error of assuming the animist childishly anthropomorphizes the nonhuman world. The animist does not perceive the water of the lake as a separate entity; the lake, from elemental to environmental, is intimately connected within the wholeness of nature. The same is true of the human child abused, the caged hen, the tortured rabbit, the clear-cut forest, the mines and quarries, the exhausted plains as they lose their topsoil to the wind. Because all nature is so intricately connected, all nature is affected when one part of it suffers disrespect.

Nor is nature irrational, as the mechanists and materialists have declared. Reason is intrinsic to nature. As human beings, we are not separate observing entities, but a part of nature, sharing and expressing its reason, its intentions, its consciousness and energy, its order and chaos, moving as we do through the tides of emergence and withdrawal, growth and decay, vibrance and stillness, as humans, as mammals, animals, breath and blood.

From the *Pagan view, there is no incompatibility between science and nature-based religions, just as there was not for the natural philosophers of our heritage. For science needs to do more than ask how; it needs to explore why, to embrace the systems it takes apart to study, to accept more of the fundamental drives that fuel our world. For when they are working well, discoveries made in their exploration (as opposed to manipulation) of nature only go to increase our awe. The Cartesian hubris that all nature will one day be known, named and restrained - and thus will be no cause for wonder - is as dangerous as the tsunami his philosophical descendants believe they will learn to control.

Hearing Nature

If all nature is inspirited, from the subatomic to the perceptible, to that too vast to perceive, is nothing in *Paganism deemed unnatural?

The answer is dependent upon the level at which we are making relationship. A table crafted of great pieces of solid timber has a presence that inspires respect and care, while one of chipboard and laminated veneer is dependent on its usefulness. A *Pagan may sense the former to have soul as wood, nourished by the intention of the craftsman's care; after its processing, the latter may have no wood soul left. At a molecular level, the chemicals are humming their own song, but it is with the wood that, as human beings, we are likely to be seeking relationship, and on that level that we seek to feel its nature.

A canal, another human construct, may feel soulless when viewed from above as a straight line across the landscape, yet in the relationships between the water and those creatures that thrive within and upon it there is evidently soul. Where the canal is sterile, barren of life as we would perceive it, it feels unnatural: there seems nothing there with which to forge relationship.

In terms of ethics, the *Pagan affirms the need to work *with* nature as opposed to *using* it as a resource. However, in order to survive we are bound to prioritize our needs over others'. When addressing nonhuman animals, Peter Singer at first attempted to draw a line between those sufficiently sentient to provoke consideration and those that could be used. In *Paganism, even beyond the realm of animals, no such cut off point is possible. The only acceptable premise for using another part of nature in a way that negates its inherent purpose is where the harm caused is *necessary* for self-preservation.

What would be sufficient provocation? There is no delineated barrier to guide the *Pagan. His ethics, instead, are dependent upon his own understanding of necessity; and, as a sliding measure, one person's decision is bound to appear extreme or slack to another. On the whole, the more capable the *Pagan is of forging sensitive relationship (experiencing the connection, awake to the inherent purpose of the Other), the less he considers necessary in order to thrive.

An ability to perceive and feel the connectedness of nature can be nurtured, as it is within most *Pagan religious practices, but everyone (except the most numb or wounded) can already feel it deep inside. It provokes empathy and compassion, embarrassment, laughter, anticipation and horror. In all humanity, the risk is ever present; however, that receptivity will be limited when it is in one's own interest to determine some creature an inanimate *thing* and thus free to be used. Or, where a culture declares it weak sentimentality to care or relate to what they would perceive as worthless or a resource - whether that is a spider or a sheep, a single tree or a rainforest. A blank face is put up, the individual's desire for acceptance within the tribe overriding the instinctive desire to engage with or protect the Other.

Of course, to imagine that a *Pagan, perceiving a snowdrop as a conscious entity, in any way anthropomorphises that snowdrop is, as I have said before, wholly to misconstrue this worldview. A plant's needs are inevitably different from a human's, its soul communicating those needs to the environment within which it lives in its own effective way. Though the cynic may proclaim otherwise, what the *Pagan perceives is not a tiny fairy that in English will inform him of some enchanting tale: he acknowledges the snowdrop's song of energy and intention, its *telos* and potential. After all, without the complications of self-awareness, the needs of nature can be simple, often obvious, thus easily communicated: a stream wants to flow, a copse of trees wants water, clean air, adequate soil and space in which to grow. Within the nonhuman world, as where humans are present, all the *Pagan is doing is exploring through experience how that tribe fits together, and thus finding his own place within the whole.

Emerson expressed it beautifully, his style as ever a gentle strolling observation: 'The greatest delight which the fields and woods minister, is the suggestion of an occult relation between man and the vegetable. I am not alone and unacknowledged. They nod to me, and I to them. The waving of the boughs in the storm is new to me and old. It takes me by surprise, and yet is not unknown. Its effect is like that of a higher thought or a better emotion coming over me, when I deemed I was thinking justly or doing right'.

Nature's Integration

For the reader saturated in scientific materialism or dualism, it may be hard to accept that their perspective is not based upon unquestionable *facts,* discovered by members of the Royal Society on behalf of the civilized West; it is simply a worldview. The alternative model of nature that I have presented here, that of an integrated world, may be hard to comprehend, let alone accept.

That I add to the model the religious elements of a Western, animistic, nature-based religion, that I have here called *Paganism, may provoke some further to distance themselves. However, I have included ideas published by various respected philosophers and other thinkers in order to place the *Pagan perspective in its broader historical and contemporary modern context, for the vision of an integrated world is neither new nor specifically *Pagan. Seekers have found it in poetry and mythology, in art, prayer and music, in religious traditions and spiritual movements, in aboriginal communities and suburban sitting rooms. It is neither Eastern or Western, for all quarters of the human world have failed to engage honourably with nature, regardless of their prophets, scientists or scriptures. It is a worldview that has instead flowed quietly within religious and non-religious mysticism, throughout time.

Writing in the mid 1850s, Henry David Thoreau spoke of the power of nature, finding for himself pockets of American wilderness, places that weren't yet soaked in human memory. In this wild nature, he found a source of spiritual truth and integrity that he regarded as essential to keep alive the spark of wakeful vitality in humanity. 'In wilderness is the preservation of the world', he wrote, for within it he ever found 'some grand, serene, immortal, infinitely encouraging, though invisible, companion'.

Such companionship is an inevitable part of the experience of accepting and feeling the web of nature's connected soul, and our place within that. The poet sat by the lough, his soul bared in his receptivity, waiting for the threads to touch him with inspiration; the artist gazing at the landscape, seeing no details yet feeling the complete picture, his brush poised above the palette; the young particle physicist, waiting, knowing he must hold no limiting expectation of what might be about to happen; the mathematician letting numbers slip through his soul, patterns emerging out of empty space; the naturalist pausing amidst the birds' song in a moment of utter contentment, the wind in the leaves above, the stillness of the dappled light on the forest floor. Everything connected, life in all its parts hums upon the course of their own currents of intent, together completely still and yet ever-moving, flowing upon the tides of nature as a *whole*.

To this worldview, the *Pagan does not impose religious strictures (he has none), but celebrates through his religious practice, feeling not only wonder and respect, but devoted reverence. In ritual he sings the prayers that rise through his soul, prayers given him by his ancestors and those of his heritage. He makes offerings of gratitude and sacrifices of himself as an expression of his commitment to *care*. He dances, drums, shedding deep tears and laughing until his belly aches, sharing with his tribe the gifts offered by the gods, pausing before each meal, each drink of water, each act of love, to give thanks to those forces of nature whose soul's expression has provided him with this opportunity to live.

Yet, though the task of this book is to explain an ethics, not to evangelize, that task is also an enthusiasm for the founding tenets of that ethics; to be devoted to nature while watching it destroyed by a careless and selfish humankind is hard to bear. As Rodman says, 'there will be no revolution in ethics without a revolution in perception'; many will find that shift hard to make, but if we are to address the crisis that revolution is essential.

It is easy to blame our governments for not addressing the crisis; yet while they avoid taxing air fuels, our people continue to fly, paying cheap fares and playing ignorant to the pollution pumped out by each flight. Governments dependent on democratic elections follow the wealthiest corporations and the media, both of whom inform and follow those streams of public opinion whose trade they depend upon: us. It is *our* attitudes and actions that make a difference. The uneducated and unthinking will believe any authority they happen to cling to, be that a tabloid newspaper or corporate advertiser, but every government office, press room and ad agency is equally filled with human beings capable of taking responsibility for their own actions.

The axiom of honour in *Paganism requires that responsibility. Every cent and penny that is spent is the most powerful expression of 'public opinion'. Acknowledging the inherent sanctity and connectedness of nature, each decision made is based upon the principle of necessity: with courage, with generosity, loyal to the tribe of his environment, the *Pagan carefully considers how necessary it is to purchase, enter, change, consume any given thing, place or spirit, awake and as informed as he can be.

In his devotion to his gods, the *Pagan forgoes the unnecessary, whether pleasure or convenience, if he perceives the cost is too high to others within the wider tribe. He may pay a few more cents for an organic apple, but the cost to the environment is considerably less than for one drenched in chemicals. Furthermore, a fresh apple hums with the soul of the apple tree, the orchard, the mud, rain and sunshine, while a processed candy bar, wrapped in plastic, has no soul within it to nourish his own. In the same way, the *Pagan will consider the use of medicines, where necessary working with herbs that sing with their own soul intention, instead of blindly ingesting chemicals he cannot properly hear, cartoned in plastic, carrying with them a heritage of animal testing and corporate dishonour.

The integrated world inspires an attitude where every interaction is, by default, *me and you*, subject to subject. There is no assumption of ownership, no assumption of consent. Understanding nature as a boundless yet wholly integrated system, stretching out through the universe and deep into the microcosm, the *Pagan worldview is not just a mental construct, but a visceral experience of living, where nothing is isolated, every action or lack of action affecting the whole. Every heavy footprint left upon our journey of life is a wound on the soul of nature, as it is on the soul of each creature who falls into it or has to walk around it.

Walking lightly, the *Pagan aims to leave only stories in the wind.

I end this chapter by returning to a frustration spoken of before: seeing Pagans, and other apparent environmentalists, continuing to support the thoughtless consumerism of our secular culture. Such people may attend the eight festivals, making prayers and offerings to the gods who turn the cycles of the seasons, but are clearly failing to forge the soul-deep relationships that make a difference. At events such as the annual Big Green Gathering in south west Britain, the car park is filled with SUVs. Supporting protest action to stop Tesco tear down trees to build a new supermarket, their kitchens and bathrooms are testament to how much money they have voluntarily given that same store. They rant about climate change, and fly to southern Europe for two weeks holiday each year.

In the next chapter, I shall address the issue of distribution of poverty and wealth, addressing more directly the problems of hypocrisy, ignorance and greed.

CHAPTER TEN

THE VALUE OF THE WEB

Three paths to peace :
receiving without need,
giving without need,
and never taking when there is no need.

Sanctity

'Secularism is like chastity': the phrase makes me smile whenever I read
it. The words are from *Straw Dogs* in which the English thinker John
Gray lays out his understanding of modern life in a stream of cutting
aphorisms. Defined by what it denies, Gray sees the secular perspective
as a response within Western culture to monotheistic Christianity. Where
a religion claims to know the indisputable truth, damning all other faiths
as erroneous and deluded, there is inevitably created a position that
opposes it. Gray talks of 'ancient pagans', but his words as accurately
apply to modern Paganism: happily tolerant of many notions of deity, the
Pagan accepts the existence of gods that can be known and gods beyond
perception or comprehension, gods who appear to care and those for
whom humanity is wholly insignificant, gods who change with the tides
of nature; amidst such open diversity, there is no need to declare oneself
an *unbeliever*. Atheism was created as a result of the inflexible
'certainties' it opposes.

Evidence of doubt about the existence of deity can be found within
texts as old as the Rig Veda, written over three thousand years ago on the
Indian subcontinent, and sketches of this doubt continue to emerge,
revealing themselves within early philosophical Buddhism and ancient
Greek thinking. However, on the whole, ideas challenging deity have
been more evidently set within the Pagan polytheistic mindset:

Epicureans, from the third century BCE, did not deny the existence of the gods, but disputed the notion that they were remotely interested in humanity and thus required reverence. Towards the end of the Roman Empire in the West, Christians were still being accused of atheism, a capital crime, but as with the earlier Greek, Socrates, the difficulty was not an absence of religious belief; they were simply not revering the *right* gods or concepts of deity. Modern atheists still dig out such ideas as ancient roots for their position, seeking to justify their belief in no gods just as religions tend to do for their creed of gods, but this is not the point. To the *Pagan, humanity holds no intrinsic authority; in other words, all human dogma on religion is questionable. Whether we are yelling for one ultimate truth or another, we risk losing awareness of our surroundings, our environment, our tribe: nature. Standing defiantly against belief in one thing facilitates dismissal or disregard of much more. Before long, nothing is sacred.

Spiritualities, as opposed to religions, have emerged throughout human culture for as long as there have been theologies. Though shying away from a notion of deity as a religious or human hierarchy, many have a clear sense of value, forging ideas of that which makes the material world a richer experience, based upon inherent or dualistic *spirit*, the 'breath' of life derived from the Latin, *spiritus*. Like many philosophies, as a framework of understanding a spirituality can be richly meaningful and effective. However, if we remove the authoritarian connotations of religion, as *Paganism does, without the experience of deity perception of what is sacred lacks *fuel*. It tends to rely upon definition, analysis, classification: the statue is considered sacred, as opposed to seething with divine energy.

If we acknowledge its Latin root, *sacrare*, the word sacred reflects its old Pagan context, for it implies both holy and cursed, blessed by gods with malicious *and* beneficial intent. In other words, helpful or unhelpful, the created or creating being is infused with a divinely potent consciousness of nature. The Old English term, *sacren*, however, shows a distinct evolution, for it means to consecrate or make holy: to draw that divinity in. The change is significant. The gods are no longer immanent; God is outside of nature, and his blessings must be invoked.

To the *Pagan, all nature is sacred. Indeed, it is tempting to risk the more generalized statement here: to Pagans, all nature is sacred. In a situation where it is necessary to explain Paganism monotheistically, to present a comprehension of one supreme being revered by all Pagans in order to clarify understanding to a monotheistic or secular audience, there is some validity in presenting nature as that single entity. The soul of nature, in its perpetual flow of creativity, riding its intemporal energy upon the flow of its ancient intent, encapsulates the totality of existence. That this soul is not venerated as the singular, or even the principal, deity of most Pagans is because the enormity of nature is hard to grasp; instead, Pagans find empathy with deities with whom it is easier to craft individual, personal, experiential relationships. The mind-blowing wonder that is evoked by contemplation upon nature as a whole leaves us blank, bewildered and overwhelmed. As Einstein said, 'Nature is a magnificent structure that we can comprehend only very imperfectly, and that must fill a thinking person with a feeling of *humility*'. Anyone who wholeheartedly seeks the patterns of nature must, he felt, be filled with this awe, which to him was a 'genuine religious feeling'.

However, if all nature is sacred, not just the altar, the scripture, the artefacts set aside for ritual, how does that affect the way we behave? If the land we have to build upon is sacred, the rain that floods the valley, the apple that abates our hunger, the virus that brings the fever, we are constantly in a position where we are (at risk of) using or abusing the sacred. The word is in danger of losing its poignancy, its purpose.

For when an entity is sacred, we are required to acknowledge its individual intention, its own journey of striving to be and to become. That is not only when we have no capability to stop that flow of intention, as with a volcano or hurricane. Sanctity charges us to consider intention, even where we could easily, whether deliberately or thoughtlessly, block it. Subject to subject, wakeful and honourable, by perceiving something as sacred, we are challenged to avoid causing any measure of unnecessary harm, instead finding the currents of its being, learning how to walk with them, crafting a relationship that is respectful, generous and authentic.

That is true of all religious traditions; in *Paganism, it extends from human life to all of nature's creativity (geological, elemental, climatic, animal and so on). As a result, the sacred is not always easy. After all, in a *Pagan sense, to be infused with a divine current or soul does not necessarily mean one is filled solely with a beautifully constructive and nurturing spirit; the gods are also brutal and destructive. The sacred is as often the quiet splitting of a seedcase at germination as the violence and cacophony of an electrical storm. The gods are not only loving care and nurture, but lust and rage. Sanctity doesn't bring with it consideration for humanity.

Needless to say, every Pagan does not treat every aspect of nature as though it were sacred, all the time. As the Christian slanders his neighbour, the Moslem idolizes an external idea of god, as the Buddhist slips back into polytheism, so does the undisciplined, unthinking and compromised Pagan behave like any other human: he *uses* nature. Trading, gathering, hoarding, stealing, abusing, consuming and wasting, without a deeply embedded knowing of sanctity, our species perceives the planet and its surrounds as a vast and free-of-charge warehouse of *resources*.

In secular terms, then, this chapter is about resources, about how we distribute their abundance and where we allow there to be a lack. As with so much of this book, I shall not cover every critical angle, instead working with just a few key issues: the selfishness and inequalities of capitalism and globalization, ownership, the myth of progress, population, distribution and the issue of need as opposed to desire. In *Pagan terms, this chapter is about the human attitude to nature, distorted by fear, that has brought us to a relationship with the earth that is no longer tenable.

Wealth and Power

Caroline Lucas, writer and Green Party MEP, has stated that 'the next forty years will be the most crucial period in the history of humankind'. I agree, yet we didn't get to this place because of an evolving stupidity within our species. Pollution, poverty and overpopulation, genocide and corruption have been an integral part of human societies for many thousands of years. What is making the difference now is simply this: the technological power we have amassed over the past few centuries means that each one of those chronic human failings is potentially now globally destructive.

For hundreds of thousands of years, the forces beneath them have been the qualities that allowed humankind to survive within the harsh and unpredictable tides of nature: with single-minded focus, we worked to satisfy our needs, accumulating with blinkered selfishness all the earth could offer, ensuring our own survival. As tribal creatures, our empathy and compassion allowed us the ability to co-operate, albeit only within the distinct if shifting boundaries of our tribe. Those qualities are as fundamental to our human nature *now* as they were five thousand or five hundred thousand years ago.

Perceiving this as human nature, the *Pagan acknowledges the innate drive for survival as a divine force; within its current lie many more gods, of jealousy, possessiveness, exchange and thievery, violence, war, greed, cunning and duplicity, perhaps even lust and love. The list goes on. Yet there is no point in saying that humanity must change. We may as well cry out that, if tigers are to avoid extinction, they must become herbivorous. Within a worldview where nature is dirty, and far from divine grace, the *Pagan perspective may feel Schopenhauerian in bleak pessimism. Yet the *Pagan does not judge nature, or human nature, as base: nature sings with sanctity, and with power. The *Pagan religious outlook encourages not resignation but acceptance, leaving each individual with the personal obligation to craft sound relationship with every one of those forces that flood through their own soul as destructively as creatively. Instead of submitting to envy, rage, hunger or desire, the *Pagan is called to ride the current wakefully, responsibly.

In Western culture, we live within a world that does not support that awareness. In urban areas, and through television, radio and print media, literally thousands of advertising messages break over us every single day, our minds - consciously and subconsciously - checking movement, reading words, taking in the associated images. Each one provokes that deep rapacious hunger within our species' nature, questioning our security, asking whether we have enough. And with each one, we judge our identity and position within the tribe, adjusting where necessary, making tiny alterations to how we ride the surging current that powers our drive to survive.

Of course, it is easy to imagine that survival used to be about no more than adequate shelter, food and warmth, but human nature has used showy frivolities and shiny weaponry to impress since the dawn of his emergence. Survival requires not just the acquiring of enough, but an overt display of having *secured* enough. We have no peacock tail, after all. Yet, once again, what was a simple survival tactic of vanity is now globally detrimental. With the recent spread of media throughout the world, particularly through television and advertising, the apparent value of the unnecessary and superficial has increased beyond all reason.

Capitalism is based on lack of necessity. It is only by producing more than is needed that wealth can be generated. The task is thus to convince others that they need what they do not. First provoking desire, with every cheap television show and expensive commercial, every magazine and towering billboard, selling notions of strength secured through vanity and superficial pleasure, success comes when that desire is transformed into a subconscious belief that the product is essential to survival. Where the drive is linked to another innate human hunger, such as the craving for sex, love and sweetness, the deception is both easier and more potent.

The globalization of markets, particularly over the past twenty five years, has been a sickening expression of this writ large across the whole world. The fastest growing companies, becoming less and less accountable and more politically powerful, amorally (even cynically) exploit these common human failings. Nestlé's now notorious campaign to sell formula milk in areas of desperate poverty, as better for babies than their mothers' milk, is a perfect example.

Assuming that increased corporate wealth will benefit nations as a whole, governments have supported the creation of these vast global companies. According to the American-based Institute for Policy Studies (IPS), over half of the world's largest economies are no longer nations: General Motors is bigger than Denmark, IBM bigger than Singapore, Sony bigger than Pakistan. In 1999, sales of each of the five largest (General Motors, Wal-Mart, Exxon Mobil, Ford and DaimlerChrysler) were greater than the gross domestic products of 182 of the world's 193 countries.

Yet inequalities continue: the 'trickle down' of wealth from the vast corporations never happens, for the wealthy hold onto the power, shamelessly continuing to exploit the rest. Smaller firms fail to compete and go under. In 2006, *The Economist* newspaper reported that the gap between wealth and poverty in Britain has returned to what it was in Victoria's reign. *Fortune* magazine relates the top one hundred salaries in the United States to be a thousand times higher than those of the ordinary American worker, while a quarter of American children live in poverty. Average incomes across the African continent are more than ten per cent lower now than they were in 1960, and almost a quarter of the world's human population live in what the World Bank defines as 'severe poverty' - those living on less than US$1 a day.

The lack of wealth shared comes not only from the extreme difference in remuneration. Technological advances have reduced human employment. While sales of those top two hundred companies accounted for over a quarter of human economic activity at the turn of the millennium, they employed less than one per cent of the world's workforce; despite a nearly four hundred per cent increase in profits over the previous sixteen years, the workforce increased by less than fifteen per cent.

Many of these huge corporations further decreased the number of people they employ directly by extricating themselves from the overheads and responsibilities of production, of factories, workers and associated legislation. Instead, they focus on selling the fantasy of their specific brand, 'outsourcing' manufacturing to contractors whom they squeeze to the lowest possible prices in order to maximize their own profits. Around the world, governments from Guatemala to South Korea, desperate to alleviate poverty and unemployment, allow the creation of export processing zones (EPZs) or special economic zones (SEZs), agreeing not to interfere with legislation, providing military protection, offering tax holidays for as long as ten years as incentives for companies who fill contracts for Gap, Wal-Mart, IBM, Hewlett Packard, Nike, Adidas, Disney, Marks and Spencer, Levi Strauss and so on. According to the Canadian writer and activist, Naomi Klein, wages in China are the lowest, where some such sweatshops pay just US¢13 an hour, days often lasting as long as sixteen hours. With no local taxes paid, settlements swell around such zones without resources for the necessary sanitation, housing, education, medical or transport facilities. Pollution is uncontrolled and crime rises. The local governments hope that workers' incomes will stimulate a supporting economy, but the global monsters buying the products pay so little to the manufacturers that they in turn pay their workers at or beneath subsistence levels. Any whispers of unions result in violence or dismissal.

In the meantime, having outsourced production to the majority world, across Europe and North America towns lose their sources of employment, creating more poverty. And a pair of trainers costing less than US$5 to make, presented in a 672 square foot advertisement as *the* gateway to freedom and achievement, are on sale for over £100.

During the 1990s, many companies were shown up as behaving wholly unethically, and as a result some changed tack, not with their ethical policies but with their brand profiles. A little 'greenwash' goes a long way when the public's loyalty for a brand is based upon vanity. A fair trade or organic option promoted with practised sincerity and marketing cunning, takes the spotlight off human rights abuses and environmental destruction, while not denting the profits. So has the marketing budget of each global corporation risen exponentially during the last fifteen years, some spending over a billion dollars a year.

Needless to say, such vast companies have tremendous political power, through government connections, special relationships, lobbying and donations. In the United States, the IPS puts corporate donations at fifteen times higher than funds provided by labour unions, making it entirely unsurprising how little social or environmental care influences the nation's legislation. Absolute freedom for business is the priority, and the big boys do just what they want. As Sarah Anderson and John Cavanagh at the IPS conclude, 'widespread trade and investment liberalization have contributed to a climate in which dominant corporations are enjoying increasing levels of economic and political clout that are out of balance with the tangible benefits they provide to society'. Companies fight to maintain their power, ensuring a sufficient lack of transparency to continue exploitation and irresponsibility; in the US, a company need not reveal information about toxic emissions, employees, wage rates or contractors overseas.

Since 2001, this unethical thrust of capitalism has been given a tremendous boost. Particularly in the US, but evident across the West, anyone expressing doubts as to the moral validity of a free economy has been labelled unpatriotic. The twin towers of the World Trade Centre in New York were a monument to Western capitalist imperialism, after all. Yet since the declaration of their 'war on terror', any protest against corporate abuse of the environment, nonhuman animals, corporate and consumer freedom, has been squashed as compromising national security and Western democratic values. So do mergers continue, creating more massive and corrupt companies, each with their marketing team assuring the public that they are socially and ecologically responsible. They aren't.

According to the American Institute of Taxation and Economic Policy (ITEP), in 1998 nearly a quarter of the top two hundred international firms avoided paying full corporation taxes. Despite enormous profits, seven of them, including General Motors, Texaco and the now discredited Enron, received more money in rebates than they paid in taxes. Without adequate taxes reaching government, and with so much power resting in the hands of the richest companies, it is inevitable that the environmental crisis is not being appropriately addressed. The Kyoto Protocol was not signed by the US and Australia who felt that it would compromise economic freedom. Indeed, *The Economist* observed the suspicion that 'attempts to control greenhouse gas emissions are part of a European socialist conspiracy to undermine the American way of life'.

In October 2006, the economist Nicholas Stern published his report on climate change. Commissioned by the British chancellor Gordon Brown after the 2005 G8 summit, Stern was asked to look at the true cost. Because of the rise in the price of fossil fuel, together with the decreasing cost of alternative technologies, he concluded that the transfer away from carbon emission would be manageable, at around one per cent of GDP by 2050, a figure agreed by many others in the field. However, to whatever extent the change in global climate is being caused by human pollution, the cost of mitigating damage, he said, was much worse than anticipated, and although the worst hit would be the poorer nations this would not deflect the impact. Basing his figures on a rise of six degrees Celsius in world temperatures, Stern calculated that world output would be up to a fifth lower over the next century or two than it would have been without the crisis. In other words, it can't be ignored.

Some writers, like the scientist James Lovelock, believe we are already too late. The Intergovernmental Panel on Climate Change (IPCC) predicts a rise in global temperatures of between 1.4 and 5.8 degrees Celsius over the coming century; if the Kyoto Protocol's aims are fully achieved, the reduction would be no more than 0.28 degrees, well below what would be needed to sustain human society. The environmentalist Jonathan Porritt still declares we have a window of opportunity within which to take actions that could 'ward off ecological and social collapse'. Either way, extraordinary change needs to happen. To continue marching blindly on is clearly insane.

Yet we are continuing blindly on. A return flight from London to New York produces around 1.5 tonnes of carbon per passenger. Miners all around the majority world are razing vast areas of rich landscape, leaving nothing but the barren rock. According to the UN, 37.5 million acres of rainforest are lost each year, three times as fast as in 1994. Much of it is burned to create short term grazing for cattle, releasing the greenhouse gases, carbon dioxide, methane, ozone and nitrous oxide into the atmosphere. Not only does this precious rainforest landscape provide habitat for half of the world's species of flora and fauna, it absorbs critical amounts of carbon dioxide.

As carbon dioxide released into the atmosphere remains for centuries, even if we were to reduce emissions to what they were before the Industrial Revolution, it is completely unknown if, when or how that reduction would show. As palaeoclimatologist, Brain Fagan writes, the levels of carbon dioxide in the Earth's atmosphere are now higher than at any time during the past 420,000 years, including the four periods of gradual cooling into freezing ice age, each ending with a sharp spike of rapid global warming. A deep ice core drilled at Vostok in the Antarctic reveals incontrovertible correlations between greenhouse gases and global temperature; over the past four major climatic shifts, carbon dioxide has risen from 180 to 300 parts per million by volume, yet currently it stands at 365. As Fagan explains: 'In duration, stability, degree of warming, and concentration of greenhouse gases, the warming of the past fifteen millennia exceeds any in the Vostok record'.

This long period of global warmth provided humanity with the opportunity to evolve from small bands of hunter-gathers to huge populations of 'civilized' and settled consumers, and so to tamper with nature's balances in a way that is far beyond our understanding or control. As we deplete the oceans of fish and the soil of its nutrients, running out of fossil fuels, fresh water and metals, vastly exacerbating the problems of natural climate change, sea levels will continue to rise, drought, hurricanes and floods worsening.

The picture is clear.

To the *Pagan, the selfishness that drives the destruction of our environment is not simply the self-sabotage of a rapacious and profoundly unintelligent species (Gray questions the term *Homo sapiens*, suggesting the more pertinent *Homo rapiens*); human behaviour is desecration. In some places, we are single-mindedly destroying the gods: clear-cutting old forests, blasting mountains apart, polluting rivers, forgetting the stories of our ancestors, the relationships they crafted, the lessons they learned. Indeed, many fear that humanity will negate the viability of all life on this planet completely. Where our impact is not proving as directly catastrophic, we are shifting the balance of ecosystems, repeatedly behaving with a consummate lack of respect. Revealing our ignorance in all its colours, we react with injured pride and surprise when nature responds in ways that don't support human ease, when depleted soil blows away, over-fished seas no longer support communities, when wild fire destroys homes, deforested hillsides slide over villages, when floodplains flood. We respond with indignance when nature reveals its lack of care.

Ancient Greek mythology tells stories of individuals whose arrogance allows them to dishonour the gods, believing themselves to be supremely capable or potent. The word used was *hubris*. Arachne boasted she could weave more beautifully than the goddess Athena; she was turned into a spider not for her lack of skill, but because of her insolence. Blinkered through pride, she forgot that Athena was a force beyond her reckoning, beyond her control or comprehension.

Aristotle spoke of hubris as an act of dishonour that shames another, writing that 'men think that by ill-treating others they make their own superiority the greater'. By belittling another person, we feel ourselves to be more important. By treating the Other as a mere object, we augment our sense of *I*, declaring our own needs the priority, the most prominent subject.

To imagine nature feels shamed by human abuse is to anthropomorphise, but there is no question that we abuse in order to belittle, to believe ourselves above nature's power; it makes us feel safe, important, wise. So do we manage the world around us - other humans, nonhuman animals and the environment - negating the validity or urgency of others' needs. Resenting any need to compromise, proclaiming our selfish desires, we assert our position as the most (or the only) important species, the most significant consciousness.

As a result, we alienate ourselves from the wholeness of nature, losing awareness of the web that connects us all. We declare ourselves the owners, and nature the slave. Whether *I* is just oneself or extends to one's tribe, *it* encompasses the rest of nature. We dismiss any notion of nature as sacred.

Indeed, within *Pagan ethics, this brings us to the next issue: ownership.

Claiming Ownership

While many strands of Paganism find inspiration in later constructs of human thought and society, the natural *Pagan consciously honours the oldest roots within us, too: for more than half a million years, *Homo sapiens* were hunter-gatherers, evolving from earlier hunting, gathering hominins. According to the most recent interpretations, especially of palaeolithic cave paintings, numerous generations of these our ancestors followed the tides of nature, thriving on an acute sensitivity to the human and nonhuman world, awake to other creatures, to the essence of the rain and frost, to the currents of the rivers, the song of the soil, in a way that most humans are now no longer capable or aware of. More easily moving through the visceral experience of relationship, of ritual and altered states of being, processing and comprehending the world more fluidly, these humans lived within communities where the tribal boundaries extended upon the natural threads of dependence into the environment through which they moved. Their ability to survive and flourish relied on every intricate and intimate interaction that expressed their integrated and wholly wakeful place within nature.

Bearing in mind the great length of that period of time in which humans had lived nomadically, the change to settled agrarian life is often described as the most significant event in the development of human society, the Agricultural Revolution. However, to use the word revolution implies it was a single and rapid transition, and one crafted as an active and progressive choice. Many thinkers are now confident that it was neither. A rise in population around fifteen thousand years ago, followed by a brief dip back towards Ice Age temperatures, is more likely to have been the motivation, provoking a sharp need to adapt. Experimentation with food production was a bid to survive. Nor did it happen overnight: in some parts of the world settling came with early farming, while elsewhere evidence points to one happening before the other, the change taking place gradually over perhaps five thousand years.

All in all, it was little more than ten thousand years ago that agriculture began slowly to seep through human societies. Yet a revolution it was in terms of the profound change it brought with it. For, while hunter-gatherers were dependent on nature thriving upon its own intentions, this new society became dependent on its ability to control nature. In its need to do so, the early farmers fine-tuned the notion of ownership.

Ever on the move through familiar territory, the hunter-gatherer does not have to take or accumulate more than will satisfy an immediate need. However, where a society invests in land, sowing seed and tending crops, that land is claimed and defended, as are the stores after harvest. For our agrarian ancestors, with more carbohydrate in the diet, tribes grew larger, women remaining fertile for longer, more children being born with shorter intervals between each one. With the need for surviving offspring, workers on the land, the value of women and children rose; they were owned. As cultivation increased the value of land, tribes stopped following the wild herds, exploring ways of domesticating animals (owning them), which in turn helped to increase the viability of staying in one place. Nonhuman animal milk became more common as mothers were for the first time habitually separated from their children to work in the fields or tend younger babies, and the first diseases started creeping across the species divide (measles, influenza, tuberculosis, smallpox). Indeed, anthropologists often state that our diet and health grew significantly worse as the shift to agrarian life progressed.

Thriving societies could support more complex structures, with chieftains, artisans and soldiers, priests and slaves. Where an excess is produced, what is unnecessary can be exchanged for other resources: so did trade increase, settled life allowing the accumulation of possessions. Yet these changes too don't automatically equate to greater happiness or fulfilment: settled communities had to work very much harder than their nomadic ancestors. Instead of an ongoing awareness of the fluidly moving tribal boundaries that were common amongst hunter-gatherers, these settled edges were proclaimed and fought. When farmed land became depleted or a tribe split, the need to move on and find new lands to conquer created more war than had the flexible edges of smaller nomadic tribes. Archaeology and anthropology reveal societies and their rituals that were more political and hierarchical. It is easy to surmise that the gradual but profound move away from an integral dependence on natural currents and tides left a fear of change, and a reliance on human governance: a step away from integrated and animistic *Paganism.

In the 1790s, the revolutionary English thinker Thomas Paine observed native American culture, both in its freedom and under pressure, writing: 'Poverty is a thing created by that which is called civilized life. It exists not in the natural state. On the other hand, the natural state is without those advantages which flow from agriculture, arts, science and manufactures.' He concluded that civilization functions 'to make one part of society more affluent, and the other more wretched than would have been the lot of either in the natural state'. His words are as poignant today, as the last pockets of viable *uncivilized* culture are worn away. Yet, as we stride through the first decade of the twenty first century, riding the currents of the latest revolution of digital information, we are clearly far from feasibly being able to dismantle the civilized world: the earth could no longer support in a 'natural state' a population grown this fat on civilization's excess.

I am not idealizing the hunter-gatherers. Our pre-agrarian ancestors were still human, grasping, selfish and thuggish. There was no golden age, no fall from grace. Nor do modern *Pagans seek to recreate their world. However, they do seek to understand what has been lost. The fluidity of edges that comes when a people are not burdened by tribal or personal ownership, the sensitivity of relationship and wakefulness to symbiosis that is necessary to thrive in harmony of nature and is possible when there is no drive to control it: these whisper of a co-operative spirit that *Pagans aim for, a freedom of spirit that is held so firmly within the web of nature, within the code of honour. In 2001, the scientist and recent president of the Royal Society, Robert May sketched it beautifully in figures that to the *Pagan speak clearly of energy and intention: as hunter-gatherers, we used about one tenth of a calorie for every calorie acquired through food. Today, around ten calories is used for every calorie we put on the table. As May said, 'In the search for an operational definition of unsustainability, that comes close'.

Although *Pagans talk of sustainability, more fundamental is the quality (and thus tenability) of our relationship with nature - with each other, with other creatures, with the earth and beyond. The same is true of equality: despite its apparent similarity to *quality*, the etymological root is different. Equality is about sameness of form or value. Perhaps because so little in nature is the same, this is not an inherently *Pagan term. Certainly the *Pagan aspires to honour equally, but in practical terms equality is not always appropriate. Relationships thrive that are based upon the most respectful, generous and *relevant* exchange: wakeful honour.

Where there is a distinct lack of equality expressed, however, a perceived lack of inherent value is underlying, and a poor relationship is inevitable. For our ancestors, the shift to agrarian society emphasized inequalities of wealth that previously would have been less prolonged or extreme. Paine wrote, 'though every man, as an inhabitant of the earth, is a joint proprietor of it in its natural state, it does not follow that he is a joint proprietor of cultivated earth'. In the late eighteenth century it was obvious just how agriculture had increased the monetary value of land, and how the 'landed monopoly' who claimed its ownership had dispossessed countless millions without adequately providing for them, producing what he called 'the greatest evil'. Globally, in this respect, the situation has not altered: inequality continues as a symptom of dismissing inherent value, a lack of acknowledged sanctity. Just as feudal estates, then the companies of the Industrial Revolution, treated their workforce as mindless machines, as means to ends, so have our nations declared ownership of tribes and countries through political imperialism, dismissing their natural value. And in just the same way, massive corporations now maintain nations in a state of submissive poverty, using those nations' resources to increase their own power, with no consideration for the invaded country, its people or culture.

The right to own private property has ever been contentious, not least because, codified into a nation's legal framework, it supports such gross inequality. Far from being a *natural* state, it is a convention developed through social agreements more often forged by dominance than respect for another's boundaries. It was not an inalienable right in the US Declaration of Independence, but first mentioned in an amendment written almost a century later: 'nor shall any State deprive any person of life, liberty or property, without due process of law'. This is over two dozen years after Pierre Joseph Proudhon's well known definition that property is theft, 'exploitation of the weak by the strong', notions that were used widely by Karl Marx in his writings of 1848.

Modern anarchist thought holds to this line. The Australian thinker Rob Sparrow explains the anarchist's aim to live without private property, for 'our needs chain us as much as our enemies'. Individual freedom can only be achieved where there is equal access to the means of production, otherwise the capitalists' monopolistic 'control of society's wealth ... enslaves us to them as surely as would a gun held to our heads'. In tune with *Paganism, he is declaring that ownership does not bring the peace of being lifted out of need, but his words still ring with a secular insecurity.

To the *Pagan, nature exists as many layers of integrated consciousness, providing a web through which we can experience that intrinsic connection. To imagine that we own (or should own) some aspect of nature's creativity is an expression of our perceived separation from nature. Where we acknowledge each creature as living in its own right, ownership is slavery. While to own a human being is widely accepted as such, to say the same is true of nonhuman animals may sound melodramatic to the non*Pagan. However, within animism, not only must this be considered, but so it must be for all the nonhuman world. Where we do not engage subject to subject, working *with* a being within an environment (river, human, tree or butterfly), with responsible care, instead claiming the right to own and *use* that creature, our ethics are based within a slave-owning mentality. Standing apart and dominating, not only are we declaring ourselves no longer an integrated part of nature, but admitting our lack of an essential and mutually nourishing relationship with nature (human and nonhuman).

A child born and raised within a household where the primary culture is *Pagan does not feel a separation from nature. His experience is always underpinned by a confidence that he belongs within nature, as an integral part of it. Held within the wider tribe that is not just his family and ancestors, but also the environment, his feet are firmly upon the ground, the wind is in his lungs; naturally he explores those tribal threads that support him, forging honourable relationships. *Paganism gathers those who have lost this inner connectedness within the walled boundaries of civilization, for whom it was broken when childhood wonder was crushed to be replaced with 'realism'. *Paganism recovers the sense of holistic belonging: not simply within a group of people who share some belief or interest, but within nature itself.

The crises endemic to so much human society are based upon this disconnection. Where we are isolated but for a handful of vulnerable human relationships, we live in fear of rejection, perpetually seeking affirmation of acceptance, following conventions, losing our honesty. Without the soul-deep satisfaction that comes with the ongoing experience that *Pagans call natural integration, human nature loses its balance within nature as a whole, and lives become tangles of drives, emotions and obsessions. Craving something that touches the soul, we chase the thrill of winning, of lust, power and ownership, and most tragically, love, never quite managing to quench that thirst for connection for more than a moment.

Like any addiction, the cravings get worse. For failing to achieve satisfaction, we chase the faintest glimmer of a kick, sure that we are on the right path but have simply not yet grasped *enough*. Where ownership is delusion, the quest for more - much more than is necessary - is perfect hubris. Not only do we steal from each other, we steal from the gods.

Belief in Progress

That craving for *more* is a crucial drive beneath the belief in natural progress.

The Lamarckian journey of human evolution as one of inherited adaptations providing constant improvement, however, has no place within *Paganism. Despite Darwin's attempt to emphasize that evolution creates diversity not improvement, the rising escalator of progress popularized by Herbert Spencer can be felt within Western culture even now. There is an assumption that life *should* or *will* get better; there are claims that access to a continually improving standard of living are an innate human right.

In Victorian England, when Spencer was writing, the rapid flow of technological progress was seen as a reflection of human evolution. The various races of humankind, from the affluent to the primitive, were seen as competing for existence in the same way as other species. In stark contrast to Paine's observation of native Americans, the economist Alfred Marshall, often dubbed the West's 'father of economics', wrote a century later, 'we find savages living under dominion of custom and impulse; scarcely ever striking out new lines for themselves; never forecasting the distant future, and seldom making provision even for the near future; fitful in spite of their servitude to custom, governed by the fancy of the moment; ready at times for the most arduous exertions, but incapable of keeping themselves long to steady work'.

So is the notion still prevalent that it is we in the civilized West that are the natural recipients of development, betterment, improvement. It is built into our expectation of economics, as crafted by thinkers such as Adam Smith. In the eighteenth century, Smith spoke of 'the natural progress of opulence', driven by man's innate curiosity and competitive spirit, together with his perpetual need to ameliorate his material condition. Seeking wealth, he believed, was part of the human condition.

In *Essays in Persuasion*, John Maynard Keynes wrote that throughout history up until the early eighteenth century, 'there was no very great change in the standard of life of the average man living in the civilised centres of the earth'. There were periods of abundance, and of struggle with famine and disease, but 'no progressive, violent change'. From his perspective in 1930, however, he decreed that 'mankind is solving its economic problem'. He predicted that 'the standard of life in progressive countries one hundred years hence will be between four and eight times as high as it is today' and that 'assuming no important wars and no important increase in population, the economic problem may be solved within a hundred years'. His argument was based upon 'the principle of compound interest' which, applied to production and capital, created self-perpetuating exponential growth. Since 1930, the average rise has already been between four and sixfold; continuing growth at the same rate would deliver between a six and 12-fold gain within his timeframe.

With the development of civilization since the Industrial Revolution, growth has been woven into the fabric of Western economies. Not only do we expect growth, but the prosperity of our nations now depends upon it. Where there is economic growth, in real terms or simply forecast, confidence inspires the necessary investment to keep it growing, wealth generating wealth for the wealthy. Where those with money have no confidence that their investment will create a larger return, they seek opportunities elsewhere (or protect their resources), leaving an economy to flounder towards recession or depression. The system is thus dependent on excess, the unnecessary, traded to generate wealth, which creates, perpetuates and increases inequality.

In nature there is no perpetual growth. A tree that grows taller than its roots can provide stability will fall in the wind; a plant growing bigger than the nourishment the earth can offer will die. To the *Pagan, the traders' obsession with economic growth is not just illusory and unsustainable, but dishonourable. The land may take generations to collapse under the demand, a nation's strength may fluctuate but hold on as long, eventually breaking under the strain of the illusion. Smaller tribes and individuals crumple more quickly.

Technology has certainly grown more complex, science has given us anaesthetics and the plough: our basic needs are being addressed more effectively than they have ever been before. Many have a prosperity that their ancestors could not have dreamed of, but levels of peace and happiness don't reveal a correlating gain. Not only has knowledge often been gained by one generation to be lost by the next, as it will be again, knowledge has not fundamentally altered who we are. History and religions across the world show that human violence, ethics and fundamental insecurities are the same as ever. John Stuart Mill, writing in 1848, that year of extraordinary change, made it clear that society needed to sacrifice economic growth for the sake of the environment and the well-being of the populace, for what economists value is clearly not the same as what is of value personally or socially.

For example, according to the WHO, suicide rates across the world have increased by sixty per cent in the last forty five years, making suicide now one of the top three causes of death for 15 - 44 year olds: that is one death by suicide every forty seconds, ninety percent of which are related to depression and the abuse of drugs and alcohol taken to escape what is an unbearable reality. Furthermore, twenty times more people attempt to kill themselves than succeed. The figures are an incontrovertible statement about the lack of improvement.

With his caustic clarity, John Gray writes: 'the idea of progress is a secular version of the Christian belief in providence'. He comments that although 'humanists like to think they have a rational view of the world ... their core belief in progress is a superstition, further from the truth about the human animal than any of the world's religions'. As Gray points out, progress was not a part of ancient Paganism; it has no place in it now.

Human Population

To own another creature, or part of nature, is not compatible then with *Pagan ethics, nor do *Pagans bank on the idea that humanity is naturally improving, growing wiser or more peaceful: progress is a myth, a story to teach us of hubris and greed. Twenty millennia ago, we may not have had the need or opportunity to hoard that came with settled living, but human society was certainly as violent and selfish; in part our survival was more tenable simply because there were fewer of us. So do we come to the next point: human overpopulation is not only a serious problem, but one that is far from being adequately addressed.

It was the single most provocative issue for a young fellow I used to know, a lad who was wasting his life, disabled by drugs and a total lack of self esteem. His irrational reaction expressed all too poignantly the underlying sense of his own meaningless life. The deep ecology movement and its protest arm, Earth First!, were torn apart on the same issue in the 1980s. For not only are we producing more rapacious consumers than the earth can support, but we are producing a redundancy. Our species does not need this number of people. That feeling of uselessness lies like a stagnant pool, particularly within young men, provoking violence, drug use and suicide, inspiring further the accumulation of products that might ease the boredom of underemployment, hyping the value of the unnecessary.

Fifteen thousand years ago, as hunter-gatherers, there are thought to have been around twenty million human beings. At the turn of the first millennium of the common era, the world's population is thought to have been around 250 million, a figure which took around six hundred years to double, reaching half a billion in the early seventeenth century. It took a little over two hundred years to double again, then eighty, then a little less than fifty, reaching four billion in 1976. In a single decade, the 1990s, it increased by half a billion, leaving us now with over six billion people. Estimates vary as to where it will go from here; the increase is slowing, with natural fertility dropping, birth rates beginning to fall. Estimates suggest that by 2050 there will be around eight billion human beings on earth.

United Nations' figures put the number without adequate safe water at over one billion. In this first decade of the new millennium, 2.6 billion are living without adequate sanitation.

In 1798, Thomas Malthus warned that population growth would always push to a point just greater than the food supply. Exploring the welfare of the poorest of English society, he knew that those in poverty are the first to suffer; yet, improving agricultural productivity or the Poor Laws (the social security of his time), he stated, would not ease the problem, for with more food or money available the population would simply grow. Famine, war and disease would keep numbers in check, but without significant change, poverty would remain an inevitable part of human society.

With his wholly Christian perspective, Malthus in part blamed the poor themselves, seeing their lack of virtue as the key hindrance to breaking the cycle. A century and a billion people later, Aldous Huxley wrote that overpopulation led inevitably to totalitarian regimes. Two billion later, James Lovelock described humanity as a plague of 'disseminated primatemania', a dangerous disease loose upon the earth.

Malthus' proposed reforms were ridiculed at the time, but change is possible without resorting to Draconian measures. What has proven most effective in reducing population is female education, not just in the majority world, but also in the West. And this is not just education about contraception; it is about teaching women to take some autonomy into their lives, so no longer do they use childbearing as their means of security through war, poverty, suppression and dependence. When a woman knows what she can do in life to generate peace, creativity, community, she will nearly always choose to have few (or no) children.

Crucially, overpopulation is not a majority world issue, but an issue for each individual human being who has the ability to reproduce. In the West, there is now a fear that a falling population will mean too few workers will have to support too large an elderly population. Yet this is the same fear that has provoked the untenable populations in the poorest agrarian cultures: children are required in order to care for the older people. Imagining that the problem will be solved by creating more children of the high-consumers of the West is profoundly deluded.

Within *Paganism, the issue is perhaps easier to discuss, for there is no overt or subconscious assumption about humanity's importance. We are not chosen by a god and especially blessed; like flocks of sheep out on the moors, we are just another mammal, overgrazing its environment to the point of self-sabotage. As anarchists, we know it is up to us as individuals to regulate our numbers. Ensuring a lifelong education about personal responsibility and relationships within the tides of nature, at least within one's own tribe, is a fundamental responsibility. Yet it is also, crucially, in the strength of our tribe that we find ways in which to ride the currents of our passionate human nature, those that cry out to be obeyed: the irrational and selfish desire to have children.

So do I come to the final point, usually called distribution: how we share what we have.

The Need to Share

For an individual within the West to abdicate responsibility through ignorance is no longer a valid option. Indeed, let me relieve you of a little more of that ignorance.

The UN has stated the aim that 0.7 per cent of a nation's gross national income should be given in aid. Five countries come close, including Denmark and Norway. Britain, France and Germany manage a paltry 0.3, while the US gives less than 0.15 per cent, with their focus of aid being countries that benefit their foreign interests. Giving the figures another perspective, in 2003 the US overseas development aid budget was $15.7 billion, while its defence budget in 2006 was $420 billion. According to the UN, the West spends more on pet food than it would take to aid developing countries sufficiently to lift those in absolute poverty away from the edge.

Aid, however, is not a solution. Africa makes up less than two per cent of world trade. Increasing that by just one per cent would bring five times more money into the continent than it currently receives in aid. Though the West promotes free trade vociferously, Western nations safeguard their economies with a tangle of protectionist tariffs, subsidies and quotas, demanded by the major corporations and lobbyists, all of which continue to suffocate the majority world, keeping it in a state of uncompetitive and submissive poverty.

To give a few examples, Oxfam reported that US subsidies protecting its own cotton producers led to a loss of over US$300 million in earnings in sub-Saharan Africa during the 2001 - 2002 season. Over twelve million people depend upon cotton in the region, the typical small cotton farmer making less than US$400 on his yearly harvest. Equally poignant, following the tsunami disaster in late 2004, Thailand's prime minister made it clear that the amount of emergency aid offered by the European Union was less than his country would gain if the EU were simply to end its tariffs on shrimps. The World Bank estimates that 150 million people would be lifted out of poverty by 2015 if the West were to stop its programme of farm subsidies and tariffs.

I could continue with more, but pull back on purpose. After all, what do these figures mean to the average reader? They may provoke a good blast of rage at the injustice of the governments, international bodies and global corporations who seem to run our world. It may seem that our civilization's success has been bought at too high a price; as Rupert Sheldrake suggests, perhaps 'the Faustian bargain is fundamental to our entire scientific, technological and industrial system.' We have sold our collective human soul to demons in order to gain this little control over nature, and now, damned like the sixteenth century magician, there is nothing we can do.

Being aware of the issues is important, and if a task of the *Pagan is to be awake to the effects of each decision he makes then such information is crucial. Stories give us an idea as to what is going wrong, but they are not a clear guide in terms of how we as individuals can best respond. The senseless reprimand thrown at me so often as a child in school, that I should eat up all that was on my plate because there were children starving in Africa, reflects a dreadful impotence: what can we do? Having seen poverty, I would have been all too pleased to share the food I had been given but couldn't eat, but how could I? It was too late.

When it comes to climate change and other environmental crises, it is increasingly clear that we can't afford to wait; we can't let it get too late. That may seem obvious, but too often the slightest glimmer that we might fail is a significant de-motivation to action. We quiver with indecision, only to resolve that it won't be worth the struggle. For many, the salient information provokes a deep dread, and fear is never a sound motivation for the kind of profoundly creative, imaginative and co-operative action that is now required. To the *Pagan then, it isn't about urgency, about last ditch attempts to save the world: what is needed is that we continue to take each step, ethically awake, with as much honour as we can draw into consciousness.

Nature is sacred. very feather and beetle, every raindrop and leaf, every clod of earth and apple tree, every seam of gold and shoal of fish, sings out with its own song, its desire to be what it is, to flourish and thrive as such, integrated within its own ecosystems in its own corner of nature. Such a perspective provides no space for a notion of *resources* available for human use. The only resources we have are those we can give of ourselves: our time, our wit and skills, our compassion and our creativity.

Nature's sanctity allows no valid notion of ownership, of land or animals, seas or skies, and the idea of separate nations weakens as a result. For while the stories of our heritage are an important part of all Pagan traditions, they speak of tribes as they have been, not as they need to remain. Nature's flow of self-perpetuating creativity is made up of countless elements, cells, organisms, creatures and environments, every one a part of some natural tribe, with tribal boundaries neither fixed nor progressive, but moving like any tide of nature. And within each tribe, we celebrate our bonds of connection, sharing who we are, protecting each other within the embrace of that tribe's morality.

The issue is not then *how* we share what we have, but why we share. The Lakota phrase is so beautiful: *mitakuye oyasin*, translating as 'we are all related'. Over a thousand years, each person has somewhere near eight and half billion direct ancestors (the world population was a thousand years ago just 250 million); it doesn't take many generations before we are indeed all related by blood and genes, memories and history. However, it is not just human connection the *Pagan refers to. When we share the same landscape, we are related, for we share water and breath in the cycles of wind and rain, we share atoms in food, through the release of decay that nourishes growth. Through an animistic perspective, we share consciousness. So the *Pagan shares not through a sense of equality, or even honour, but because we are related and, awake to the web, we cannot help but give and receive.

Such poetry finds its feet in gentle simplicity. For each decision we make is based upon our awareness of - and the extent to which we are willing to be aware of - the other beings that make up the world around us and within us: nature. Being awake to how an Other fits into the web of its own world allows us better to understand its needs and in what way we can be a part of satisfying those needs. For it is only when we are not gripped by need that we find peace, whether that need is our own or one we perceive as making demands of us. Yet the first point is always to ascertain what need is.

Near the beginning of this chapter, I referred to that human failing so well exploited by advertising: as human beings, too often we confuse need with desire, both in ourselves and in others. As a result, necessity, that essential ethical touchstone within *Paganism, can be hard to apprehend. The confusion can run deep, further complicated by the fact that we are often extremely skilled at justifying an emotional craving with intricate reasoning. So is the *Pagan obligated by his ethics to understand himself, that he may stand fully in his own feet, in the immediacy of a moment, present to each relationship, awake to the stories of each soul around him, finding his place within the web, confident in what Sartre calls *authenticity*. Only then does he have a chance to understand where necessity truly begins and ends.

It is because it is not always (or often) easy that we speak of *Pagan honour using key words - courage, generosity and loyalty - drawn from the heroic tales of our Western Pagan heritage. In each of the old stories, the hero is seeking something magical, something ordinary that, drenched in the sacred, is extraordinary. Whether a golden fleece, a cauldron or grail, an ancient ring or even home and tribe, each hero is compelled by their own quest as a warrior in search of some quality of immortality. Yet the mythologies do not hold their validity in the detail: it is because the individual, whether part or fully human, finds the strength of his honour that the stories continue to shine with such poignancy, even after thousands of years. It is for that reason that they are still so important to Pagans. There is no single hero revered, one who sacrifices all for the people of his tribe: there are many heroes, each one finding the steps to do what is needed.

Within *Paganism, the individual knows that sitting on his backside and blaming the government is as useless as awaiting the flying entrance of some modern superhero who will fight for justice on his behalf. Just as the old stories tell, the *Pagan must find the courage to act for himself, fuelled by his certain loyalty for his tribe and his gods, willing to give of his own soul with true generosity: he must be the hero. After all, knowing that all nature is sacred, and walking that understanding, requires the honour of the hero.

So does that ethos of honour require us to pause at each crossroads of decision in this increasingly busy world. Instead of chasing life at speed, grabbing every opportunity, we stop, for a moment stepping off the rush of the highway, and consciously allow ourselves the time and space to remember the foundation of nature's sanctity. With sufficient stillness, we acknowledge again the sacred, feeling the threads of connection, the web of nature naturally supporting us, and there find the generosity to accept where another's need is greater than our own. It can take courage to receive less than we wanted, but the visceral experience of the web supports that. Without rushing, the *Pagan perceives the intrinsic weave of connections, of empathy and symbiosis, of co-operation and shared stories.

That web nourishes, naturally. With no external supernatural force, no separate God who prevails as the overwhelming authority, there is no dependence upon something outside of the web for guidance or strength. Each environment is drenched in deity, created through deity, shining with deity, allowing the *Pagan's experience of life itself to be saturated with the divine mystery of deity, of myriad gods.

So does the *Pagan find an honourable balance on the age-old scales of equality and liberty, between what he wants for himself and how that might impact another's opportunities, whether that other is human or nonhuman. He does not quest more, allowing growth to be tidal with decay. He does not submit to his desires, but experiences the currents of his human nature aware of their creativity and their power to destroy, allowing the energy to flow where the intent is respectful. In each situation, he acknowledges which of his tribes (his blood family, the local community, the local environment) upon this web has the most relevance in terms of need, and which is the most at risk of unnecessary harm, and to this tribe he commits his loyalty, holding to the morality of its shared ethics, always remembering that all nature is sacred.

A point made in an earlier chapter bears repeating: if we feel we need to make a choice, we haven't yet all the information to hand. When we do, the path becomes clear. There is no doubt. The weave continues.

PART THREE

WALKING THE PATH

In the Pagan Federation's triad of defining beliefs, the second tenet speaks of the Pagan's 'positive morality': the individual explores his own nature, in order to discover how he might live in harmony within the currents and tides of nature. Doreen Valiente, that key figure in the development of mid twentieth century Wicca, asserted that Pagans were not pacifists, sitting back and letting others fight the good fight: she observed how often it is said 'that to allow wrong to flourish unchecked is not *harming none*. On the contrary, it is harming everybody'.

In this book, I have laid out my understanding of 'wrong' from the perspective of a nature-oriented animistic Pagan, or *Pagan. In this final chapter, I shall explore just why it is that we, as human beings, so often do nothing about those wrongs, and what it is that motivates us to step forward, out of the crowd, with courage, taking responsibility. What is it that inspires us to act through our personal ethics and tribal morality? We can talk of rights theories, of utilitarianism, rationalism or ethics sourced religiously, and these may be necessary when reaching decisions through extended debate, but they seldom motivate the individual in terms of actual behaviour. As human beings, it is not only valueless but fundamentally hypocritical to proclaim philosophical, spiritual or religious axioms and fail to transpose their tenets into praxis. The question is crafted in Paganism as: do you walk your talk?

Deeply suspicious of purely speculative thinking, Kant's maxim was: 'ought implies can'. In other words, any who are able to act morally have a responsibility to do so. A century later, the philosopher Hannah Arendt concurred with her compatriot, criticizing philosophers for the degree of importance they too often confer on abstract thinking. Blaming the mechanists and materialists of the Renaissance and the Enlightenment for creating an abstraction of nature through mathematics and scientific analysis, she felt humanity had been disconnected from earth as a result. 'Action,' she wrote, 'no matter what its specific content, always establishes relationships and therefore has an inherent tendency to force open all limitations and cut across all boundaries.'

To Arendt, it was not just action that was required; it was only through the individual achievement of *public* action that the necessary space and relationships were realized for effective, respectful and responsible creativity: ethical living. Without such discourse, the 'public spaces' within which we freely make and realize our choices would diminish, dangerously limiting opportunities for action. Her experience was based on being a Jew in Nazi Germany but, even having fled to the US in the 1940s, she spoke of the paradox that in America allowed 'the co-existence of political freedom and social oppression'.

Her notion of public action is beautifully in tune with *Paganism, for it articulately weaves together the importance of relationship and co-operation, with the inspiration and support that come with witnessing and being witnessed. However, human nature provides a gap between our freedom of thought and practical action, and that momentary gap is all the time we need to fail to act at all. In *Pagan ethics, as for Arendt and Kant, however noble our ideas, apathy equates to immorality.

We are measured not by our ideas, after all, but by how we behave.

CHAPTER ELEVEN

INTEGRATION AND INTEGRITY

Three drops of inspiration touch the tongue :
the first wakes the soul, the second fuels the soul,
and if the soul does not sing its song, the third is slow poison.

Anxiety is rising like steam through my soul, drenching every thought so that, sodden and heavy, it falls to the bottom of my belly with the muted weight of dread. What had yesterday felt reasonable, sustained by threads of viable relationship, today seems entirely unsupported, and though I keep telling myself that I am simply tired, the collapse of my confidence is taking down with it empires of dreams, possibilities that I had not even been aware I was holding. It now seems inevitable that I shall not only fail in this enterprise, but lose everything I value in the process. The apocalypse, quiet and un-dramatic, is so effective that, within half an hour of failing to convince myself the worry is just tiredness, I have lost my ability to concentrate on anything else. I am at risk now of making some truly stupid decisions. Abandoning my task, I murmur to colleagues that I am taking a break, and head out.

The sun is warm, the wind bringing a chill that cuts straight through me, but it is easy enough to find a quiet spot sheltered by the wall, and I sink to the grass, aware that even as I look out over the garden I am seeing very little, my soul's focus taken up by the slow cyclone within me, and I smile through the storm, giving thanks to the ancestors of my religious heritage, to my teachers who have made it now impossible for me to accept this kind of self-centred, self-sabotaging isolation.

The soil is warm beneath my fingers as I place my hands on the ground before me and, closing my eyes, I begin the prayers, singing softly to the earth with the words of respect, at first painfully aware of how closed I am, able to do little more than acknowledge its divinity, this goddess of earth, ancient mother. The lack of trust is like a veil that separates me, and in my song I call to my ancestors, all those who, generation after generation, managed to make an honourable bond with the land, forging a relationship that was strong enough to sustain both themselves and their families.

Slowly, I breathe, and with each breath I find a little more courage to dissolve the veil that separates me, relaxing my body with each exhalation, feeling the roots of my soul, of my people, more and more clearly, running deep in the earth. And as I give of myself, offering my breath and my trust to the earth, with each out-breath I find the ability to breathe in through those roots. I breathe in the rich dark mud of the land, breathing in my heritage, and every soul who has lived and loved with respect for the earth hums in my breathing, touching my soul, as through those roots I find the sweetest deep nourishment.

When I open my eyes, the grass is shimmering in the early autumn sunshine, in vibrant conversation with every living creature beneath, within and above it, and I smile, watching the wind chasing an occasional falling leaf that ducks and dives, resting for a moment then rising to play once more. A blackbird looks up at me, eyes sparkling as he listens for my song before returning to dig out the worm, his feathers as rich as tar. My whole soul smiles, feeling again the wonder of life, supported by the fertile earth of these lands of home, held by the old gods in their dance of nature. This is not a moment's meditation I need lose as I walk back into the fray: this is who I am, a part of nature, connected into the web of life, of my people, our ancestors and the gods of this land. I give my thanks.

And as I move across the grass, I can't help but be more aware of every step, my soul touching and being touched by the earth. There is a peace between us once again. I am no longer asking for too much. I have all I need. I must walk that remembering.

* * *

Natural Selfishness

Life is not easy. It never has been and I have little doubt that it ever will be. Even in the comfort of Western culture, not currently crippled by war, with adequate employment, housing and social security to support the majority, vast numbers struggle with disabling depression, with stress and illness, and the passive indifference of living without hope or satisfaction. For millennia, religions and philosophies have tried to inspire us to live in ways that their adherents assure will help us find value, but the producers of recreational drugs and modern toys are out there too, pushing buttons in our souls with their captivating advertising, offering inspiration in the form of a thousand paths of escapism. As human beings, when it comes down it, we don't tend to think very carefully about the choices we make. Our core priority is to look after ourselves, seeking out the assurance of immediate solutions and pleasures, focussing on establishing security within the pales of our tribe.

For those who do think, those selfish decisions can feel wholly rational and justifiable: we drive, for example, because public transport would take more time and energy than we can clearly afford; we buy cheap food and clothes believing it is all we can afford, despite knowing that others have suffered in its production. Very often, however, that selfishness is inexcusable, even where we justify it with the stiff scaffolds of reason; and it seldom takes much insight to recognize it as such. Hungry for a sugar rush, a burst of instant calories, we buy the unethical chocolate bar because its high sugar and dairy content is comforting, and - we convince ourselves, albeit superficially - we *need* a little comfort. We may know about slavery in the cocoa trade, about how badly Nestlé behave or who owns Kraft, but we choose to shrug that off and do what we want.

We leave lights on in empty rooms, we drive our cars and drink bovine milk as if to do so were a human right. We fly across the world unnecessarily, we use clean water as if it were free, even though we know all too well that nature can't support this level of demand. We fill our cupboards with detergents, perfumes and drugs that we know wear down our natural resilience, pollute the air we breathe and support industries that torture nonhuman animals. We've heard the statistics, the reports about melting ice sheets that will raise sea levels high enough to flood Western (let alone majority world) cities; whether the climate's warming is entirely provoked by human actions or not, the way we treat the earth is not sustainable given the inevitable changes. We know that bird 'flu, BSE and salmonella are rampant amongst poorly kept livestock. We are aware that the price of multimedia components is falling in part due to the sweat-shops in which they are increasingly made. But still we play along, giving our money to the corporations that continue to create and perpetuate the problems.

Sure, we like to present ourselves as if we are doing *enough* to allow us to call ourselves environmentally and ethically aware, but we don't. Even when we have the information, we don't. Why not? What is it that stops us from putting our ethics into practice?

Fear and the Currents

The first answer is fear. We are afraid.

The reasons for our fear come as a thick catalogue of human insecu-rities, from those specific to our human self-awareness, our ability to expect past trauma to repeat itself, to the more instinctive crises of antic-ipated scarcity and abandonment. We fear we are not good enough, not quick enough or attractive enough, not rich enough or slim enough. We fear we don't have enough. We tiptoe around each tribe that we crave to be a part of, stomping within it immediately we feel we have been accepted, always anxious about whether we might lose our position. We are human animals, playing with reason but carried upon the white water currents of our constitutional emotions.

Because the fear is such a familiar part of who we are, most of us are barely aware of it, or the ongoing strategies we use to deal with it. Finding sufficient consciousness to be awake to it requires us to understand the foundational attitudes and assumptions we have about life, a clarity of self-knowledge, a willingness to explore our own perceptions not only about the world around but about ourselves as well. Without that self-knowledge, the fear remains a hidden but affecting, self-protecting guiding force. And if we are shaken, it floods us. Instead of acknowledging it, facing it and overcoming it, again and again, we use it simply to justify our inaction, our lack of ethical action.

As forces of nature, the fears within our human nature are divine currents. To the *Pagan, they are forces that require reverence but not submission, understanding and not acquiescence. Seeking out those fears that entangle us in the chains of passivity, though some primary causes may appear to emerge, even where they don't it is the acknowledgement of those currents that is more important. With respect for their power within the wide web of nature, the *Pagan's task is to be awake to the experience of their consciousness within his own being. So does he learn to forge relationship with these gods, finding a way to ride their currents, courageously, responsibly, creatively, dealing with all those brutally disabling human insecurities.

Indeed, with courage such a fundamental constituent of honour, I am not convinced that our ancestors would have got away with the fear-based apathy that is so common today. That our Western society allows it is expressed through the 'nanny state', where those who don't break through the fear are mothered by supporting systems set in place by the government: where there is no apparent need to find one's own strength, there is no need for true courage. Apathy is acceptable, the fear agreed as inevitable; social mothering is *expected*. It is easy to be physically, intellectually and spiritually lazy when you know you won't starve.

That may sound harsh, but it does not remove the ethical requirement of a tribe to care for those who genuinely cannot cope. However, while the generosity of care is crucial to *Pagan ethics, so is courage. Each individual is personally responsible for everything he or she contributes to the tribe; those not *willing* to do their part are naturally not supported.

If we are to live ethically, we have a responsibility to be aware of our fears, and to grasp the honour that allows us to move through those fears, so that we can fully live.

Habit and Change

Another reason for inaction is the power of habit.

Although holding to habitual behaviour may be provoked by fear, often it is simply a blinkered perception of the world that stops us from adapting and exploring. We stick to a familiar course, even when it is clearly unethical. It is easy to continue buying the same old shampoo, staying with the bank we've had all our adult lives, reading the newspaper we've always read, even when we know that the specific companies are morally bankrupt. It is easy to maintain a lie, to hide from the truth, to keep pretending we are something we are not, when that's how we have always behaved.

In *Utilitarianism*, John Stuart Mill stated that, 'both in feeling and in conduct, habit is the only thing which imparts certainty'; because the need to make a decision relies on us finding a surety that our choice is the right one, we rely on habit. 'Will is the child of desire,' he wrote, 'and passes out of the dominion of its parent only to come under that of habit'; in other words, that need for certainty is so profound that as human beings we are prone to continue with an action even when we no longer wish it. Habit provides a very real sense of safety.

In all nature, but most especially within temperate climes, change is a constant. In these islands of Britain, on the edge of the world, between the vast eastern land mass and the western ocean, the changes are overt not only throughout the course of each day of cloud, rain and sunshine, but seldom accurately predictable, and further emphasized by the surging and receding tides that are the seasons of the year. All around us, the nonhuman world is in a continuous state of responding to the changes, adjusting to the moving parameters of light and darkness, of warmth and cold. In a theology that reveres these forces of change as divine, nature is perceived as offering us beautifully articulate teachings on how we too can adapt, moment by moment, allowing our human nature to be as flexible as is needed to thrive, never resting blindly in complacency, always ready to move with the wind. Change, then, is not only integral to nature, but learning to embrace it is a fundamental part of *Pagan ethics.

Where the response to nature's wild and perpetual changing is to become entrenched in fixed views, habit is a side effect that provides dangerous blinkers. Instead of adapting, we become brittle, disconnected from the web of our environment and thus no longer sufficiently rooted to be nourished. Our position becomes untenable, requiring more and more determination until, blind to those around us we break, most often flooded by the rage that has fuelled our intransigence. We may believe that our loyalty to one position is honourable, but without the generosity or courage to *give*, our ethics will be flawed by disconnection. Day by day, it is necessary to sacrifice a little security and flexibility in order to behave ethically.

In worlds of change, a cultural mindset that believes the human species is special within nature fuels that instinctive human response to hang on tightly, to control the immediate environment and everyone in it. Because to the *Pagan we are not special, there is an inherent levelling which provides a natural humility and a willingness to compromise, accommodating others' needs, giving in to the flow, adjusting our own consciousness in order to find a harmonious way of sharing life.

How much we are fully able to make the adjustments by choice, and how much the *Pagan's ease of adaptability comes from an acceptance of his own place within the larger tribe of nature, brings us to the issue that has been debated within philosophy and theology for millennia: free will.

Free Will

Within the context of this book, the importance of the idea rests with the degree to which we are morally responsible for our every action (and inaction). Exploring just how little human beings do tend to practise the ethics they proclaim, it is pertinent to question just how much each individual can be held accountable for the decisions they take.

Perhaps because as a species we are so easily inundated with emotion, losing our feet in the flood of energy, taken up in the currents of rage, of lust and fear, thinkers for millennia have repeatedly held reason to be the source of our salvation. The base premise is simply that it is our ability to reason which makes human beings moral agents, and in this we are unique within nature.

In his 1690 *An Essay Concerning Human Understanding*, Locke observed how our human 'power to suspend the prosecution of any desire makes way for consideration'. Commentators interpret his words as a cry for rational deliberation, but I am not so sure the great thinker was that blinkered. Controlling our desires with Enlightenment notions of duty and virtue, or indeed suppressing our emotions through Victorian manners or modern drugs, is not the *Pagan way. In common with the teachers of many traditions, *Paganism holds self-knowledge to be our primary guide. Locke's contemporary, Baruch Spinoza, felt what most benefited humanity was maximizing the understanding of God: 'knowledge of God is the mind's greatest good'. As a monist, and a monotheist, he believed that nothing existed but God, thus nature itself was God, so the deeper our comprehension of God the more we understand the world. His perspective is very *Pagan: 'reason demands nothing contrary to Nature', and thus, he wrote, it is through this striving for knowledge of an integrated and sacred reality that we find satisfaction, minimizing conflict, freeing ourselves from the chains of our destructive passion. As Locke wrote, it is our ability to pause and examine the situation in its wholeness that provides 'the liberty man has'.

Yet the question remains as to how much we can ever truly know. This is where the deterministic view of free will strides in, suggesting that cultural and biological influences are so strong as to make impossible any independent choice; further, through the notion of natural causality, each step that we take is fully determined by what has preceded it, the inherent patterns of natural law crafting the course of every action.

Hume declared the problem 'the most contentious question of metaphysics', yet his own contribution to the debate was poignant. He pointed out that without some measure of determinism ethics are irrelevant. Every action, in other words, has its specific context. Without acknowledgement of the contextual connections, actions must be seen as random and therefore can carry no responsibility. Taking into account the influences that move around and through us, we have a chance to exercise our free will.

Writing earlier than Hume and in an age more saturated with the theological presence of a single divine creator, Descartes wrote of the liberating quality of free will. 'It is free-will alone or liberty of choice which I find to be so great in me that I can conceive no other idea to be more great.' Indeed, he believed it to be 'this will that causes me to know that in some manner I bear the image and similitude of God'. With such a definition, by its very nature free will 'can never be constrained'. Because of this gift of free will, human beings are prone to error, but this is simply poor use of a freedom that requires breadth and clarity of knowledge before being implemented. In fact, he felt sure that a compulsion in one direction or another was a better expression of free will than was indifference, which he attributed to a lack of knowledge.

Schopenhauer's perception contains no gods. In his beautiful piece, *On the Freedom of the Will*, he went more deeply into the human condition. Acknowledging that 'I am free if I can do what I will', he questioned whether we are ever free to *will* what we will: what provokes the will, the wanting, in the beginning? This led him to consider necessity, for if we are driven by need then we cannot truly be free to will. Defining necessity as 'that which follows from a given sufficient ground', on that basis he explains that everything we do is bound within the chains of necessity. Forged through the immediate and natural necessary reaction to each stimulus, our character determines how we act and react, which in turn continues to forge who we are. So is our freedom naturally disabled.

Schopenhauer's understanding of the Will is as the essential force that lies beyond and beneath perception. Indeed, in as much as we can ever perceive it, we feel it as a stream of true freedom within us. Though he didn't imagine it a divine gift, he was in agreement with Descartes in his sense that, through its unqualified liberty, the Will has no inherent morality. Its force can change how we think and what we crave, but no amount of thinking can adjust the current of the Will. Thus, albeit subservient to the Will, it is the intellect that must step in and take responsibility for how we engage with this untamed force moving through us.

Because the Will as such has no specific object or goal, it can never be satisfied, thus to Schopenhauer the only answer was to disconnect from the rack of desire through means of transcendence such as music or meditation. Although Nietzsche was hugely inspired by Schopenhauer's perspective, he could not concur with this call to renounce the world: for him, the goal was to achieve power over oneself. Instead of being overwhelmed by the world, crucially the individual needed to grasp the impetus of self-governed action. This *wille zur macht*, or will-to-power, he defined as the ability to access nature's inherent creative impulse. Dismissing Darwin's theories of adaptation or self-preservation, Nietzsche declared that nature's principal drive was to thrive, to express itself through abundance: life lived to its fullest. Glorifying the dance of riding the current of one's own creative potential, fuelled by the innate strength of life's essence, he wanted to free the human will to choose its own values, not blindly to follow social conventions. In other words, Nietzsche declared it our own responsibility to find and use our will to power, our will to act: our free will.

Writing in the twentieth century, the dunes of human understanding having shifted with the influences of science, Jean-Paul Sartre's perception of the will was not so much as a force of nature as a state of being. He saw freedom as fundamental to human existence. It is only by using our freedom to choose that we create ourselves: with each decision and each action, we construct value on what is otherwise the 'nothingness of being'. Indeed, to Sartre, the only limit to freedom is freedom itself, for we 'are not free to cease being free'. In this way he emphasized what others had said before him: our free will not only leaves us responsible for every action we take, but responsible for what we make of our lives and, indeed, *who we are*.

The American scientist Benjamin Libet added another element into the debate with experiments carried out initially in the 1970s. Libet measured an average half second delay between initial brain activity and awareness of intention. In other words, what we tend to think of as conscious decisions are preceded by a neural electrical build-up that implies pre-conscious intention. The ramifications of this in terms of free will are significant, for if there is to be any valid responsibility or accountability, definitively free will requires there to be fully conscious awareness. While we may stall an act that was initiated unconsciously, in reality we can never know if that command has been taken on board or we are in fact responding to further stimuli we haven't been aware of, the change having been initiated beneath the conscious mind.

Certainly the percentage of our consciousness that is accessible is very small, the vast majority of our being lying deep beneath our awareness. According to the English philosopher John Gray, we process around fourteen million bits of information per second; the 'bandwidth of consciousness' or awareness is around eighteen bits per second. As Gray says, 'Our acts are end points in long sequences of unconscious responses'. On that basis, and with glimpses of physiological process offered by Libet, doubt as to the validity of free will is unsurprising. Yet the notion that we are not fast enough to respond consciously to anything in our world is uncomfortable to accept. Further, it is that belief in our ability to act as moral agents that allows us to take credit for our creativity and achievements, as well as rightly to take the blame for acts that cause harm.

So what is the *Pagan view? Of the many thinkers throughout Western philosophy who have debated the issue, these I have mentioned because their attitudes help to explain the *Pagan perspective, Hume initially perhaps most distinctly. Inimitably accepting of human nature, within his clarity the importance of integrated perception shines through. In *Paganism, hearing the stories of an individual's life and tribal connections, both ancestral and environmental, provides the context within which each individual is capable of choosing. It is with the generosity of honour that we listen, not just with our intellect, but with the soul as a whole, allowing ourselves to feel and understand the other's position. It is the loyalty integral to honour that further compels us to do so, knowing that we are all related, constantly influenced by and influencing the world that we live in.

Freedom is a god, just like the wild wind on the currents of the ocean, and like all *Pagan gods it is glorious and dangerous, nurturing and destructive. There are times when it batters us, times when its energy exhilarates, filling our sails with potential, times when its force is behind us and we race upon our course with its exquisite support, and times when it simply blows too hard, turning us over. Yet freedom is also the softest breeze, both when we crave gentle guidance and when we are calling out for a gale: it barely lifts the hair from our face but will carry a dandelion seed for miles and miles.

Like any *Pagan deity, it is an inherent part of nature, not only around us but also within us. The *Pagan's task is to find that breath of wind within his soul that is his free will: his own will to freedom. For to do so is an act of reverence, a way of giving thanks to the gods and the ancestors, stepping forward in appreciation of all he has been given and all that he can be. Each individual, as a part of the web of nature, senses it within himself uniquely, influenced through blood and landscape, heritage and tribe. Discovering what it feels like inside, he explores how it can be breathed into his fingers, his feet, his heart and his voice, into his thinking, into his every relationship. If he perceives himself isolated, that freedom can tear through his life and his tribe, with the harshly cyclonic wind of selfishness. When he crafts it with honour, the *Pagan weaves his experience of free will into his perception of the web of life, the connecting threads of nature guiding him as to how to express that freedom, with responsibility, with respect, in all that his consciousness and energy touches.

The issue of free will in *Pagan ethics can be further clarified by recognizing that there is no sense of it being a specifically human characteristic. Free will is as much a part of nonhuman as human nature: the divine current of freedom that Schopenhauer called the Will exists within all nature. After all, it is clearly debatable how much (what we sense to be) our freedom, or how we are able to use it, is based upon either our human reason or conscious awareness.

While in Western culture most human beings do have what appears to be a peculiarly acute awareness of self, this is not a superior or wholly beneficial attribute; it compromises our ability to remain aware of the world around us. Within *Pagan ethics, the task of working honourably within this current of freedom is thus more clearly to understand ourselves, but also to be more wakeful to our environment. In other words, it is placing - or indeed, *locating* - our own free will within the web of life that most effectively inspires us to let it flow, and through honourable interaction. This does not require conscious awareness: it requires the simple experience of nature's integration.

Just as some declare the human ability to remember the past and anticipate a future is unique to our species, so some say is the ability to predict and recognize the consequences of our actions. Yet the mess human beings have made of this planet, the suffering we create mismanaging relationships in our lives, does not inspire confidence in our skill to judge those consequences or act accordingly. Nonhuman animals appear naturally more aware of the web of connections, not stopping to consider systematically the effects of each possible action and how an action may be justified, but pausing to increase the level of wakefulness to all present within a given moment. Faced by the consciousness of an Other, an animal makes his choices, weighing up the ease of interaction with his own priorities, his sense of value and necessity, and his drive for freedom.

It is when we are detached from the web, disconnected, that we fail most hopelessly to act either appropriately or honourably, whatever our species.

Empathy or Sympathy

Libertarians may proclaim that they have clear knowledge of the environment, human and nonhuman, and yet still hold to their right to do as they wish. It may be that those most affected by their actions are individuals whom they consider less worthy of respect, further down some medieval chain of being: animals they eat or hunt, workers in factories overseas. Their lack of care, however, from the *Pagan perspective, is simply the prejudice of ignorance, and considering the information available now to all, such ignorance is inexcusably founded upon a determined denial of others' value, upon a lack of care asserted in order to retain selfish pleasure and security.

There can be no defence for valuing others' wellbeing as lesser than one's own desires. The only reason one might acceptably give for doing so is a lack of empathy. It is unwillingness or inability to empathize that underlies all sociopathic and psychopathic disorders. It is that unwillingness that blocks dialogue and leads to conflict. And here we find what is perhaps the most crucial quality that flows as a current through *Pagan ethics.

Empathy is a fascinating quality, and one well honed by human evolution. As a core characteristic of our species, a basis of humanity, it has allowed us to live in tribal bands, in close quarters, without perpetually untenable levels of violence. Seeking out the natural currents, and learning to ride them both effectively and creatively, *Pagans hold this quality of empathy not just as a guide for decision-making, but as a fundamental *motivation* of ethical behaviour.

Kant talked of the moral impetus being founded upon what he saw as a universal drive of reason which, beyond individuated desire, creates an obligation or duty within us to live by that reason. Hume could not agree; to him, our understanding of the world is indeed crafted of reason, but equally of our experience of stimuli and natural *sympathy*. Indeed, our sense of right and wrong, of moral approval and disapproval, he saw as based upon sympathy, which he depicted as a physiological process through which emotions or 'sentiments' are communicated. The nearer or more similar a person is to us, the easier it is for us to receive this communication, so that not only are we observing the person's situation but we too are feeling it. So do we experience another's 'passion'.

The German thinker Max Scheler, writing around the turn of the twentieth century, clarified this philosophical notion of sympathy, laying it down in a more modern era. Scheler outlined four distinct kinds of sympathy, and they so articulately add to my exposition of the *Pagan perspective that I shall explain them by transposing them in part into *Pagan terms.

The first is *emotional infection*; this is the herd instinct, when emotion becomes a subconscious contagion. The collective euphoria or fear that is felt at a protest rally, a football stadium, a party, is a recognizable example; having lost any sense of our individuality, we are identifying ourselves as the larger being. Sharing its consciousness and energy, we are swept up into its response, moving within its cohesion, feeding into it and being fed by it. This doesn't only happen in large crowds where there is high passion: through our naturally shifting boundaries of self, this merging is always happening, quietly but surely, most often when we are barely aware of it.

The second sympathy is *emotional identification*, where that instinctive connection is more consciously shared. Here, though we are retaining our sense of individuality, deep memories of having lost our edges provoke us to perceive and experience the feelings another is expressing. Watching a film, we are moved to tears by the grief expressed by an actor, even if we ourselves have never been in a similar situation: we feel - we experience - a degree of the emotions ourselves, just as if we are remembering having shared the same consciousness.

It is this sensitivity that allows the compassion Scheler describes as the third kind of sympathy: *shared feelings*. Here we are responding to a situation in accord with the other (or others). In *Pagan terms, because we now know how, whether consciously or subconsciously we choose to let go our defensive edges and emote together with that other person. This is an important step, for though emotional infection or identification may create a tribe, that tribal cohesion may be momentary; it is through the mutual experience of choosing to share the feelings that a tribe is more firmly established.

The fourth sympathy is *fellow feelings*. Not only are we here sharing an emotional response, but we are aware of each other's emotions; we are experiencing our own and the other's feelings. It is this level of receptivity that holds a tribe together. Indeed, it is only when we are able to reach this degree of awareness of pleasure and suffering in others that the morality which emerges within a tribe has genuine validity. Based upon an emotional unity, agreed tenets of behaviour are forged not simply through reasoned judgement; they have a foundation of shared experience. The connection is visceral, not only mental.

Crucially, to the *Pagan, this is not only relevant between human beings. Because the *Pagan is spiritually open to the nonhuman world, perceiving all of nature as inherently valuable, as 'people', he *feels* the hillside after the forest has been clear-cut, the flock of ewes when the lambs have been taken to slaughter, the last whispers of life in the polluted river. His natural sensitivity and love of nature may allow an initial receptivity to the emotional infection or identification, but his understanding of tribal boundaries means that he chooses to share the experience of being. To share trauma can be brutal, but we can't morally chose only to share the exhilaration of beauty.

It is poetry to speak of the poisoned earth as grieving or desolate, and poetry is an important craft of communication. Yet, attributing 'emotion' to nonhuman nature can imply a projection of human beliefs and thinking.

However, that is not the *Pagan understanding, nor indeed the natural *Pagan perception; when the integrating web of nature is a foundation of how we see the world, any projection of self onto others is immediately uncomfortable. Instead of emotion, it may be easier to understand this notion of empathy with the nonhuman world as the infection, identification and sharing of consciousness and energy, of essential vibration and intention, and mutually felt response.

An articulate and insightful mystic in much of his thinking, William James encouraged deep introspection, believing (perhaps experiencing) that it was through this process of self-knowledge that we find an ethical base. Describing nature as a sharing of consciousness, and God as 'the mother-sea of consciousness', he wrote of the way in which we can achieve an intimacy of connection through the intuitive empathy of this sharing. As such, his was a wholly *Pagan understanding, and beautifully articulated.

Although Lyall Watson's book *Supernature* has its critics, much of what he speaks of is in tune with natural *Pagan experience. Watson outlines experiments carried out in the late 1960s where the polygraph expert Cleve Backster used the machine to measure responses in plants. He began without expectation, in many ways just playing around, but when he realized he was seeing marked reactions he began to take the idea seriously. What was most fascinating was that the plant clearly responded to the *intention* to inflict harm more than to harm itself. Extending the idea, Backster dropped live shrimps into boiling water beside the plant, recording the polygraph needle jumping each time; the same thing occurred when he set up a machine to drop the shrimp, randomly, with no human present. If the shrimp were already dead, the plant did not respond. 'Backster has found that fresh fruit and vegetables, mold cultures, amoebae, paramecia, yeast, blood, and even scrapings from the roof of a man's mouth all show similar sensitivity to other life in distress.'

The experiments have been replicated by others, but cynics are quick to laugh, taking the implications to absurd limits in their endeavour to discredit such findings. Although scientists declare themselves highly skilled in objective observation, all too often where experimental evidence doesn't fit the scientific paradigm it is wholly dismissed. To the *Pagan, Backster's results are interesting reading, whatever their scientific validity, for they display what is understood as self-evident within *Paganism. Consciousness or mind does not come with being human; inherent within every part of nature, along with energy, consciousness hums within its tiniest building blocks. It doesn't take much in terms of relationship, atom to atom, cell to cell, to generate a response to a force that might threaten that relationship. It would make sense for such responses to be alarm calls that others in the vicinity could pick up. Sympathy, then, is an essential, intrinsic and foundational element of life.

While the word *sympathy* has been in use for many centuries, *empathy* is a more modern term, brought into our language through the German thinker Theodor Lipps and the English psychologist E G Titchener, both of whom used it in their theories of aesthetics around the turn of the last century. I use the term not just because it is better understood, but because the word sympathy has come to imply a weakness of benevolence. We might wonder how that change may be indicative of a growing selfishness in Western culture, but I would pose the simpler idea of the inevitable flow of language changing. Empathy, however, side-steps the connotations of weakness; and it does require courage. To feel empathy, we must be emotionally engaged.

The Tribe and the Wanderer

Observing his late twentieth century world, Zygmunt Bauman wrote of the ways in which humanity too often fails to engage or make relationship, limiting its investment not only with people but with the environment. Using the metaphors of *vagabond* and *tourist*, the former, he writes, is kept on the move by 'disillusionment with the place of last sojourn and the forever smouldering hope that the next place .. may be free from faults which repulsed him in the places he has already tasted'. At sea within and yet holding onto his core uncertainty, this traveller is committed to nothing but perpetual seeking and disappointment. Equally 'extraterritorial', the tourist is constantly urged on by his desire for amusement; for this individual, 'glorified by the chorus of commercial exploiters and media flatterers', the world is given meaning through his own experience of pleasure. His right to live in this way is not open to debate. He does pay for his freedom, but not with care or commitment: 'the right to disregard native concerns and feelings, the right to spin their own web of meanings, they obtain in a commercial transaction'.

While we may think of the tourist as an individual travelling away from home, it is those who have no sense of home that Bauman speaks of, those whose ability to invest in their surroundings has been destroyed or never nurtured. In the same way, commonly cited examples of relativism refer to practices such as female circumcision in distant lands and tribes, our Western understanding questioned, and thus our right to intrude upon another culture's traditions. Yet within our daily lives, it is relativism that is used to justify moral apathy: "it's not my business". Tribal boundaries are perceived or created all around, providing the necessary reasons not to understand or get involved.

As Bauman writes, in another of his typically pertinent indictments, the trick is to achieve a physical closeness while remaining spiritually remote. Both tourist and vagabond 'move through the spaces other people live in', ensuring 'the briefest and most perfunctory of encounters' with the locals, for their most fundamental concern is to evade entirely what is perceived to be 'cumbersome, incapacitating, joy-killing, insomniogenic moral responsibility'. There is no relationship. There is no tribe but that peopled by other drifters who too have no investment

If such people were uncommon, this world, and indeed our species, would be very different. However, as Bauman points out, it is this attitude within our society that sets 'the standard of happiness and successful life in general'. It is because so many behave this way that it is perceived as acceptable. Yet just because *everyone does it* doesn't make it ethically sound.

Empathy requires us to see the other, face to face. We cannot empathize with an abstract such as *humanity*, or with a conceptual Other. Morality is based upon relationships and social bonds. The closer we are to someone, and the more we are willing to listen to the other's soul (their energy and consciousness), and be receptive to what they are expressing, the more we can understand. Of course, not uncommonly it can be difficult; the other feels alien to us, and we aren't able (or don't wish) to acknowledge there is anything that we share. However, the defensive boundaries we raise are often unnecessary, and it is selfishness or apathy that stops us from accepting that we do indeed share a tribe, even if that is as broad as our gender, species or landscape. Further, because each and every tribe is bound by the pales of its own morality, it is in that action of finding and accepting what it is that we do share that we are able to perceive a shared morality, its values and concerns. So do we break through the barricades that provoke prejudice and conflict.

When it comes to empathy, facial recognition is an important factor. Where we know a face, we sense a connection with that person; the vegetarian quip of not eating anything that has a face conveys a deep animal instinct. A face allows us to establish with some certainty whether the individual is a part of our tribe or not. The modern cult of celebrity is built upon the dissemination of photographs through our rapidly expanded media, allowing faces to be recognized: we feel we *know* someone when their face is so often in our home. The media, politicians, indeed anyone with a *cause*, will use faces to elicit support or horror. A person's reputation, voice and actions are in many ways secondary to how we feel about their face.

As we come to recognize the face of a pet, that nonhuman animal becomes special to us, but beyond our pets species recognition is a significant measure of empathy - or our lack of it. Most are tugged by a natural empathy with gorillas and chimpanzees, whose facial expressions are so poignantly close to human. There is an association between the big brown eyes of a fawn or puppy and a human child that makes them a less easy target than a pig or fish that are clearly far from human. When we can't see any human features, our empathy all too quickly slips away, and for good reason in the context of our evolution. After all, through the slow journey that took us from small furry creatures to Homo sapiens, we needed to kill others to eat. Without denying this instinct, *Pagan ethics requires us to reach for an empathy beyond this heritage of our animal instinct; instinct alone will not ensure a tenable future.

In the same way, relationships where there is no (or not sufficient) empathy are self-focused. Our desire for the other is forged of need, welded by our fear that we will lose them. When we have found true empathy, the feeling is of a deeper connection; we not only relate to the other, but feel related to them, soul to soul. We are willing to travel at the same velocity, moving upon the same path.

We must open the bounds of our tribe, and live by honour.

Impotence and Connection

The final reason I shall raise for the failure to live by our own ethics is a belief in the impotence of our personal insignificance. I have left this one until last because it is both simple and fundamental.

In the self-centred mindset that places humanity in a privileged position within nature, especially where that is accompanied by a deity who listens and cares about his extra-special bipedal creation, any sense of one's own insignificance must equate to a disconnection from that belief. In *Paganism, such a perspective is equally based upon personal isolation: it comes from the self-absorbed and conceited delusion that one is separate from nature's web of life. For within that web, not only *can* we each make a difference, but we *do* - with every idea and assumption, with every wave of emotion that breaks through us, with every action and step we take, influencing the world around us with our breath and sweat, with our words of support and our apathy, our energy and our consciousness.

The distinct task of the *Pagan is to be ever exquisitely awake to the web in order to ensure that the difference he is making is always appropriate and positive: honourable.

Simply by changing the way that we live as individuals creates ripples of change, each person adding to the pattern and momentum of those ripples with their every small action. When we no longer expect constant growth, learning to thrive with just what is necessary, we stop our complicity in the demand for a perpetual state of harvest. Informed and careful every time we vote in this global democracy of capitalism, with each penny we spend we learn to speak with crucial awareness to those who have real power: the vast corporations whose money controls this world. Making relationships on the understanding that each creature, each part of nature's ongoing creativity, is a subject in its own right, crafted of life, we allow interactions that are naturally and easily nourished by consensual reciprocity, rich with wakeful care.

*Pagans aren't looking to 'go back to nature' - as some ill-informed clichés still proclaim - but nor do they see the answer to our current state of crisis and decline purely in the elusive salvation of science and technology. What is needed within Western culture is a new philosophy, one that is founded not upon human arrogance but integration. That change comes through each of us working with how we individually perceive and engage with the world, attending to our own inspired relationships and inspiring creativity. Listening to the stories of nature, awake to nature's currents within our own being, we can find both the will and the way needed to create a sustainable human society. As Mary Midgley says, it requires us to focus on 'the nature of our imaginative visions'; and it *will* take creative effort and imagination. It will take wakeful loyalty, sincere generosity and true courage to sufficiently shift our intent away from the habitual comfort of fetid Western consumerism, to find the path of freedom and honour, blessed with sated needs, not with greed.

Mill asks his reader to 'take into consideration, no longer the person who has a confirmed will to do right, but him in whom that virtuous will is still feeble, conquerable by temptation, and not to be fully relied on; by what means can it be strengthened? How can the will to be virtuous, where it does not exist in sufficient force, be implanted or awakened?' His answer was to ensure that doing the right thing was adequately associated with pleasure, and wrongdoing with pain, 'by eliciting and impressing and bringing home to the person's experience the pleasure naturally involved in the one or the pain in the other', for when this is sufficiently embedded, we inevitably act to provoke pleasure and avoid pain, without needing to think.

Though his words are beautifully sound, to the *Pagan this utilitarian argument is unnecessarily theoretical. By focusing upon relationship, where there is openness to the experience of sincere empathy, with reverence for life, interactions come naturally to be forged with honour. The profound experience of connection that underlies *Pagan religious practice provides both the guidance and the fuel for ethical behaviour. It inspires care.

So what inspires us to make those relationships?

The poet David Whyte speaks of the importance of 'moments of exile', when we are poignantly aware of being disconnected from nature, from the tribe. We feel lost in an ancient fog of meaninglessness, a landscape made barren to us by our inability to touch or be touched by it, lost in a crowd of people who don't appear to see our truth or know just who we are. Whyte celebrates the desolation of these moments as integral to the experience of being human. Indeed, it is the brutally conscious effort of stepping from this grey mire that crafts the beauty of our humanity.

Reaching out for the wizened hand of his grandfathers, his grandmothers, the *Pagan takes that step, no longer willing to live passively, blindly reactive and weary. He reaches for stones and roots, pulling himself to his feet, and shrugging off his coat, pulling off his shoes, beginning to feel the wind on his skin, the sunshine upon his face, striding forward, he knows that as he does so he takes on the responsibility of awareness. By sacrificing the ignorance and separation of his apathy, nature becomes as awake to him as he is to nature. Shimmering with life, seething with the vibrant energy of the gods, the world is suddenly the stage of myriad encounters, the mist stroking the water, the wind flirting with the leaves, the earth opening to be touched by the exquisite warmth of the sun. The *Pagan closes his eyes in the embrace of the goddess of night's darkness, waking each morning to whisper songs of devotion to the dawn. He sinks to his knees before his lover, flooded by the surging tide of his adoration, reverential in the presence of his gods.

His honour is, in other words, utterly inspired by the wealth he experiences in every wakefully empathetic relationship he crafts within nature.

~ ~ ~

A badger is shuffling home along its path behind me. I close my eyes, drawing my soul in so as not to be perceived. The first birds are breaking the air, finding their songs, and I look up, watching a small group of deer move through the softening darkness. It was black dark when I made it up here, to the ridge that marks the edge of my valley, and watching the shapes of the trees emerging, hearing the songs that move with the wind, I've been singing beneath my breath, giving them voice once again, the songs of the old dead of this ancient place. With my gloved hands, then bare fingers growing muddy, I touch the earth beneath me as I make my prayers, and like the air and the birds, each creature around me, every part of me feels the changing, waiting, breathing. Now and then I let my gaze rise to the ridge that marks the horizon, waiting, quietly calling.

When brilliant pale gold touches the clouds above, my heart lifts through my soul. Barely aware of breathing, I feel the ridge top as the first tip of light breaks over it in golden rays, and I am transfixed, rising, silently, until the moment when the circle breaks free of the horizon, flooding the sky with light, filling my heart with its inimitable strength.

Every cell in my body wakes to it, opens to it, seeking warmth and such an ancient reassurance ...

My voice hardly touches into sound as I lower my head in the poetry of my devotion. "Sacred Lord," I whisper, "know that you are honoured here!"

~ ~ ~

An Expression of Devotion

This is not about love, or not in any romantic sense of the word.

This intensely sacred relationship with nature, with the land and the gods that most Pagans do strive for, that is at the heart of animistic *Paganism, is a powerful awe. Inspiring attention and care, it calls to us to listen and understand, to sacrifice our own desires, compromising for the sake of the other. It is a compulsion. It brings the raw desolation of impotence when the other is harmed beyond our control. It brings exhilaration at times of ecstatically wakeful sharing. Indeed, in that it is *not* about our own human needs, it *is* about love.

And it is that deep visceral love for nature and its gods that draws the *Pagan to understand the bounds of his tribe, embracing not just his family and community, but his ancestors and his descendants. It is that love which compels him to open his soul to the nonhuman beyond. Accepting who he is and what he has been given, he perceives himself as a tiny moment within the integrated web of nature, as nature, within nature, of nature.

And with his soul naked to the gods, sharing the experience of life with those who share his life, he makes his decisions. Upon their currents, he learns to live with honour.

BIBLIOGRAPHY

Books

Abram, David : *The Spell of the Sensuous* (Pantheon Books, 1996)

Akers, Keith : *The Vegetarian Sourcebook* (Putnam, 1983)

Arendt, Hannah : *The Human Condition* (University of Chicago Press, 1958)

Ariès, Philippe : *Centuries of Childhood* (Random House, 1965)

Aristotle : *Nichomachean Ethics* (http://classics.mit.edu/Aristotle/nicomachaen.html - written 350 BCE)

Ayer, AJ : *Language, Truth and Logic* (Dover, 1952 - first published 1936)

Bates, Brian : *The Way of Wyrd* (Hay House, 2005 - first published 1983)

Bauman, Zygmunt : *Postmodern Ethics* (Blackwell, 1993)

Bentham, Jeremy : *An Introduction to the Principles of Morals and Legislation* (http://utilitarianism.com/jeremy-bentham/index.html - written 1781)

Blackburn, Simon : *Being Good* (OUP, 2002)

Blackburn, Simon : *Think* (OUP, 1999)

Blake, William : *Laocoön* (http://penn.betatesters.com/blakelao.htm - printed 1826-7, now in private collection)

Boersma, Hans : *Violence, Hospitality, and the Cross* (Baker, 2004)

Buber, Martin (trans Walter Kaufmann) : *I and Thou* (Free Press, 1971)

Campbell, Joseph and Moyers, Bill : *The Power of Myth* (Doubleday, 1988)

Carr Gomm, Philip (Ed) : *The Druid Renaissance* (Thorsons, 1996)

Carson, Rachel : *Silent Spring* (Mariner Books, 2002 - first published 1962)

Clark, Henry : *The Ethical Mysticism of Albert Schweitzer* (Beacon, 1962)

Crowley, Vivianne : *Wicca* (Aquarian, 1989)

Darwin, Charles : *On The Origin of Species* (Penguin, 1968 - first published 1859)

deGrazia, David : *Animal Rights* (OUP, 2002)

de Quincey, Christian : *Radical Nature* (Invisible Cities, 2002)

Derrida, Jacques : *Of Grammatology* (Johns Hopkins University Press, 1997 - first published 1974)

Diamond, Jared : *Guns, Germs and Steel* (Norton, 1997)

Dukas, Helen and Hoffman, Banesh (ed) : *Albert Einstein: The Human Side* (Princeton University Press, 1979)

Emerson, Ralph Waldo : *Nature* (http://www.vcu.edu/engweb/transcen dentalism/authors/emerson/nature.html - written 1836)

Fagan, Brian : *The Long Summer* (Granta Books, 2004)

Farrar, Stewart : *What Witches Do* (Hale, 1991 - first published 1971)

Frazer, James : *The Golden Bough* (Penguin, 1998 - first published 1890)

Gardner, Gerald : *The Meaning of Witchcraft* (Weiser, 2004 - first published 1959)

Gilbert, William : *De Magnete* (Dover, 1958 - first published 1600)

Goldman, Emma : 'What I Believe' *New York World* (1908)

Gore, Al : *Earth in Balance* (Earthscan, 1992)

Graves, Robert : *The White Goddess* (Faber, 1961)

Gray, John : *Heresies* (Granta, 2005)

Gray, John : *Straw Dogs* (Granta, 2002)

Greenfield, Susan : *The Private Life of the Brain* (Penguin, 2001)

Harris, John : *The Value of Life* (Routledge, 1985)

Hegel, Georg : *The Phenomenology of Spirit* (OUP, 1979 - first published 1806)

Hegel, Georg : *The Philosophy of History* (Prometheus, 1990 - first published 1818)

Heidegger, Martin (trans John McQuarrie and Edward Robinson) : *Being and Time* (Blackwell, 1962)

347

Hobbes, Thomas : *Leviathan* (http://www.infidels.org/library/historical/thomas_hobbes/leviathan.html - written 1651)

Hume, David : *A Treatise of Human Nature* (Hard Press, 2006 - first published 1740)

Hutton, Ronald : *Triumph of the Moon* (OUP, 2001)

Hutton, Ronald : *Witches, Druids and King Arthur* (OUP, 2006)

James, William : *The Will to Believe / Human Immortality (Dover, 1956 - first published 1897 / 1898)*

Jay, Peter : *Road to Riches or The Wealth of Man (*Weiddenfeld and Nicolson, 2000)

Kant, Immanuel : *The Metaphysics of Morals* (CUP, 1996 - first published 1785)

Kennedy, James : *Herbert Spencer* (Knight, 1978)

Keynes, John Maynard : *Essays in Persuasion* (Macmillan, 1984)

Kierkegaard, Søren : *The Sickness unto Death* (Princeton University Press, 1941 - written 1849)

Klein, Naomi : *No Logo* (Flamingo, 2001)

Lamond, Frederic : *Fifty Years of Wicca* (Green Magic, 2004)

Laurie, Erynn Rowan : *'The Truth Against the World'* (http://www.seanet.com/~inisglas/ethics.html)

Lévinas, Emmanuel (trans Michael Smith and Barbara Harshav): *Entre Nous* (Athlone, 1998)

Locke, John : *An Essay Concerning Human Understanding* (Penguin, 1998 - first published 1690)

Leopold, Aldo : *A Sand County Almanac* (OUP, 194*9)*

Lucas, Caroline : 'Low Carbon Future' *Resurgence* (September/October 2006)

Lyotard, Jean-François : *The Postmodern Condition* (Manchester University Press, 1986)

Magee, Bryan : *The Story of Philosophy* (Dorling Kindersley, 1998)

Marshall, Alfred : *Principles of Economics* (seventh ed., Macmillan,

1916)

Matthews, Eric : *Twentieth Century French Philosophy* (OUP, 1996)

May, Robert : *'Are we in Crisis?'* (http://www.nhm.ac.uk/nature-online/environmental-change/fathom-areweincrisis/science-the-natural-world-and-public-opinion-are-we-in-crisis.html)

McGinn, Colin : *Minds and Bodies* (OUP, 1997)

Midgley, David (Ed) : *The Essential Mary Midgley* (Routledge, 2005)

Midgley, Mary : *Science as Salvation* (Routledge, 1992)

Mill, John Stuart : *On Liberty* (Penguin, 1974 - first published 1859)

Mill, John Stuart : *Utilitarianism* (Hacket, 2002 - first published 1863)

Moran, Dermot : *Introduction to Phenomenology* (Routledge, 2000)

Moran, Dermot : *The Phenomenology Reader* (Routledge, 2002)

Myers, Brendon : *'The Ethical Paradigm of* Druidism'
    (http://www.druidry.org, 1996)

Myers, Brendon : *The Mysteries of Druidry* (New Page, 2006)

Naess, Arne (trans David Rothenberg) : *Ecology, Community and Lifestyle* (CUP, 2003)

Naess, Arne (trans Roland Huntford) : *Life's Philosophy* (University of Georgia Press, 2002)

Neuberger, Julia : *The Moral State We're In* (Harper Collins, 2005)

Nietzsche, Friedrich : *A Nietzsche Reader* (Penguin, 1977)

Nietzsche, Friedrich : *Beyond Good and Evil* (Penguin, 1973)

Nussbaum, Martha C : *Frontiers of Justice* (Belknap Harvard, 2006)

Paine, Thomas : *Common Sense* (Penguin, 2004 - first published 1776)

Paine, Thomas : *The Rights of Man* (Dover, 1999 - first published 1791)

Passmore, John : *Man's Responsibility for Nature* (Duckworth, 1974)

Pearson, Keith Ansell and Large, Duncan (Ed) : *The Nietzsche Reader* (Blackwell, 2006)

Plato : *Phaedo* (http://classics.mit.edu/Plato/phaedo.html - written 360 BCE)

Rawls, John : *A Theory of* Justice (rev. ed. Belknap Press, 1999)

Regan, Tom : *Animal Rights, Human Wrongs* (Rowman and Littlefield,

2003)

Rodman, John : *'Four Forms of Ecological Consciousness Reconsidered' Ethics and the Environment* (Prentice-Hall, 1983)

Rousseau, Jean Jacques : *The Social Contract* (http://www.consti tution.org/jjr/socon.htm - written 1762)

Ruskin, John : *Fors Calvigera: letters to the workmen and labourers of Great Britain* (George Allen, 1884)

Ryder, Richard : *Painism:A Modern Morality* (Centaur Press, 2001)

Sartre, Jean-Paul (trans Hazel Barnes) : *Being and Nothingness* (Routledge, 2003 - first published 1943)

Safranski, Rüdiger : *Nietzsche: A Philosophical Biography* (Granta, 2002)

Schopenhauer, Arthur (trans E Payne) : *The World as Will and Representation* (Dover, 1966 - first published 1819)

Schopenhauer, Arthur : *On the Freedom of the Will* (CUP, 1999 - first published 1839)

Scruton, Roger, Peter Singer, Chrstopher Janaway, Michael Tanner: *German Philosophers: Kant, Hegel, Schopenhauer and Nietzsche* (OUP, 1997)

Sessions, George (Ed) : *Deep Ecology for the Twenty First Century* (Shambhala, 1995)

Shakespeare, William : *Richard* III (Arden/Methuen, 1985 - written 1592-3)

Sheldrake, Rupert : *The Rebirth of Nature* (Century, 1990)

Singer, Peter : *Animal Liberation* (Pimlico, 1995 - first published 1975)

Singer, Peter (Ed) : *Ethics* (OUP, 1994)

Singer, Peter : *Practical Ethics* (CUP, 1993)

Smith, Mark J (Ed) : *Thinking Through the Environment* (Routledge, 1999)

Sophocles : *The Theban Plays* (Penguin, 1947 - first published c. 440 BCE)

Sparrow, Rob : *'Anarchist Politics and Direct Action', Versions of*

Freedom: An Anthology of Anarchism (Visions of Freedom
Collective, 1996)

Spinoza, Baruch : *Ethics* (Penguin, 2005 - first published 1677)

Thoreau, Hentry David : *The Portable Thoreau*, Ed Carl Bode (Viking
Portable Library, 1977)

Wallis, Robert and Johnson, Nathan : *Galdrbok* (Wykeham Press, 2005)

Warburton, Nigel : *Philosophy: The Classics* (second ed. Routledge,
2001)

Warnock, Mary : *Making Babies* (OUP, 2002)

Watson, Lyall : *On the Nature of Things* (Sceptre, 1990)

Watson, Lyall : *Supernature* (Anchor Press, 1973)

Wittgenstein, Ludwig : *Tractatus Logico-Philosophicus* (Routledge,
2001 - first published 1921)

Wittgenstein, Ludwig : *'A Lecture on Ethics' Philosophical Review 74-1*
(1965)

Wollstonecraft, Mary : *A Vindication of the Rights of Women* (Penguin,
1972 - first published 1792)

Wordsworth, William : *'The World is too much with us; late and soon'*
(http://www.everypoet.com/Archive/Poetry/William_Wordsworth,
1804)

Valiente, Doreen : *An ABC of Witchcraft Past and Present* (Hale, 1994 -
first published 1973)

Velmans, Max: *Understanding Consciousness* (Routledge, 2000)

Young, Julian : *Schopenhauer* (Routledge, 2005)

Websites

The Druid Network : http://druidnetwork.org

The Great Ape Project : http://www.greatapeproject.org

The Order of Bards Ovates and Druids : http://druidry.org

The Pagan Federation : http://www.paganfed.org

John F Wright's Compilation of Triads : http://gamall-
steinn.org/Leabharlann-org/triads.htm

INDEX

abortion 65, 215, 217

adolescence 171

advertising 94, 140, 226, 235, 293, 315

Agricultural Revolution 301

anarchy 41-43, 94, 120, 174, 184

ancestors 18, 49-52, 127-8, 137, 206,
    222, 269, 300-4, 314

animal testing 230, 254-5

animism 3, 14, 15, 29, 56-7, 146, 204,
    216, 223, 240, 249-50, 278, 281, 305,
    315

anthropomorphization 14, 252, 283

Antigone 90

apathy 100, 119, 138, 151, 246, 319,
    324, 338

Aquinas, Thomas 80, 232

Arendt, Hannah 318-9

Aristotle 53, 69-70, 89, 173, 231, 252,
    261, 278, 299

Assisi, Francis of 232

atheism 82, 272, 288-9

attachment 177-9, 183

Augustine 53, 261

authenticity 142, 197-8, 203, 205, 217,
    243, 315

authority 36, 39-42, 79, 80-1, 83, 87, 89-
    91, 103, 119, 125, 161, 165, 172, 286,
    289

autonomy 36-9, 44, 104, 125, 201, 203,
    311

Ayer, AJ 192-3

Bacon, Francis 263-4, 267

Bates, Brain 33

Bauman, Zygmunt 151, 155, 159-60,
    162, 137-8

becoming 194, 196-9, 205

belief 4, 9, 12-3, 26, 63, 65-6, 69, 81-2,
    128, 133, 168, 177, 191, 215, 235,
    289, 306, 309

Benedict XVI, Pope 119

Bentham, Jeremy 77-8, 100, 221, 232,
    241

Bible, The 4, 80, 112, 144, 187, 231, 260

birth 24, 79, 200, 216, 277, 310

Blackburn, Simon 63, 235

Blake, William 23, 266, 268

Boersma, Hans 160

boundaries 65-6, 69, 175, 181-2, 188,
    220, 237, 253, 275, 280, 301-6. 314,
    334-5, 338-9

Bowlby, John 177

Brehon law 106, 120

Brentano, Franz 146

Bruno, Giordano 263

Buber, Martin 160-1

Buddhism 13, 288

Campbell, Joseph 202

capitalism 43, 265, 291, 293, 296, 341

care 4, 11, 14, 77, 80, 217, 235-9, 245, 254-5, 324, 342, 344

Carr Gomm, Philip 29

carrots, killing 250

Carson, Rachel 270

Categorical Imperative 75, 161

Celtic 15, 106, 108, 126, 159

certainty 45, 76, 80, 105, 189, 198, 325

Chain of Being 258-61, 264, 33

change 13, 16-7, 20, 21, 39, 45, 49-51, 55, 92, 120, 140, 183, 253, 256, 258, 260, 267, 270, 292, 302, 325-6, 341

childhood 71, 172-4, 177, 306

children 20, 51, 84, 86, 114, 149-50, 168-74, 213, 215, 294, 301-2, 311-3

chocolate 148-50, 322

Christianity 3, 21-2, 24, 25, 28, 52-4, 80-3, 135, 138, 195, 231, 258, 263, 267

Civil War 24, 28, 87, 89, 127

climate change 270, 287, 297-9, 313

commitment 184, 186, 196, 338

communication 57, 156-7, 161, 184, 283

community 10-12, 19, 43, 60, 64-6, 84, 104, 108, 136, 175, 206, 221-2, 229, 236, 244-6, 253, 275

compassion 73, 109, 195, 292, 335

complacency 38, 78, 220, 247, 271, 326

complicity 6, 43, 138, 182, 206, 221, 229, 248, 254, 341

connection 3, 23, 42, 58, 129, 146-7, 152, 156, 161, 169, 175, 177-8, 186, 278-80, 305-6, 314, 316, 334-6, 340, 342

conscience 68, 71, 87, 92

consciousness 39, 52-60, 141, 143-7, 181, 194, 197-201, 204-5, 216-8, 223, 239-43, 249-53, 278-81, 315, 324, 330, 334, 336-7

consent 181, 207, 217

consequentialism 79

consumerism 5, 34, 92, 271, 287, 296, 310, 341

contract theory 89-91, 238, 258

contraception 215, 311

Copernicus, Nicholaus 255, 262-3

counter-culturalism 23-4, 36, 40, 44, 99, 116, 118, 266

courage 66, 108, 116, 127-30, 138-9, 142, 147, 174, 179-80, 186, 206, 210, 253, 276, 280, 315-6, 324, 326, 337, 341

cows 149, 235,

creation 82, 232, 258-61

creativity 13, 18, 51, 55, 58, 138, 141, 171-2, 185, 197, 246, 270, 278, 290-1, 305, 311, 314, 317, 319, 330, 341

creator, divine 69, 133, 135, 138, 190-1

Crowley, Aleister 25, 99, 101, 115-6

Crowley, Vivienne 32

Crowther, Patricia 103

cunning folk 21-3, 26-7, 111, 114

cycles of nature 12, 25, 30-31, 32, 135, 141, 315

dairy 149, 249, 322

darkness 3, 10, 39-40, 50, 325, 343

Darwin, Charles 90, 233, 266-7, 270, 273, 306, 329

da Vinci, Leonardo 233

death 49-51, 137, 139-143, 182-3, 203-6, 210-11, 229, 243, 255, 309,

decay 39, 53, 140, 223, 315

Deep Ecology 274, 310

deforestation 269-70, 299

deity, Pagan 12-5, 26, 32, 57, 113, 133, 191, 211, 288-90, 316-7, 331

deity, Christian 15

Dennett, Daniel 145

de Lamarck, Jean-Baptist 266-7, 306

de Quincey, Christian 144-5

Derrida, Jacques 45

Descartes, René 72, 143-5, 199, 232, 264, 269, 276, 281, 328-9

determinism 327-8

devotion 10, 14, 34, 80, 81, 286, 344

disconnection 52, 132-5, 195, 199, 271, 306, 319, 326, 333, 342

diversity, Pagan 11-2, 15, 16, 35, 46, 104, 120, 288

diversity, through evolution 75, 267, 273, 277

divorce 124, 185

Dostoevsky, Fyodor 83

drugs 6, 38, 66, 79, 137, 203, 210, 212-3, 223-4, 227, 229, 243, 248, 255, 271, 309-10, 322-3

Druidry 5, 15, 24-31, 46, 104-7, 109, 112, 115, 118-9, 126, 156

dualism 52-4, 143-5, 151-2, 199, 204, 261, 264, 277, 284, 289

duotheism 15, 26

Dworkin, Andrea 26

ecstasy 47, 58, 88

Eden, Garden of 53, 269

edge 10, 21, 55, 57, 85, 108, 111, 119, 137, 156, 160, 175, 181-2, 216, 302-3, 334-5

education 11, 24, 77, 91, 92, 173, 232, 265, 295, 311

Einstein, Albert 44, 69, 268, 290

embryo 79, 213-7

Emerson, Ralph Waldo 266

emotion 54, 71-4, 76-9, 134, 156, 179, 193, 203, 216, 238, 248, 266, 323, 327, 334-7

empathy 73-4, 127, 134, 147, 157, 175, 195, 209, 292, 333, 336-7, 339-40, 343-3

energy 25, 42, 52, 55-9, 70, 72, 73, 145-7, 156, 181, 200, 208-9, 217, 278-9, 334, 336-7

Engels, Friedrich 93

Enlightenment 28-9, 31, 116, 266, 318, 327

environment 36, 38, 43, 130, 198, 212, 218, 226-8, 240, 243, 248, 257-8, 274-5, 278-81, 283, 286, 296-300,

305, 316-7, 332, 333, 337

Epicurus 83

equality 86-8, 91, 93, 155, 172, 179-80, 182, 245, 275, 291, 294, 303-5, 315, 317

euthanasia 78, 148, 205-8

evil 40, 42, 78, 81, 132-40, 151, 255, 304

evolution 90, 243, 266-7, 269, 306-7, 333, 340

existentialism 94, 138, 196, 205

experimentation 214, 219, 229-30, 237, 262-3

face 126-7, 130, 135, 137, 138, 142, 155-7, 160-7, 172-3, 178, 283, 339

family 64, 66, 84, 86, 119, 157-8, 183, 186, 213, 280

Fawkes, Guy 127

fear 21-2, 39, 50-1, 63, 65, 78, 89, 92, 103, 128, 133-5, 138, 177-9, 188, 211, 225, 229, 231, 270, 273, 306, 323-5

feminism 15, 26, 113-4, 136, 263

fertility 10, 26, 51, 212, 310

festivals, Pagan 30-1, 50-1, 203, 287

food 141, 148, 150, 219, 221-7, 240, 246-7, 303, 322

Frazer, James 24-5, 32

freedom 23, 38, 47, 64, 71, 74, 85, 89-90, 92-5, 120, 125, 128, 137-8, 161, 175, 183, 188, 197, 199, 202-3, 232, 252, 265, 296-7, 303, 305, 319, 328-

9, 331-2, 338, 341

free will 138-9, 196, 326-32

future 183-6, 217, 243, 307, 340

Galileo 262

Gardner, Gerald 15, 26-7, 30, 99-102, 115

generosity 86, 109, 127-30, 138-9, 147, 159, 160, 172, 174, 179-80, 186, 200, 206, 210, 253, 280, 315-6, 326, 341

Genesis 231

ghost in the machine 143, 145, 239

Gilbert, William 262-3

Globalization 93, 149, 152, 291, 293

Goldman, Emma 93-4

Grail 199-201, 315

Graves, Robert 26

Gray, John 76, 234, 288, 299, 309, 330

Great Ape Project 244

habit 138, 172, 182, 325-6

handfasting 185

Harris, John 207-8, 236

Heathen 15, 31-2, 107-9, 120

Hegel, Georg 58, 63, 93, 182

Heidegger, Martin 142-3, 155, 183, 197-8, 201, 204

Heraclitus 55

heresy 41, 44-7, 66, 94, 115, 197, 258

hero 14, 128, 164, 171, 315-6

hierarchy 40-3, 165, 174, 231, 246, 258-61, 302

Hinduism 10, 31, 102

Hobbes, Thomas 72, 89-90, 94

homicide 125

honesty 3, 117, 130, 139, 143, 147, 151, 159, 167, 169-75, 186-8, 200, 253, 280

honour 124-30, 139, 147, 160, 162-3, 165-7, 172, 177-84, 186-9, 197-203, 205-11, 216-7, 248, 253-5, 276, 286, 304, 314-7, 324-5, 331-3, 340, 341-4

honour killings 125

hospitality 108-9, 160

hubris 281, 299, 306

Hume, David 31, 72-3, 77, 118, 238, 330, 333

hunter-gatherer 49, 51, 169, 260, 298, 300-3, 310

Hurricane Katrina 37

Hutton, Ronald 116, 118

hypocrisy 5, 43, 66, 184, 186, 228, 254, 287, 318

identity 16, 55, 57, 100, 105, 107, 124, 129, 142, 156, 169, 175, 181-2, 196-7, 204, 206, 216, 221, 249, 275, 280, 293

industrialization 172, 270

Industrial Revolution 23, 265-6, 298, 304, 308

I-it 161, 164, 172, 179, 181, 191, 210, 227, 239, 276

imagination 197, 240, 264, 266, 341

intention 42, 47, 55-60, 69, 141, 146-7, 156, 175, 184-6, 190-1, 199-200, 204, 217, 251-2, 255, 278-83, 286, 290, 301, 303, 330, 336

intuition 68, 143, 150, 190, 266

Iron Age 28

Islam 43, 53, 81-2, 111, 225, 258, 261, 263

I-Thou 160

IVF 211-5

James, William 160, 266, 278, 336

Jealousy 54, 134, 179-81, 292

Judaism 155, 187, 225, 258

Kant, Immanuel 58, 66, 71, 73-5, 82, 128, 130, 161, 232, 239, 278, 318-9, 333

Keynes, John Maynard 307

Kierkegaard, Søren 182

Klein, Naomi 295

knowledge 17, 21, 23, 54, 72, 80, 98, 105, 107, 193-4, 264, 308, 327-8

Kyoto Protocol 272, 297

Lamond, Frederic 101, 103

language 4, 7, 45, 54, 142, 146, 192-3, 198, 207, 220, 239, 240, 242-3, 245, 262, 277, 337

Laurie, Erynn Rowan 109, 111, 126

Leopold, Aldo 275

Lévinas, Emmanuel 80, 154-7, 160

Libet, Benjamin 330

Linsell, Tony 108, 111

Locke, John 24, 46, 87, 89, 236, 242, 327

love 3, 12, 14, 34-5, 52, 58, 80, 101-3, 105, 169-70, 175-81, 183-4, 186-7, 269, 306, 344

Lovelock, James 269, 271, 273, 297, 311

love thy neighbour 5, 80

loyalty 86, 108, 109, 116, 126, 127-30, 139, 147, 159, 174, 178-80, 185, 186, 253, 280, 296, 316-7, 326, 331, 341

Lucas, Caroline 292

lust 13, 52, 134, 139, 211, 291, 292, 306, 327

Lyotard, Jean-François 45

MacIntyre, John 101, 103, 246-7

magic 4, 16-7, 21-3, 25-6, 33, 51, 99, 103-4, 112, 114, 261-2

Maimonides 54, 232

Malthus, Thomas 310-11

marriage 124, 126, 158, 184-6

Marshall, Alfred 307

Martin, Richard 233

Marx, Karl 82, 88, 93-4, 305

materialism 145, 191, 235, 267, 268, 277, 281, 284, 318

Mathers, Samuel MacGregor 25, 116

McGinn, Colin 219, 234, 250, 255-6

me and you 161, 163-67, 170, 175, 179-80, 184, 187, 286

meaning of life 104, 145, 155, 189-96, 198-202, 338, 324

means to an end 161, 165, 178, 232, 304

meat 222, 224-5, 246, 249

memory 42, 156, 204, 216, 243, 251, 271, 284, 314, 334

Midgley, Mary 75, 77, 108, 144, 153, 221, 237, 264-5, 273, 276, 341

Mill, John Stuart 78, 100, 154, 198, 276, 309, 325, 341

monogamy 187

monotheism 9, 31, 36, 45, 80, 258

mother 6, 26-7, 172, 175, 181, 217, 230, 302

Myers, Brendan 105, 107

Mythology 14, 15, 17, 24, 28-9, 31, 46, 99, 199-202, 231, 260, 263, 299, 316

Naess, Arne 274-5, 280

Native American 16, 33-4, 302, 307

natural law 69-71, 80, 83, 87, 89, 327

nature - defined 276-7

necessity 213, 246. 248, 250, 282, 286, 293, 315, 328, 332

Neuberger, Julia 173

New Age 3, 34

Newton, Isaac 44, 72, 115, 266, 268

Nichols, Ross 30

Nietzsche, Friedrich 82, 91, 136, 195, 201-2, 209, 273-4, 329

Nine Noble Virtues 107

nonhuman animals 136, 213, 219-56, 267, 278, 296, 305, 323, 332

Nussbaum, Martha 201, 252, 278

object 56, 155, 160-7, 170-1, 178, 182, 232, 239, 277, 300
objectivity 7, 15, 152, 267, 337
occult 16, 25-6, 102, 115-6, 262, 283
Order of Bards Ovates and Druids, The 104
Other 154-7, 159-63, 166-7, 169-70, 174-5, 178-81, 183, 198-9, 255, 282-3, 300, 315, 332. 339
ownership 106, 181, 202, 286, 291, 300-6, 314

Pandora's Box 260
Pascal, Blaise 196
Pagan Dawn 103, 246, 248
Pagan Federation, The 12, 248, 318
pagan, Latin definition 41
pain 50, 76-9, 85, 100, 203. 205-7, 215-6, 224, 227, 230, 232, 242-3, 245, 250-2, 274, 342
Paine, Thomas 87-9, 302, 304, 307
painism 78
pale 136-8, 157, 206, 222, 237, 322, 339
paradise 53, 128, 139-40, 260, 263
paradox 9-10, 187, 319
parent 71, 113-4, 168-72, 177, 217, 222, 224, 237, 252
patterns of nature 5, 19, 29, 38, 44-7, 49, 51-3, 55-9, 69-70, 93, 115, 181, 216,

240, 243, 268, 290, 327, 341
PEBBLE 112
people 65, 241, 335
persecution 26-7, 111, 113-4
person 79, 133, 157, 159-66, 170, 179, 215-6, 234-43, 245
Pert, Candace 216
Pets 221, 228, 237, 312
Pigs 85, 101, 223-5, 228, 340
Plato 52-3, 55, 81, 89, 94, 139-40, 143, 260-1, 269
play 174
pollution 76, 226, 269, 272, 285, 292, 295, 297
polyamory 187
polytheism 12, 15, 31-2, 141, 191, 266, 288, 291
Popper, Karl 44, 94
population, human 13, 117, 140, 212, 224, 226, 249, 269, 292, 298, 301, 303, 307, 309-11
postmodernism 29, 44, 151, 155
poverty 84, 140, 173, 234, 265, 292, 294-5, 302, 304, 310-3
prejudice 69, 111, 136, 167, 220, 222, 237, 240, 245, 251, 254, 276, 333, 339
presence 161-2, 171, 197, 198-9, 202-3, 205, 210, 217, 243, 276, 281
primates 86, 136, 177, 221, 229, 235
progress 36, 38, 88. 94, 209, 264, 306-7, 309

property 87, 185, 231, 233, 237, 304-5

protein 222, 225-6, 249

Proudhon, Pierre Joseph 83, 304

psychotherapy 3, 6

Rawls, John 91

reason 70-74, 76-7, 87, 130, 139, 143-5, 199, 203, 209, 236-41, 247-50, 267-8, 323, 327, 333-4

reason, divine 58, 71, 80-1, 144, 232, 263-5

reason, natural 4-6. 28-9, 54, 70, 134, 211, 231-2, 281, 327

reason, universal 58, 74-5, 153, 333

rebirth 32, 39, 50, 141

reciprocity 160, 180, 184, 210, 238, 341

Regan, Tom 240, 254-5

relativism 75, 81, 118-9, 338

Renaissance 25, 72, 103, 172, 191, 318

resource 37, 54, 138, 142, 144, 174, 177, 183, 208, 212, 215, 219, 234, 254, 255, 264, 282-3, 291, 314

respect 4-6, 51, 66, 130, 138-9, 160, 165-7, 171, 174, 178, 180, 187-8, 232, 252, 278, 304, 317

responsibility 6, 42-4, 68, 71, 91, 94, 104, 130, 138-9, 140, 147, 149-50, 162, 168, 171-4, 178, 180, 183, 196, 198, 202, 217, 236-9, 255, 280, 286, 311-2, 318, 325, 328-30, 338, 342

rights 77, 85-8, 90, 93, 98, 113, 160, 213, 227, 233, 238, 244-5, 250, 258, 296, 318

Rodman, John 275, 278, 285

Roman 21, 26, 27-8, 41, 42, 53, 81, 116, 289

Romantic 23, 25-6, 36, 265-6

Rorty, Richard 45

Rousseau, Jean-Jacques 24, 73, 84, 90

Royal Society, The 264-5, 284, 303

Ruskin, John 270

Russell, Bertrand 4

Ryder, Richard 78, 85, 241-2, 274

sacred 19, 52, 54, 57, 60, 90, 145, 174-5, 211, 215, 263, 265, 278, 289-91, 300, 314-7, 344

sacrifice 10, 22, 24, 83, 285, 309, 316, 326, 344

sadomasochism 182

Sartre, Jean-Paul 94, 138, 192, 194, 196-9, 315, 329

Satanic abuse 114

Satanism 40, 112-4, 133

Saxon 31-2, 129, 135

scarcity 142, 323

Scheler, Max 334-5

Schopenhauer, Arthur 73, 82, 101, 194-5, 199-200, 203, 292, 328-9, 332

science, new 22, 44, 72, 116, 144, 262-3, 265-7, 276

secrecy 111, 117

secret societies 25-6, 28, 116-7

secular 2, 10, 37, 38, 54, 64, 83-4, 98,

140, 192, 265, 287-8, 309

selective treatment 207

self 73, 119, 141-2, 154, 181-2, 195,
    197, 201, 275, 332, 334, 336

self-knowledge 324, 327, 336

Seneca 17, 26

sentience 19, 85, 133, 22, 224, 232, 241-
    2, 245, 258, 274, 282

separation 54, 57, 60, 74, 105, 143-4,
    151, 156, 176, 181-2, 224, 263, 279,
    305, 343

Sessions, George 271

sexuality 49, 51-2, 65, 81, 117, 125, 247,
    277, 293

Shakespeare, William 71, 262-3

sheep 224, 247, 283, 311

Sheldrake, Rupert 268, 313

simplicity 100, 139, 142-3, 240, 315

sin 135, 172, 213

Singer, Peter 78, 136, 223, 225, 229,
    236-7, 241, 244, 250-1, 254, 274, 282

social law 10, 43, 75, 78, 83, 85, 93, 95,
    144, 150, 186, 188, 277

song 3, 10, 55-8, 60, 137, 138, 141,
    145-7, 156-7, 161, 190, 204, 206,
    221, 240, 251, 279, 282-3, 300, 314,
    343

Sophocles 90

soul - defined 55-9

Sparrow, Rob 42, 305

Spencer, Herbert 91, 266-7, 269, 270,
    295, 306-7

spirit 27, 54-5, 57-8, 101, 145, 204, 259,
    286, 289, 303

stem cells 214-7

Stoicism 17, 70, 89, 134

story 44, 130, 134, 137-8, 151, 154,
    165-7, 190, 206, 217, 252-3, 279, 309

stranger 160, 162-5, 171, 173, 175, 182

subject 155, 161, 167, 175, 179, 187,
    196, 239-40, 253, 286, 291, 300, 305

subjectivity 15, 71, 89, 118, 142, 145,
    152, 194, 201, 255, 277

submission 14, 38, 83, 139, 159, 182,
    211, 324

suffer 73, 78-9, 100, 144, 194-5, 203-7,
    212, 215-6, 223, 233-4, 237, 240-3,
    247, 249-51, 256, 274, 310, 322, 332,
    335

suicide 50, 90, 202-3, 205-10

supernatural 42, 54, 111, 128, 133, 164,
    191, 316

superstition 21-22, 37, 39, 103-4, 113,
    137, 177, 262, 268, 273, 309

survival instinct 119, 211-2, 292-3

sympathy 72-3, 160, 252, 333-5, 337

telos 69-70, 278-80, 283

Thoreau, Henry David 266, 284

Threefold Return, Law of 102-3

time 20, 32, 68, 73-4, 142-3, 147, 197,
    205, 243-4, 319, 322

tourist 337-8

transplant 216

triads 106-7, 109, 120

tribe 43, 64-6, 75, 85-8, 104-5, 107-9,
    111, 113, 120, 124-30, 135-7, 141-2,
    146-7, 157-60, 165-7, 171, 174-5,
    183, 205-6, 208-10, 213, 217, 221,
    235-9, 271, 275-6, 283, 286, 292-3,
    304, 314-7, 324, 335, 337-40, 342,
    344

trust 84, 103, 104, 117, 159-60, 165-6,
    175-6, 182-4

truth 44-6, 87-8, 105, 107-8, 118-20,
    167, 171, 182, 190-2, 197-9, 202,
    284, 288-9

tsunami 37, 133-4, 313

Tutu, Archbishop Desmond 157

uncertainty 151, 157, 204, 338

UN Declaration of Human Rights 88,
    213

universalism 45, 54, 58-9, 70, 74-5, 81,
    118, 136, 152

utilitarianism 77-9, 241, 250-1, 274, 318,
    325

vagabond 337-8

Valiente, Doreen 101-2, 318

value 11, 24, 37, 57, 59, 63, 66, 75, 79,
    104-5, 114, 118, 145, 165-6, 173, 187,
    190-6, 198-202, 207-10, 217-8, 251,
    274-9, 293, 302-4, 309-10, 329, 339

value, inherent 161-2, 218, 231, 235,
    238-9, 241, 244, 246, 251-2, 275,

    277-9, 304

veganism 221-3, 226-7, 246, 250, 274

vegetarian 221, 246, 255, 339

Vegetarian Society, The 233

Wallis, Robert 108

Warnock, Mary 194, 213

water 57, 59, 147, 204, 226-7, 249-50,
    275, 280-3, 299, 310, 314, 322

Watson, Lyall 336

web 42-3, 47-8, 55, 60, 79, 146-7, 156,
    201-2, 213, 218, 221, 240, 249, 259,
    279, 280, 284, 288, 305, 315-7, 326,
    331-3, 336, 340, 344

web of wyrd 32-3, 43, 135

Velmans, Max 146

Whyte, David 342

Wicca 15, 26-7, 29-30, 32, 99-105,
    107-8, 111-2, 115, 118-9, 318

Wiccan Rede 120, 139

Wilderness Society, The 270

will 16, 25, 73, 91, 101, 103, 194-6,
    199-200, 203, 325, 328-32

Wilson, EO 271

Wilson, Steve 112-3

witch 15-16, 20, 22-3, 26-7, 99-100,
    102-3, 111-4

Wittgenstein, Ludwig 2, 193

Wollstonecraft, Mary 233

Wordsworth, William 23, 266

zoos 228